About The Author

Dr Prasad Modak holds BTech (Civil Engg) & MTech (Environmental Science and Engg) from Indian Institute of Technology (IIT) Bombay, and Doctor of Environmental Engg from Asian Institute of Technology, Bangkok, Thailand. He joined the Centre for Environmental Science and Engineering at IIT Bombay as a faculty member in 1984. He left IIT Bombay in 1995 to set up Environmental Management Centre LLP. In 2012, he established Ekonnect Knowledge Foundation - a Section-8 not-for-profit company. He served as Dean, IL&FS Academy for Applied Development (IAAD) and functioned as Chief Sustainability Officer at IL&FS Ltd. He is currently, Adjunct Professor at the Centre for Technology Alternatives in Rural Areas at IIT, Bombay

Dr Modak has worked with almost all key UN, multi-lateral and bi-lateral developmental institutions in the world. Prominent amongst these include UNEP Geneva, Paris and Osaka offices; UNDP and UNDESA, New York, UNIDO, Vienna; DFID, London; GIZ and CDG, Germany; Asian Productivity Organization (APO), Tokyo; SIDA; Embassy of the Netherlands, New Delhi; FAO; the World Bank;, IFC; Asian Development Bank and the New Development Bank, China.

Apart from Government of India and various State Governments, Dr Modak has advised the Governments of Bangladesh, Egypt, Indonesia, Mauritius, Thailand and Vietnam. Recently he was inducted on the India Resources Panel (for secondary material flows) by the Ministry of Environment & Forests and Climate Change, Government of India.

Dr Modak has published books with the UN University on EIA (translations in Chinese, Japanese), Tokyo; Oxford University Press; UNEP, Paris on Textile Industry and Environment and Centre for Environmental Education in India on Waste Minimization. He served as Hon. Editor of the Journal of Indian Water Works from 1998 to 2004. He coordinated the chapter on Waste Management and Recycling in UNEP's Green Economy Report; contributed a chapter on Waste and Resource Management in UNEP/ISWA's Global Waste Management Outlook and assisted UNCRD to establish IPLA - International Partnership for Expanding Waste Management Services of Local Authorities. Currently he is working as Principal Author of the Asia Waste Management Outlook for UNEP IETC.

Dr Modak has been a recipient of the Distinguished Alumni Award of AITAA in 2010 for Significant Contribution to International Affairs. He was elected to the Board Certified Member at the American Association of Environmental Engineers in recognition of his work in research & practice. He is now the Founder President of Indian Society for Indoor Environment.

Music, Education, Travel and Environmental Movements are some of his passions in life

BLUE GREEN

and
Everything in Between

Musings on Life, Love & Sustainability
Dr Prasad Modak

301/302, Third Floor, Godrej La Vista,
MB Raut Road, Shivaji Park, Dadar,
Mumbai 400028 Maharashtra, India
+91-9820126074
prasad.modak@emcentre.com

Copyedited by Mrinalini Patwardhan
Copyediting assistance by Sonal Alvares
Book and Jacket Design by Kedar Prabhavalkar, Studio Inspira
Illustrations by Manish Rangnekar
Author's photo by Harshad Parashare
Bhushan Bhaud (DTP)

First published in India in 2016
Typeset in Palatino Linotype and Amatic SC

ISBN: 978-1541318915

Table of Contents

Foreword

In my life, I have been fortunate enough to become a Professor, practice as a Consultant and establish an organization as an Entrepreneur. Furthermore, my proximity to the Government, International Development Financing Institutions and Corporates, gave me unique exposure and experience. Indeed, these multiple roles have helped me acquire a holistic perspective on environmental management and sustainability. My extensive travel across continents has added yet another dimension of professional and personal experience that I really cherish. I met amazing people as I globe trotted and made wonderful friends in this process.

I started writing posts on my blog site since 2014. The focus of the posts was to raise issues of concern on environmental management and sustainability relevant to India. Today there are more than 1300 followers and more than 45000 views. Enthused by this response, I released a compilation of 60 select posts early this year captioned "SIXTY SHADES OF GREEN". This book has been well received.

The second book presents 25 posts that reflect my personal experiences (I call them BLUE) and another 25 posts that continue to deal with issues regarding environmental management and sustainability (the GREEN). It is really hard to put the posts in the separate boxes such as GREEN and BLUE as there are several overlaps and intersects that represent various SHADES of BLUE and GREEN.

In all the posts, like before, I use humor and satire and tell the "stories". Most of the 'stories' are not necessarily real ... but created from my experiences and suitably crafted for the purpose of sharing.

'My Professor Friend' is a character I have created, essentially to provide another point of view. I simply adore this character and often wish that he was real! Sometimes I cite names of people, only to project "real world" and a feel of "authenticity". No offence is intended to anyone. And I do hope that the readers understand this perspective. The messages of the stories are the key takeaways. But these messages are often hidden.

One of the characteristics of the posts is that while narrating these stories, knowledge is embedded in an implicit manner. Sometimes references are cited for further reading. The book could potentially be used as a supplement to a course on Environmental Management & Sustainability. Some of the posts could be used to open up group discussions or formulate assignments.

I do hope that you enjoy this collection of 50 posts of the shades of BLUE and GREEN

Visit https://prasadmodakblog.wordpress.com/ and stay tuned.

SHADES OF BLUE

01

This post shares some of my life's sentimental experiences. As usual, the story is a carefully crafted blend, with altered names and locations. Even today I am not sure which parts were real and which parts were imagined but is it worth knowing?

I don't know why I feel like sharing such stories with you – to vent? to make you jealous? or to see if they strike similar chords in your lives?

I am sure you all would like to have a friend like Byke in your life. And if you don't then I suggest you look for someone like her. Don't ever lose the envelope if ever you get one!

I met Byke for the first time in the Chemistry Laboratory of Environmental Engineering Program at the Asian Institute of Technology (AIT) in Bangkok. She was a new student. It was 10 pm at night. She was doing a titration that was needed for some analyses. She was all alone as she had missed the regular laboratory session. I was in the lab reading a book. The air in the lab was chilly with a sweet aroma of chemicals.

Somehow Byke was missing the end point of the titration. "Shit, not again!" she used to scream when a miss would happen. She had to redo then the entire set up of solutions once again. That was quite a pain. When this miss happened for the third time, she looked around helplessly and found me (smiling).

In the utter frustration that she had, Byke looked really cute. With her straight short hair, a dimple on the cheeks, a bright red Tee shirt and white shorts, she looked like a pretty doll. I walked across and stood close to her, removed the earphones she was wearing and pulled out the Sony Walkman that she had belted on her waist. I said "My Dear Friend, You look like a true Music Lover", I then put the earphones on me and heard the song she was playing – "Simply the Best" a hit song by Tina Turner

"Come on, how can you

get the end point with such a great Tina Turner song going around?" – I tapped on her head lightly. "Now do the titration without your Walkman – you are not going to miss the end point this time."

And she did not.

"I am Byke! And you?" She said in her Pilipino accent in an excited tone.

"I am Prasad and I love Tina Turner too", I said

With this short introduction, we became best friends thereafter.

Byke – not her real name, was from the Philippines. Philippino names are just as complicated as our south Indian names. Everybody called her Byke and I never asked her full name.

I taught Byke engineering design and Byke taught me how to dance. She used to take me out on the town with her Philippino friends and after all that dancing, we used to end up at Niu's on Silom road. Niu's (now closed) was a famous Jazz Club & Italian Restaurant with great choice of wines.

Byke had a good voice. Sometimes she used to sing on the stage. "Inspire me Prasad!", she would say as she used to punch my chest with her fists. I used to play the keyboard and so there were occasions when I accompanied her for some soulful numbers, especially those by Carole King. "Now it's too late" was one of her favorite songs.

Byke wanted me to teach her to play the keyboard and so we spent our evenings in the Piano room of the AIT Center. Although she made a serious attempt, she could never pick up the keyboard. "You are wasting your time my dear friend." I used to say and she used to retort "No wasting of time when I am with you Prasad. I enjoy every moment we spend together in this Piano room."

I knew Byke had several close friends like me. That was her nature. Her friendliness was not to be confused with anything more. Some did and suffered in the process! In fact there was a rumor that she had a rich boyfriend who she was going to marry after returning to Manila. Once I coaxed her to show me his picture and she was very upset with me. She didn't speak to me for the entire day! "I don't like such questions Prasad – especially from you."… she said this when we patched up later.

When we graduated, Byke and all our "music friends"

had reserved a table to dine together. We really had a ball during the dinner party remembering all the good times. Most knew that we may never meet again and so we exchanged addresses with a promise that we will meet once again after 25 years! This was 1983.

"Prasad, you lousy friend – I am going to be tracking you…" Byke said, pulling me out of the dining hall under a tree outside the foyer. "…as I still need to learn keyboards from you." she was panting and gasping for breath. It was nearly 12 at night.

She stared at me for a while and then inserted an envelope in the front pocket of my shirt. She gave me a good long hug and kissed on my cheeks. I could smell the scent of jasmine. "So long Prasad!" she whispered and then went on running to disappear –cutting me from her life with surgical proficiency.

I opened the envelope when I reached my room and all it contained was a short note that read, "Ask me before you marry."

I returned to Mumbai and got into the mess of my career. Kiran was introduced to me by the families and we got married.

Even though I had misplaced Byke's envelope/note by then, the fond memories of our close friendship however remained. I would remember her everytime I listened to Tina Turner or Carole King.

I did ask about Byke's whereabouts through my friends and was told that she had moved away from Manila.

Years went by and one day I received a letter from the Hong Kong Productivity Council (HKPC) inviting me as the Chief Resource Person, to help them conduct a five day training program on Green Productivity. When I communicated my acceptance, I was told that one Ms. Rodora S. Natividad from HKPC will be contacting me for all the travel logistics and the technical details.

Ms. Rodora was quite efficient in all the arrangements. Her response to my emails (queries) was quick. My flights were booked perfectly and the hotel for my stay was an excellent choice - the L'hotel Causeway Bay Harbor.

I got to Hong Kong early morning by Cathay Pacific, checked in, showered and came down to the hotel reception as instructed by Ms. Rodora. Ms. Rodora had sent me the full program and we were to begin the program with a morning meeting of the resource persons on Floor 3, the Mandarin Room; followed by Days 2 to 4 of lecture sessions ending with a field trip on Day 5. Day 6 was reserved for the wrap up. I was all set, carrying all the papers for this opening meeting with the Resource Persons.

When I arrived at the reception, I was shocked to see Byke standing there. Dressed in a smart skirt, Chinese style top and a silk scarf, she looked magnificent - a lovely woman in her mid-thirties blending youthful charm and maturity. I was simply floored!

When Byke saw me, she came running and hugged me and said, "So, I got you here Prasad."

Before I could ask her how she was in Hong Kong as Ms. Rodora, she said, "Now shut up! I am going to tell you everything later– but the most important thing I want you to know is that there is no resource person session today. The program actually starts tomorrow. I got you to in Hong Kong one day early just to spend the day together. The program I sent you was fake – the real action starts tomorrow and the resource persons will arrive only tonight"

I was zapped. "What a woman

this Byke!" – I said to myself

"So?" I tapped on her head lightly – like I used to "What then today?"

Byke had worked out the entire day's schedule for us – and so very meticulously. Everything was planned well in advance.

We drove first to the Lover's Rock.

Situated on Bowen Road, this rock stands close to 30 feet high and is said to possess magical powers. It is decorated with oriental red and beautifully crafted drapes especially during the Maiden's Festival held each year in August. As it was already August, the festival was underway. During the festival, young unmarried girls pray for a suitable husband and lifelong good fortune.

When we were at the rock, Byke softly said, "Prasad I made my wish at this rock that I will see you one more time again. See my wish got fulfilled and there you are in front of me today." I was really touched and did not know what to say. "I too remembered you Byke so many times" I said this but in a voice that seemed faded and miles away.

We lunched on the street-side remembering the good old times. Byke then drove me to the Sundaram Tagore Gallery. The Sundaram Tagore Gallery is devoted to examining the exchange of ideas between Western and non-Western cultures. The Gallery focuses on developing exhibitions and hosting not-for-profit events that encourage spiritual, social and aesthetic dialogues.

When we reached the Gallery, we found that there was exhibition of mystic paintings of the world going on. As we walked around, Byke stopped in front of a painting that showed an angel like girl sitting on the branch of a barren tree. There was something deep and magical about the grey blue of the sky with a contrasting mat of green leaves under the tree. The face of the angel looked lost and a bit sad – as if she were longing for the Earth.

"I know this artist" Byke said. "Don't remember the name though".

"Many a times I feel that the angel is me." Byke said this staring at the painting that was hung on the wall.

Then she turned around and looked into my eyes and said slowly, "Prasad, when I returned to Manila, I married Rudy – who was part of one of the wealthy and influential families of Manila. But in a year, we split as we had differences. Then I decided to leave the Philippines and look for a job elsewhere. And that is how I landed at the HKPC." Her voice was broken. Her eyes were moist. I could feel the pain.

"Sorry to know this Byke." I said. "Oh don't feel sorry Prasad – I am now alright." Byke said this in a very matter of fact sort of voice.

We stepped out of the

Sundaram Tagore Gallery quietly.

Byke had some errands to run for the next day – i.e. the first official day of the training event, so she dropped me back at my hotel and went to the nearby supermarket. "Take a shower and come down in 30 minutes – we are going to the Wanch tonight." she instructed.

Historic, friendly, unpretentious and international, The Wanch is quite simply a Hong Kong institution. It has been the home of live music in Hong Kong since 1987, offering original music showcase nights, the top local cover bands and jam sessions. There is live music every night. The walls are decorated with a medley of very old photographs of Hong Kong and music posters reflecting The Wanch's iconic status at the heart of Hong Kong's music scene.

We were greeted very warmly by the owner of The Wanch. Byke seems to know him well and we got the best seats in the house. When the band started playing 80's music, , Byke really got excited. "Let us do one number together – I will sing and you take on the keyboard. Let me speak to Wong." Wong was managing

the live music and it was around 12 30 am before Wong let us on the dais. Byke sang her old time favorite "Now it's too late" by Carole King and I backed her up on the keyboard. We must have done pretty well because someone shouted "Encore!" when we finished. I felt that I was re-living my earlier life.

Byke drove me to the hotel and as we stopped in front of the entrance, she hugged me once more, brushed her lips on my cheeks lightly and said, "So I was able to steal you from your wife at least for a day. We had a wonderful time today Prasad."

I got down from the car, stepped aside and waited to say good night. Then all of sudden, Byke opened the door, got out and walked towards me. Punching blows on my chest with her fists (like she used to do), she held me close and said, "You never reached me before marrying – You scoundrel!" Before even I

7

could attempt an excuse, she said, "How could you? I never wrote down my telephone number for you Prasad. I should have. My mistake.".

And then almost like stabbing me with a knife – she said, rather sharply "But you not getting back to me was quite a disappointment Prasad". Then she turned back to the car and drove home.

The next day morning we met officially in the Mandarin Room on third floor. Byke was reading out short introduction of the resource persons. It appeared that she could not locate my profile. "Dr. Modak, will you please introduce yourself?" she said.

"Well, Ms. Rodora, I think you know me well enough to introduce" I said.

"Not really Dr. Modak, I don't know you that well enough. May I request you once again to introduce yourself please?" I saw Byke's face and the tone different with hardly any resemblance to yesterday

I realized that one day early in Hong Kong was over.

I had told my wife Kiran, who is a ceramic potter, about Byke. So when I returned home, I told her about my encounter with Byke in Hong Kong. She had a good laugh. "You fool, you never understood Byke and I feel sorry for you both." she said and she continued her work on her pottery wheel.

In 2007, when I had my angioplasty and when we were home Kiran said, "I guess this stent belongs to your long lost friend Byke." I looked at the mischief in her eyes but saw the deep trust in me at the same time – that was so comforting.

"You know everything – what can I say?" I said this moving to my shining Rolland Keyboard.

02
The Secret Life of Dr. Modak

This post is based on "The Secret Life of Walter Mitty[1]" – a short story by James Thurber[2]. This story first appeared in The New Yorker on March 18, 1939 and is considered one of Thurber's acknowledged masterpieces. It was made into a movie in 1947[3] and once again in 2013[4]. The movies bore the same name but the stories were very different from Thurber's original story.

The name Walter Mitty and the derivative word "Mittyesque" have entered the English language, denoting an ineffectual person who spends more time in heroic daydreams than paying attention to the real world.-- Wikipedia

I have been a great fan of James Thurber and especially of the story of Walter Mitty. This is my attempt at sharing with you, my own secret life as a salute to James Thurbur.

As always I am sure that you (the discerning reader) will pick up on the messages I wish to highlight through my story laced with its usual seasoning of humour and satire.

A Professor friend of mine called me one morning asking for a ride to the office of the Ministry of Environment and Forests and Climate Change (MoEFCC). He had been called to chair a meeting on the review of research proposals for MoEFCC's funding.

The Professors' car plates were odd-numbered and since on the day of the meeting odd numbered vehicles were banned from city streets, he wanted me to pick him up from his house in my car (which had even numbered plates) and drop him at the MoEFCC. To make my time worth however, he said that he

---

1   See https://en.wikipedia.org/wiki/The_Secret_Life_of_Walter_Mitty
2   You can read the original story on-line at http://www.fraumuenster.ch/wp-content/uploads/2013/09/The-Secret-Life-of-Walter-Mitty.pdf. Please don't miss it.
3   See https://en.wikipedia.org/wiki/The_Secret_Life_of_Walter_Mitty_(1947_film)
4   See https://en.wikipedia.org/wiki/The_Secret_Life_of_Walter_Mitty_(2013_film)

had spoken to the concerned Joint Secretary and had me included as an Observer on the Committee.

"I will have your gate pass ready" he assured me as sometimes getting a gate pass to the MoEFCC took a lot more time than the meetings! I agreed to be the Observer as there was no work to be done except to be present.

"Please pay attention when in Jor Baugh. There was not much congestion on the streets – thanks to Chief Minister Kejariwal's Odd-Even vehicle policy. The Professor wasn't speaking as he was busy reading the research proposals that were submitted for review. Apparently, he always skimmed through such proposals in the car while going for the meeting – "Not worth spending too much time on such stuff", he used to say.

you drive. Lately, I see that you have become a day dreamer and you don't concentrate", instructed my wife as I left my home and headed for the Professors' bungalow in Noida. And she was indeed right. Lately I had become almost Mittyesque with my day - whether I was busy with something or doing nothing at all. Often I would day dream my way into my 'secret world'.

When I arrived at the Professor's bungalow, he was waiting at the gate and soon we started driving towards the MoEFCC office

I overtook a tanker that was blocking us for a while near the IGL CNG Station. While overtaking, the HazChem signage on the truck caught my attention. And I entered my secret world…

There was a huge commotion at UniChem India's tank farm near Ghaziabad. The tank farm had a storage tank of Ethylene Oxide (EO) of 100 Metric Tons (MT). EO is highly toxic and flammable. It has to be stored in steel vessels maintaining temperature in the range of 100 to 15°C. If this temperature exceeds then polymerization happens that is exothermic leading to fire and explosion.

On his routine rounds at the tank farm, one of the junior engineers noticed that the temperature gauge on the EO Tank was at 18°C and quickly moved to 19°C. The engineer immediately sounded the alarm.

When the sirens blared, I was sitting in the office of the managing director (MD). The Health Safety Environment (HSE) Head Chopra rushed to the Tank Farm with his team. No one dared to get close to the EO Tank. Everyone clearly understood the gravity of the situation but nobody was clear on what action to take. The guidebooks/manuals were as usual not proving very useful. Perhaps this was one of those unforeseen and consequently unplanned emergencies. A fireball resulting

from the explosion of this 100 MT EO Tank would be impossible to handle putting people located in the 2km radius around it into a zone of acute toxicity. Soon the MD and I had also reached the spot.

Chopra was an experienced HSE Head with 20 years of experience in handling hazardous chemicals. But at that time he looked very scared and helpless with beads of sweat on this forehead. He looked at me with a sigh of relief, "Dr. Modak, Good to see you here. Guess the runway reactions are already setting in." Only Chopra knew that I was one of the most regarded Safety Expert in the Asia-Pacific region.

I decided to step in. There wasn't any other option. I looked at the pressure gauge and volume indicators of the tank; and monitored the oscillating needles of the temperature, pressure and volume gauges over two minutes. After some quick calculations on my iPhone, I looked up the ambient temperature with my handy iPhone App. Then I started taking slow and steady steps towards the tank! Everybody tensed up

11

as they stood frozen watching me taking such a risk. The MD of UniChem called out in a low and cracking voice, "No Dr. Modak, please don't go too close!"

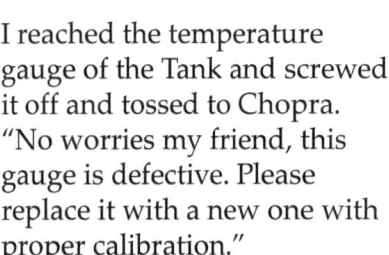

road. I have never seen you driving so recklessly before. What is wrong with you today? Please watch the gauge."

The Professor's warning brought me out of my secret world. "Sorry Professor, my mistake." I said this nervously with my mouth running dry. I was that Ethylene Oxide Storage Tank hero no more.

I reached the temperature gauge of the Tank and screwed it off and tossed to Chopra. "No worries my friend, this gauge is defective. Please replace it with a new one with proper calibration."

Everybody was shocked. They could not figure out how I had detected the error in the temperature gauge. Chopra almost screamed, turned to his Team and said to the MD, "Only he could do this Sir, only Dr. Modak." There was great applause and the MD patted my back.

I suddenly felt someone tapping my shoulders. It was my Professor friend. He seemed very perturbed.

"Dr. Modak, please slow down! Take a look at your speedometer. You are driving at 140 km/hr. Do you want to be caught by the traffic cops, get held up and pay a hefty fine? Besides the car tire could burst on this not so well done

We drove a few kilometers in silence and when we were close to the shopping mall of the Great India Place, the Professor asked me to take the service road. "I need to buy some fruits for my wife. Why don't you park the car and wait for me? I will not take more than 10 minutes" he said. But I knew he would take more than 10 minutes.

Finding a parking space in the shopping mall was not easy but I found one on the second stage ramp. I had to negotiate a spot next to a fish van.

The workers were pulling out large trays of Kingfish, Black Pomfret and Emperor Fish. There was quite a stench and so I rolled up the car windows and put on the AC. Having secured a proper parking space, I was free to dive back into my secret world…

Divers on the ship Vijayanta were visiting an isolated site, some 300 miles south west off the Gujarat coast, to survey the marine floors for an Oil Exploration company. The team consisted of 12 divers.

I was with Subra Iyer – the Captain of the ship. I was to do some monitoring to understand relationship between marine iron concentrations and the phytoplankton. It was noon when the dive team came across an injured whale shark. The divers saw a thick metal rope wrapped around the shark, cutting into her skin threatening the pregnant female's life and that of her unborn pup. The divers made two trips down to the whale shark to check its condition and tried to remove the rope. All their attempts failed.

On hearing the divers screaming, we rushed to the deck. When some of the senior divers saw me, they whispered amongst each other, "Oh, Dr. Duck is on board – he is one world famous marine diver who has made animal rescue as his mission."

I was affectionately called Dr. Duck by the diver community. "Dr. Duck is also an internationally acclaimed campaigner against marine debris", one senior diver told his junior.

I realized that there was no time to think. We needed to act immediately.

"Subra," I snapped, "what sort of diver suits you have on board?"

"We have ADS 2000." Subra said. I turned to one of the divers, "What's the diving depth?"

"200 meters Sir!" he said.

"Then the ADS will be just fine. Get me in." I dropped my T-shirt and the trousers and spread my hands wide.

"Aye aye Sir!" said the divers and two of them helped me to get into the ADS 2000.

"And get me a set of Scuba Deep Sea Hammerhead Stainless Steel Diving Knife." I ordered.

"Get the Doc that knife." Subra shouted.

"Getting one, Sir!" said one of the divers and rushed off.

I dived with two divers to guide me to the 'spot.'

We got to the whale and it broke my heart to see the poor and helpless creature. It was going to be very difficult, not to mention dangerous to rescue her but I felt compelled to help the animal despite the great risk to my own life.

I moved around the struggling animal and found a thinner section of the rope that I could cut through using my Hammerhead knife. I succeeded and even managed to unravel the rope from around the whale shark. Finally she was free. My two fellow divers gave me thumbs up for victory and I knew they must be thinking; "Only Dr. Duck could do this!"

I was jolted back to reality when I heard a number of knocks on my side window. It was the Professor. I lowered the window.

"Where the hell were you, Dr. Modak?" The Professor asked angrily.

"It took me 15 minutes to find you. And why were you hiding behind this fish van?" The Professor was obviously not happy with the smell. "Open the dickey and let me put the fruits in there."

14

I noticed that that Professor's fruit bag looked like a fish net. But instead of a pregnant whale shark, it only had fruit!

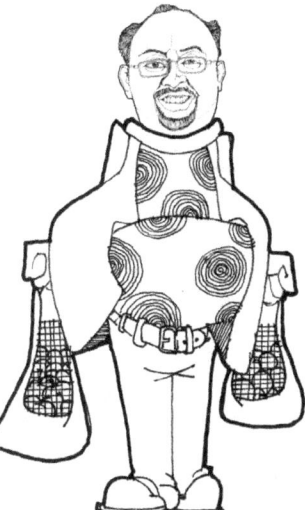

We drove out of the parking lot. I was that world famous diver Dr. Duck no longer.

We were close to Lajpat Nagar when traffic was blocked by a crowd of protesting students. Initially I thought that the protest was about the incidence that took place on the campus of the Jawaharlal Nehru University (JNU), however to my surprise the student were protesting the universities' non-implementation of the Supreme Court directive on compulsory Environmental Education (EVS).

Just to give you the background on this directive: The failure on the part of universities and colleges in introducing environmental studies modules for undergraduate courses despite repeated reminders, prompted the University Grants Commission (UGC) to issue an official notice. According to this notice, the UGC had prepared and provided a six month EVS module for all undergraduate courses in 2003. This was a follow up to the 1999 Supreme Court order directing all Indian universities and affiliated colleges to take appropriate steps to introduce EVS into their curriculum.

The students protesting on the streets were demanding corrective action, given the precarious state of India's environment. They were carrying banners that read "Hame Chahiye Paryavaran ke Shiksha – Wahi dega Deshko Suraksha" – Ab Aur Deri Nahi Challegi!" (meaning -Environmental Education will provide security to India and its Resources. We don't want any further delay in imparting environmental education). One young college student was giving an impassioned speech on a loudspeaker

lashing the UGC, Ministry of Human Resources and Development (MHRD) and the National Green Tribunal (NGT).

I was overwhelmed to see the yearning to learn about environment displayed by the new generation. "There is some hope!" I said to myself. I wanted to share my sentiments with the Professor but he brushed me aside – saying that he was busy adding the evaluation scores of the research proposals and did not want to be disturbed. He simply said, "Don't take these protests seriously!"

I asked the traffic policeman about the traffic jam. He said "Sir, relax on the wheel. You won't be going anywhere for the next 20 minutes. The roads are blocked by students for over a kilometer." So, back into my secret world I retreated...

A public hearing for a Coal Fired Thermal Power Plant project in the State of Orissa was underway. This hearing was conducted by the Orissa State Pollution Control Board as a part of its Environmental Clearance process. Nearly a thousand people had gathered and a pandal (stage) had been erected complete with a

number of standing fans to try to beat the heat.

The local Collector was presiding over the hearing and a Consultant representing the Project Proponent was making a presentation. The crowd

consisted local residents, member of some of the tribes who were to lose their land, environmental NGOs and a large technical team that was brought in to answer questions. Media and local police were also present.

There were hoardings all around the venue, describing the benefits of the project. Handouts in Oriya (the local language) were being circulated amongst everybody present. There was a food stall set up along with a place to get water and a place to wash faces and hands. The arrangement closely resembled a wedding reception.

I was sitting in the second row of seats in front of the pandal. In the large crowd assembled and all the hulla-gulla my presence had gone unnoticed -- even by the Collector.

As I watched the Consultant give his presentation, I realized that he was blatantly lying and giving incorrect information. Those asking questions were making unreasonable demands and there seemed to be no transparency or feeling of trust amongst the participants of this hearing. Allegations were being made freely and I got the sense that the lobbyist (on the payroll of rival industrial houses) and activists were mainly interested in milking the proponents for all they were worth.

The Collector was present, only because it was his job to do so without having the least bit of interest in the proceedings. The situation seemed to be worsening with voices getting louder and an imminent threat of a physical assault or even a riot.

Deciding to get involved, I got up and walked on to the stage. When the Collector saw, he stood up and said, "Sirji, I did not realize that you were present. It is our great honor to have you here." The industry proponent came forward and called to his cronies to garland me on the stage.

Most knew that I was the Ramon Magsaysay Award winner of 2015. This annual award was established to perpetuate former Philippine President Ramon Magsaysay's example of integrity in governance, courageous service to the people, and pragmatic idealism within a democratic society. This award is considered as the "Asian Nobel Prize".

I spoke extempore about the project, its need and the benefits. I also elaborated on the impacts and the risks, touching on the concerns related to land acquisition. I summarized at the end that we were all present there to know how the project proponent was planning on addressing the project's downside while ensuring economic development and livelihoods of the locals. The audience was quiet and everybody was listening intently. When I finished, there was a 30 second silence followed by... Applause!

"Move boss. MOVE!"

It was the traffic policeman I was talking to earlier. The traffic was moving already as students had dispersed and those behind my car were honking with a vengeance. I started the engine apologizing to the policeman and drove off as an ordinary human being and not the famous Ramon Magsaysay Award winner.

We reached the gate of the MoEFCC and the Professor told me to wait while he went in to sign the entry register and get our gate passes. He said it would only take 5 minutes but it took longer.

When he returned, his face was red and he looked upset."Dr. Modak, the instructions to make your gate pass did not reach the entry gate in time. So no gate pass was made for you. I tried to speak to the Joint Secretary but his cell phone is switched off."

He looked at me apologetically and said, "Sorry Dr. Modak, would you mind spending an hour at the nearby Khan Market and come back to pick me up? The meeting should not take too long."

I realized that there was no other alternative.

"Do some book shopping at Bahri's." advised the Professor as he headed through the gate.

Turning the car around, the amazing and invincible Dr. Prasad Modak, drove towards Khan Market, looking forward to once again slipping into his secret world. This world was much more thrilling and enjoyable than the mortal world he lived in.

03

Reading Faces – Scanning of Minds

It was 1993 and I had boarded a flight from Lucknow to New Delhi along with my friend Chris Messner. It was a hopping flight, operated by Indian Airlines and flying from Kolkata to Patna, then to Lucknow and finally to Delhi and there was no fixed seating arrangement.

Chris and I were looking for two empty seats next to each other, but as the aircraft was already partially full of passengers who had boarded at Kolkata and Patna, we were unable to find two seats together.

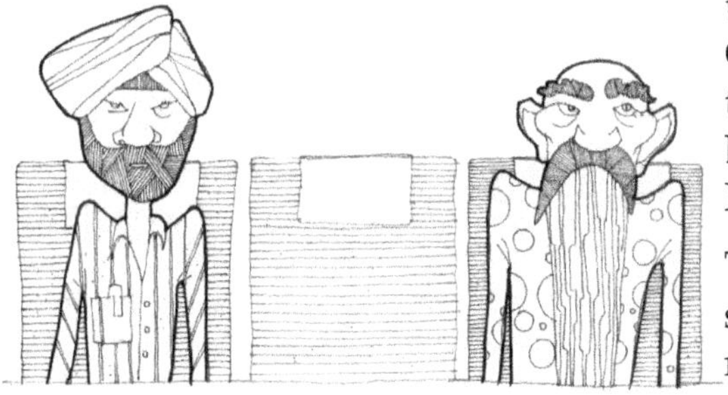

Looking around for a place to sit, I was almost halfway down the rows of seats when I felt a strong gaze, almost as though I was being scanned. This alarming sensation made me uncomfortable and also very curious at the same time.

I looked around and spotted a man with a white beard, dressed in a kurta and pyjama with powerful shiny eyes. He had a magnetic personality – and I could sense that there was something special about him. I told Chris to go ahead and find a place for himself and sat down next to the mysterious stranger. He was sitting in the aisle seat and the window seat was occupied by a Sardarji (Turban headed), who as I found out later was the Deputy Governor of the Reserve Bank of India.

The middle seat in that row was vacant and as soon as I took the seat, the man held my hand and said very warmly, "So you got my invitation?"

The aircraft was moving

19

already and as an amateur student of phrenology (reading faces) , I attempted to read this man.

"Trying to read me?" he asked and it was then I realized that this stranger was truly gifted.

The Man took the air sickness bag from the seat back pouch in front of him, took out his pen, drew a circle, made quadrants, gazed at me once again and made a few scribbles over the quadrants. This was strange!

Then, in a matter of fact tone, he spoke – telling me what was essentially my life's story. He told me the reason for my travel; details about my education, my profession, my family (i.e. my wife, children and three sisters) all of which was true and he didn't even ask me .if he was right or wrong. It probably did not even matter to him as he was so confident.

By that time, the aircraft had taken off and we were cruising. When the "fasten seat belts" sign was switched off, the Man got up and went to the loo leaving me sitting there dazed and speechless.

I then turned to the Sardarji next to me and said, "Sir, do you know what this person said? Everything he told me was true. I am shocked!"

The Sardarji smiled and said "Well, before you there was someone from Patna and earlier somebody else sat here from Kolkata. They experienced exactly the same thing that you did. What do you expect when you are sitting next to the great phrenologist Anil Sharma (name changed)?"

I was familiar with Anil Sharma's books. They were based on the Samudrika Lakshana written by the Samudra Raja (King of the Sea). It was thrilling to know that Anil Sharma was sitting right next to me and that he had read me!

The Art and Science of Phrenology

Phrenology is one of the most traditional techniques of predicting a person's character, personality, behavior, their attitude and their success in life. All our future, present or past may well be defined and determined by our own facial structure. Face is the index of the mind. It tells all about our character, our destiny and your future. Comparing the human face with that of animals and birds is one method in which the reading is done. Watching the walk of the person helps greatly in identifying the ruling animal or the bird.

There are a few blessed souls

who by merely looking at people can predict with high levels of accuracy. To some, it comes as a siddhi (power), and for a few it comes out of experience. The art or science of face reading is an age-old method of predicting human lives, and has been used by people as a reliable method of astrology.

When Anil Sharma returned to his seat, I introduced myself and told him about my interest in face reading. "I have just started reading your books Sir." I said. I also told him that I was a great fan of his and felt honored sitting next to him. Anil Sharma only smiled.

During the flight, Sharma spoke of several aspects of face reading that are not generally mentioned in the books. Not wanting our chat to end, I kept wishing that the flight would take more time to reach Delhi which, given that I was flying with Indian Airlines was not entirely unlikely.

As we began our descent to Delhi, Anil Sharma said, "I know you don't have any checked-in baggage but I do."

"How did he know?" I wondered.

"I want to gift you my book of notes and sketches." He continued. "It is an unpublished work and therefore is special and only for a select few. Would you mind waiting with me to collect my luggage?"

"Of course I will wait Mr. Sharma. It will be my pleasure and great honor." I said, pleasantly surprised.

At luggage belt, Anil Sharma opened his suitcase and gave me his book and a parting message, "Don't share this treasure with others. Just keep with you, study hard and practice!"

And I have done just that. Soon I was hooked on to face reading or should I say mind scanning. I would practice all the time - at meetings, at the airports, at parties, in classes while teaching students and even when I would meet strangers. I would actually be happy when a flight was delayed as it would give me more time for people scanning!

Initially, my reading and assessments were all wrong but it was a fun learning experience. Soon I got better and eventually was quite adept at reading people. A bizarre incident at the International Airport in Jakarta proved that I was soon becoming quite a proficient phrenologist!

I was working as a GTZ consultant for a cleaner

production project - ProduksiH Bersi in Indonesia. The project require me to be in Indonesia every two months and while there I travel across the country – developing demonstration projects, holding in-company training sessions and advising BAPEDAL – the then Ministry of Environment. During this time, I was famous amongst the Indonesian professionals and Academia, more for my face reading hobby and skills than my expertise in Cleaner Production!

During one of the trips, as I was clearing the immigration and customs checks at the Soekarno-Hatta International Airport, a Customs officer took a look at my passport turned to his colleague and spoke in Bahasaand then looked at me sternly.

"Well, we have to question you Dr. Modak." He said. "Please come with us upstairs for interrogation. It is part of our routine check. "

I was shocked and a little scared. I tried to tell the Officer that I was an innocent and frequent traveler to Indonesia and that he was wasting his time investigating me. The officers were however firm and I was taken to an upstairs lounge and told to wait. As I sat these tense and

unsure of my future, one of the customs officers (whose name, I later learnt was Rudy) smiled and said, "Oh Dr. Modak, don't worry. You are not in any trouble. I met your friend Professor Nurul of the University of Indonesia for dinner yesterday and he told me about you and your amazing face reading skills. So when I asked Professor Nurul how I could meet you, he said that you are busy and that I should try meeting you when you flew out of here today. He gave me your flight details and that's how we found you! Now, can you read my face Dr. Modak, Please?" Rudy said all this and proceeded to order me a glass of beer.

I was speechless. Ideally, face reading should not be forced; it has to be a natural process. But I realized that I did not have any choice and thought that it would be in my best interest to give it a go.

I thought of Anil Sharma, his shining eyes, his special book of notes and of all the time I had spent practicing.

After looking at Rudy for a minute, I said, "Rudy, you have an elder brother. Your parents live in Yogyakarta. You send money every month to them to help them to look after their health expenses. Your elder brother unfortunately does not help at all and despite all your good work, your parents still love your elder brother much more than you." My tone was calm and matter of fact – just like Anil Sharma's had been when he read me.

Saying all this was so simple and straightforward –I just told Rudy everything he already knew! Rudy was shocked. "You are absolutely right Dr. Modak, but how did you know?"

The girl who got me a glass of beer had been watching and listening. "How about me Sir?" she asked.

I looked over at her and said, "You my friend are in a difficult situation. You have fallen in love with two men at the same time – one lives in Indonesia and the other is abroad. That's your dilemma and the problem." I had not just observed her face but had also scanned her walk as she brought in the drink. The girl blushed on hearing what I had to say about her.

This incident really boosted my confidence. I now understood that face reading and scanning of the minds is possible – and it really does work. I also realized that this was a skill worth honing as it allowed one to not only read/scan a person or situation but also understand them better. It also made it easier to take decisions and sometimes even gave the decision maker the upper hand.

For example, if I was to meet a stranger for a contract, then I would reach the venue 10 minutes earlier to be able to observe this person's walk as he/she approached the meeting table. This would give me a sense of how much I could trust the newcomer. A person's walk tells you about the ruling bird and animal behind the person. Then I would focus on other aspects such as the eyeballs and the nails, etc.

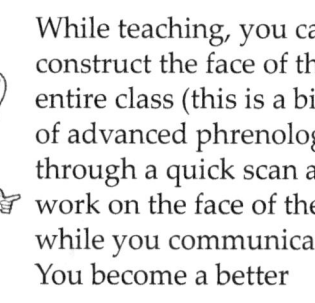

While teaching, you can construct the face of the entire class (this is a bit of advanced phrenology) through a quick scan and work on the face of the class while you communicate. You become a better teacher and more effective communicator in the process. I like to ask people to introduce themselves before I begin speaking so that I get some time to construct face of the class.

Does phrenology work for predicting the future? Sure it does – with some limitations of course.

In 1998, I was working on the Ho Chi Minh Environmental Improvement in Saigon. My project manager Bert, a 76 year old man, had fallen in love with a 22 year old Vietnamese girl! Bert had asked me to have dinner with them and I was to sit facing the girl and read her mind. I wasn't keen for this kind of dinner but Bert simply insisted. After dinner later that night, as we were walking towards my hotel on the Bon Sen Street, Bert asked me for my assessment. I didn't want to say anything as something weird had come to mind when I scanned her. But Bert was insistent and he simply wouldn't let me enter the hotel until I told him!

"Bert, this girl is going to kill you!" I said almost unwillingly. When Bert heard this, he laughed loud and said "Not a good joke Dr. Modak but I let you go."

Three weeks later, Bert called to tell me that the girl attacked him with two knives while he was slept. He had survived miraculously but lost three of his fingers!

"How did you know?" he asked.

"Well it was all there in her eyes." I told Bert.

For past 20 years, I have been successfully running my consulting outfit the Environmental Management Centre, LLP (EMC). So far, nobody has left EMC with any grudges or bad feelings. Those who left us for other reasons are still a part of the EMC family and our professional associate network. Do you think this happened because I used to read the faces and minds of every new entrant to EMC?

Sometimes it can be quite fun to read a person's mind and find that what they are saying and thinking are two completely different things. Once a colleague, who was resigning from EMC, told me that her mother in law has been unwell and she needed to quit her full time job to look after her. I could see from her face that she was all set to join another consulting firm (a competitor) and was feeling awkward to tell me this frankly. I accepted her reason and resignation but was quite amused to see how people bend the truth and put on pretenses because of the various constraints, uncertainties and risks that they perceive. It is as though we wear a mask. The following week after she received her relieving letters from EMC, this former colleague informed me that she had joined our competitor firm and she had found/employed someone to take care of her mother-in-law!

One often gets the opportunity to meet other mind-readers in the course of one's life and sometimes one may even across some mighty-minds. While mingling in a crowd, fellow mind scanners can spot each other and on making eye contact they often smile in recognition and acknowledgement. I have found this to also be a lot of fun.

I once met a sage who was thought to be over 150 years old. I found this hard to believe. This aged sage looked very strange and almost ape-like with his hands almost touching his knees. He looked at me with his shining/dazzling eyes. There was such a force of light in his gaze that even though I tried to resist, I soon realized that it was best to surrender and let him enter my mind. During the few minutes of silence between us, I felt as though he had opened all doors and windows of my mind-house and wandered around to feel and understand me. All this while, he had a warm smile on his face.

I told my Professor friend about my experiences and suggested that we should introduce phrenology as a course or offer training programs, especially for our environmental fraternity. In the environmental field, we are constantly connecting with people, meeting folks of diverse backgrounds, resolving conflicts and attempting to align visions for the sustainability of this planet. Armed with phrenology, we could perhaps build the more effective communicators and change-agents that this world needs!

Not everybody can learn this science and a certain degree of interest/ inclination, intuition and most importantly perseverance is necessary. Each one of us possesses some phrenology skills. However, most don't cultivate this power on a systematic and serious basis.

The Professor lit his cigar as he heard my recommendation said, "Well, I must say that you are a very good story teller. All your stories are rather entertaining Dr. Modak, but they really hard to believe. I don't know how much of you said is real and how much is fiction or your imagination. I do like your idea on coaching our environmental folks on face and mind reading. But why limit this education to the environmental fraternity – we should have such courses open for all."

Extinguishing his cigar with a deep puff, he added, "But please don't introduce this skill to people before they fall in love. If you teach them face reading too early, then nobody is going to fall in love. Relationships will be looked at rather analytically or shall I say clinically, through the lens of deductive sciences such as phrenology. Love should simply happen. Face reading or mind scanning will interfere with this natural process." He said with his typical mischievous smile and in a manner that I found quite charming.

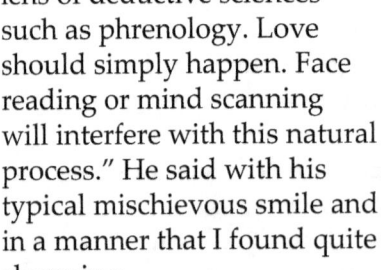

"You are absolutely right Professor." I responded

"I learnt phrenology only after marrying my wife Kiran. Not before – and I don't regret it at all!"

04

Driving (Me) Crazy

We have been living in the great city of Mumbai for over two generations. In this span of nearly 80 years, we have had several individuals who have been a support to our living/lifestyle and a part of the family. This included a barber who used to show up every morning for 30 years and shave my father (in fact he gave me my first shave – leaving some bruises behind as a memory). Then there was an Aya (maid) who looked after me for 25 years and was like my second mother. I always miss Tanubai (her name).

In this ecosystem, there were car drivers who worked with my father for years. These drivers did not just drive our cars but functioned as butlers too, doing anything and everything for us. We looked after them well, respected them (never treated them like servants – a term I hate to use) and supported their families. The young generation of today will probably not understand the warmth of these lifelong relationships that we enjoyed as an extended family. Life is so different today.

I am writing this post about my driver Siddhu Kolekar who worked with me for 10 years. Through this narration, my attempt is to reflect a few sensitivities laced with some humor in the form anecdotes. Pardon me as there are no musings on sustainability in this post!

One Sunday morning my doorbell rang and when I opened the door I saw a short (and a bit stocky), dark skinned man grinning at me with a paan in this mouth. He almost looked like a chimpanzee.

"Saheb, I was told that you are looking for a driver." He said.

I was indeed looking for a new driver at that time as my earlier driver had retired. But I was surprised as to how this chimpanzee knew about it.

27

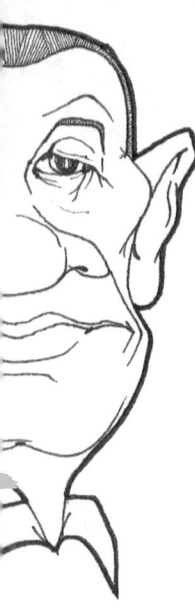

The man simply got in (almost pushing me) and took a seat on the sofa. He looked around the drawing room as if to get the measure of his potential employer. He took out his (dirty) handkerchief and wiped sweat on this forehead

"I can start working for you from tomorrow." He said in a matter of fact tone.

I was both amused and irritated.

"Who are you Mr....?" I asked in not so friendly a tone.

"I am Siddhanath – but you can call me Siddhu."

Siddhu looked like an experienced person – I guessed that he must have been nearly 50 years of age.

"Where did you work before?" I asked.

"Well, my first job was with the Chief Minister of the Government of Maharashtra – Shri Vasantrao Naik. That was for 10 years. Then I worked for more than 10 years with Mr. Soman, Inspector General of Police of Maharashtra. You should know these people – both good."

He saw my gaping face and continued.

"Someone told me that you are looking for a new driver. Many told me that you are good man. So I have decided to work with you"

(So I was going to be the third important and fortunate boss of Siddhu!)

I tried to explain to him that he cannot assume that I have selected or appointed him. I am looking for options and he could well be one of them.

But Siddhu did not listen and gave me an impression that he did not understand my point of view.

"I will come tomorrow morning at 8 am. You have Maruti Esteem right. I know this car very well." He said while getting up from the sofa. While opening the door, he turned around and said "I decided my job with you so now you decide my salary – I leave that to you."

With that the man left.

At 8am the next morning, he showed up, slightly better dressed and asked for the car keys.

I accepted him. Not that I had a choice in the matter as the Man had already decided.

Since that day Siddhu came to work for me every day at 8 am

sharp for the next 10 years.

The first thing I had to do was to get a strong and pungent air spray for the car so as to neutralize Siddhu's body odor. He was a shepard by birth – and smelt of sheep and the soil. The air spray used to work for the day.

Siddhu was a decent driver and knew how to take care of my car. He could negotiate well with the car mechanics and speak to them like an automobile engineer with authority and experience. He had a number of stories to tell about his driving skills – especially the story of the award – a silver badge – he received from Larsen & Toubro to bring down one of their massive 12 wheeler from the hills in Chambal Valley – a valley that was rampaged by the dacoits.

Siddhu had an uncanny skill of attracting women. Whenever I used to go for meetings and return to the car, I would see him chatting with women – this included waste-pickers, vegetable sellers and the like. He used to be sitting like a Krishna amidst them.

But there were many more interesting episodes with this chimpanzee that I must narrate to you.

When I used to go to my office

at IL&FS, the security guards at the Gate would stand by and salute me. I never liked this saluting practice and so I told Siddhu to tell them to stop this nonsense. Siddhu laughed at me and said "Saheb, do you think they are saluting you? They are saluting me – as they come from my village. I am like their Mama (uncle)". I was simply speechless.

I realized later that Siddhu's village must be a really big and important place. I remember that once he jumped the traffic signal near Worli in Mumbai and we were promptly stopped by the Traffic Police. The policeman took his driving license and asked him to appear in the court next day and pay fine. I was quite upset and told Siddhu that firstly he should have not jumped the signal and secondly he must report to the Court, apologize and pay the fine, the very next day.

Siddhu said, "No worries Saheb. A policeman with a handlebar mustache will come to your house at night and return my driving license. All the driving licenses collected in the Central part of Mumbai go to him at night. This man is from my village and once he sees my license – he will come to your house and return the license." I was shocked with his confidence.

And sure it happened just as he predicted. At night around 10 pm, a policeman with a handlebar mustache appeared at my door step. While handing over the license, he said, "Saheb, there has been some mistake. Please give this to Mama when he comes tomorrow and convey my regards."

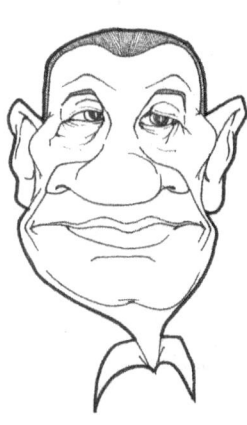

Siddhu once told me that he has been blessed by a sage that he will not die in a car accident. "It's good for you to know this." he said. I however told him to re-check with the Sage whether his blessings were limited only to him or if they were also applicable to someone sitting behind - me! He laughed. "I will check." he told me.

The laughter reminds me of another incident. I had taken my good friends Richard Ackermann and Hari Sankaran out for dinner at the Copper Chimney restaurant in Bandra (Mumbai) and was dropping them back. First we were going to drop Hari who lived on Carter Road and then to Taj Lands End where Richard was staying. At the time, Richard was Sector Director of Environment at the World Bank and Hari was Joint Managing Director of IL&FS. The conversations in the car were extremely intellectual laced by Richard's sophisticated sense of humor that would make all of us laugh. Whenever we would do so, driver Siddhu would also laugh. I was surprised and also irritated to see him laughing.

"How come this guy laughs when he does not know even a sentence in English?" I thought to myself.

When we were returning home, I could not resist asking him, "Why were you laughing Siddhu? I am sure you understood nothing of what Richard was saying."

Siddhu replied "Saheb, doesn't it look bad if three in the car laugh and the fourth doesn't? Isn't it bad manners? So I joined you all in laughing."

I didn't know what to say. Whether to laugh or cry!!

I paid Siddhu his salary in cash every month as he did

not have a bank account. Once day while counting the notes, he told me, "Saheb, don't take this the wrong way, but I just wanted to tell you that I am much richer than you are. I have 4 acres of fertile land, four deep wells, 30 sheep, 4 cows and 2 bulls. Also I live in an open sunny place with lots of fresh air."

He was absolutely right I thought, especially in the latter, Mumbai always had overcast sky, poor ventilation and more of carbon monoxide than the oxygen. "Then why do you work for me Siddhu?" I asked. He was about to finish his counting of the notes and so took a pause and said "Saheb, I have everything I said but no cash so I am here just for that."

Indeed, many from rural areas of Maharashtra are in Mumbai because of the hard cash this sin city provides.

Siddhu was quite popular with my office colleagues and friends as he used to often give everybody his free advice and practical wisdom. One day, Santosh Shidhaye, one of my colleagues at IL&FS gave me a cassette of Marathi loksangeet (folk songs). He said that one of the singer's voice in the cassette resembled Siddhu's voice. I left the cassette in the pouch of the car and forgot about it.

One day, while on the Western Express highway, I remembered what Santosh had said and I asked Siddhu to play the cassette. After a few songs, which were all good, there came a song about a shepherd. The moment this song started, Siddhu got visibly excited and pulled the car to the side of the Express highway, rather abruptly. I thought we just missed a fatal accident. "What are you up to Siddhu?" I said, almost shouting.

Siddhu turned to me and said in a chocked voice, "Saheb, this is my song. I recorded this at the HMV (His Masters Voice) studio at Marine Lines, some 10 years ago. They never gave me the cassette but I get every year a money order of Rs.25/- This came as a great surprise to me. I checked the inside cover of the cassette and it did have the name of the singer -- Siddhanath Kolekar and Party. So, Siddhu was an accomplished singer as well.

Siddhu however continued to speak – now recalling his memories. "Saheb, I not only sang but wrote this song. This song is based on a folk tale about a shepherd."

I got curious and asked Siddhu to explain.

"Well the song tells a story about a railway tunnel project in the ghats (mountains) during the British times." He said. "A British engineer was trying to figure out the right alignment of the tunnel that would connect both sides with the minimum excavation/blasting and generation of spoils. He was not able to come up with a good solution. Locals in the area told him that he must speak to the old shepherd who tends sheep on the mountain. Only he will know – most people said. The British engineer met the shepherd and learned from him, how to plan the best tunnel route.The tunnel got built and gave the best result.

The British engineer met the shepherd and learned from him, how to plan the best tunnel route. The tunnel got built and gave the best result. The British engineer was now worried that the credit will also go to the shepherd so he had him arrested and cut off his hands so that he could no longer go up the mountain to tend his sheep. This was done in all possible brutality.

On the day of inauguration, the train left the station from the city with an engine whistling and smoking proudly and catching a good speed to reach the tunnel. As the engine reached the beginning of the tunnel it suddenly stopped. Despite all efforts from the engine driver and the mechanic, the engine would not move.

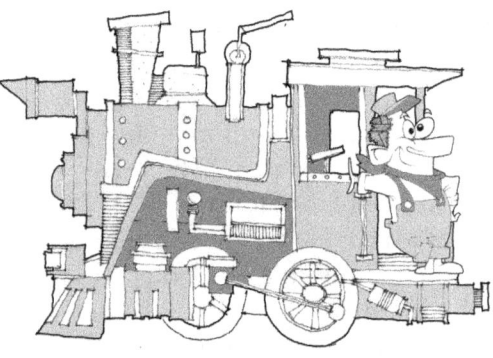

It looked like the engine was in the tears remembering the tragedy of the shepherd. It did not want to cross the tunnel of injustice! The song ends with this touching tale where someone not human cared for the poor human being."

"So you wrote this song Siddhu, about a story to remember and ponder?" I exclaimed. Then in a voice that was still chocked Siddhu said, "Saheb, in this world and in

this city, I see many like the British engineer and many like the shepherd – people innocent and compromised." We did not speak a word in rest of the journey.

One day while accepting his monthly salary, Siddhu declared that now is the time to quit. When asked he reminded me that he had told me when he joined that he will leave me on his own – no questions to be asked. "I want to go to my village and get back to farming." he said.

I let him go as he was clear and firm on his intention to leave.

Many told me later that Siddhu had decided to quit as his eyesight was getting worse due to a cataract. He used to have difficulties in driving me around at night, especially on the Mumbai-Pune expressway. So apparently he left for my safety – knowing that the Sage whom he had met had assured him of his safety but not of the person sitting in the rear seat!

I have not seen Siddhu again.

05

Changing the Course

There is a lovely thick tree growing on the edge of Shivaji Park (Mumbai) that we can see from our apartment.

Early one morning I was sitting out in the balcony, getting ready to check my emails on the laptop. Just then face of Yaksha appeared on the tree!

Yaksha is the name given to a broad class of mostly benevolent nature-spirits, who are caretakers of the Earth's natural treasures. Yakshas occupy trees, groves, forests and water sources.

"Dr. Modak, I thought you had decided to change the course of your life?" I heard Yaksha say to me.

I told Yaksha that I did indeed intend to do so and was very serious about it, but… from tomorrow.

"Well, it doesn't happen that way." Yaksha said "You change now and today."

"For this, you have to listen to the nature, birds and the animals around you. More importantly, you must understand what they think of you and your life. They will always speak the truth and that will be enough to guide you as you assess yourself and accordingly change the course of your life."

"But my dear Yaksha," I smiled and said, "Do you think I know the language of the birds and animals?

The sounds they make are sometimes interesting and sometimes most irritating. Nothing more."

Yaksha said, "As you know, I can converse not just with the birds and animals but also with the trees and the insects. I can lend you my powers for a day, starting from now till 8 pm tonight. Would you like to try this out?"

I thought this proposition to be very interesting and agreed.

The Yaksha said, "Tathastu!" (let it be), gave me his blessing and disappeared.

Soon after, two parrots flew by and perched on the tree. They saw me working on the laptop checking my emails and the male parrot said to his mate, "Look at this fool, I see him every day sitting in this balcony looking at that stupid machine. Don't you think this man should get out of the house and take a nice walk across the park? The sun is just about to rise and there is such a lovely breeze out there. Surely he can work on that contraption later."

I felt like a fool and immediately got out in my track pants, put on a smart T-shirt, wore my brand new Reebok shoes (straight out of the box) and armed with a headset to listen to my favorite Mark Knopfler, I set off for a walk.

The walk was great. I saw few of my old friends – some just waved at me and others actually stopped and asked, "How come you're out walking today? We thought we lost you!" It had been almost a year since I last walked in the park and I realized that even after a gap of a year, the Shivaji Park walkers were the same.

"Phew! These folks seem to be so regular - why can't I be this way?" I said to myself.

My secretary Kermeene called to remind me about a meeting with the Secretary of Environment, Government of Maharashtra at the Sachivalaya, down town. I was an invited member on a Committee for Environmental Clearance of Very Sensitive and Controversial Projects and I considered it to be a quite prestigious honor to be part of this committee.

As I stepped out of my car at the Garden Gate of the Sachivalaya to collect my entry pass, I saw a street dog looking at me as he sat next to a tree.

"Oh my friend, you continue to fall into the same trap over and over again!" said the dog. "The Government invites you on these committees not just because of your good professional credentials, but because they are looking for respectable scapegoats. You feel great as you can proudly advertise this membership on your CV and become known within your professional circles – as someone important and powerful. You get quoted in the newspapers sometimes and get invited to speak at

seminars. But is that worth anything? – Since in most cases decisions are political and are taken apriori. You simply agree and sign up?"

I was certain that the dog on the street was absolutely right and deciding to skip the meeting, asked my driver to take me to one of the by-lanes of the Fort area. Years ago, when I had the time, I used to visit an old/secondhand book seller there and buy a variety of books such as, Yogi in Himalayas or books on face reading. I found the spot but

soon discovered that old man who used to be there selling books and giving all of us good advice was no more. His son had now taken over the business and I told him about my memories of his father (he was really touched) and bought a book titled How to select antique furniture. The book was a bit yellowed but was leather bound and had golden embossed lettering. I didn't haggle for the price, so the son gave me a pocket edition of Around the World in Eighty Days, for free.

"Just for you Sir, keep it! It's a rare one to get" he said.

Book seller on the Street

Meanwhile, my secretary Kermeene, was chasing me, frantically texting, "Meeting with the Overseas Development Corporation (ODC) to start in another 20 minutes at the Taj Chambers."

"Oh, how could I forget," I muttered and asked my driver to take me to the Taj. I was supposed to be there to support my client in securing a long term cheap fund. Key was adherence or compliance to ODC's environmental and social management framework.

As I was about to get into the heritage wing of the Taj Mahal Hotel, a horse carriage loaded with tourists was waiting there. The horse looked at me and neighed (and thanks to the Yaksha, I was able to understand what he was trying to say!).

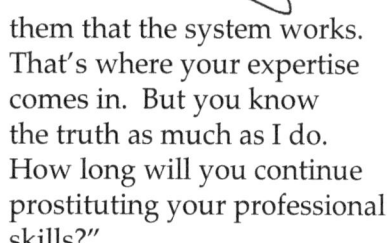

The horse said, "Do you know that the meeting you are about to attend is to assess the environmental and social performance of the company you are a consultant for? You know very well that while the company's top management is fully committed to the environmental and social matters, the executives below are least sensitive, bothered or committed. The ODC is going to ask questions and I know you will elaborately and elegantly argue to convince them that the system works. That's where your expertise comes in. But you know the truth as much as I do. How long will you continue prostituting your professional skills?"

The horse stopped neighing. I didn't like what I heard, especially the last part, but I realized that the horse was right. I was indeed selling my soul to corporate paymasters. I decided to skip the meeting and told Kermeene to say that I was sick and unable to attend.

Instead, I strolled across to Café Mondegar (fondly called as Mondie) - a great place for a draft beer and egg bhurji (akuri) on pav (bread) with Musca (butter). The most interesting part about Mondie is the walls completely covered by cartoons (done by Mario Miranda). As I was picking up a table, I spotted an old buddy of mine who had returned from the US after 30 years. What a great coincidence! Soon we were sharing a table together and chatting about all the fun we used to have. When I asked him what he was up to, he said that he had made enough money now to do as he pleased.

"How about you? You must be well off seeing as how you are loitering around Mondie's in the late afternoon on a working day." He said, as we parted.

I knew I had to be in my office in time to supervise and submit a tender for developing a Green City Action Plan for Nasik. My team at the office had prepared all the documentation and I was to review and sign off on it. As I reached the office, a pigeon sitting the air conditioner saw me and said, "Are you sure you want to submit that bid? These bids are generally pre-decided but I know you have a high chance of getting selected as your company has good credentials. But think about this a bit more – you will never be paid on time and you will be required to bribe the officials to get your money. Also your Action Plan will never be implemented and the reports will be stacked somewhere left to gather dust."

The pigeon was right! I told my team that we still have some time and I wanted to rethink the bid. I got into the car and my driver started driving towards Taj Lands End in Bandra. I was to deliver a valedictory address at the National Environmental Association. As the car was approaching Taj Lands End, I realized the futility of speaking at this event. First, I was scheduled to speak at the very end of the event when there would hardly be any people present; and those who were, would be in a hurry to catch their return flights/ trains. My talk was on one of the interesting perspectives on sustainability (specifically whether recycling was worth the effort?) but I thought the audience may not be interested in anything serious at that time. The talk would be preceded by the usual of welcome flowers and long introduction and would be followed by the President of the Association thanking me profusely saying with the standard pleasantries ("thank you for sparing your valuable time despite your busy schedule etc.")

I noticed we were close to one of the quaint lanes of Bandra that I used to frequent years ago to learn piano from Freddie Braganza. Freddie played music for nobody but himself and was a teacher par

"Cathy, is that you?" I asked. Cathy was Freddie's daughter and many of us had simply adored her not just for her grace and looks but more so for her musical talent and skill on the keyboard. I was very fond of her and after Freddie's piano lessons were over, we used to go for long walks on Carter road holding hands.

So there was Cathy, still stunning even with the slightly white and grey hair. I thought that this added even more grace to her charming personality.

"Oh Prasad, come on in. It has been such a long time." said Cathy.

excellence. I told my driver to take me to his old house – I thought I would meet him for old times' sake. It was already past 7:30 pm.

When I rang the bell in the verandah, a woman in her mid-forties opened the door.

I learnt that Freddie passed away last year and Cathy had been in Lisbon (her Portuguese family connection) for the past 10 years. She had returned with her husband after Freddie's death. Her husband was a ship's Captain who was on-shore and off-shore every three months (at that time, he was away). Cathy still played the piano.

"Let me get you some wine." said Cathy opening the bar chest. Her kitten (Dora) jumped up and settled on the cushion of the cane chair, gazing at me.

We chatted and reminiscing about the old times. "You were quite the flirt with me Prasad." Cathy said jokingly. I am sure I was – And I told her so quite candidly.

It was nearly 8 pm and as I got up to leave I said, "I have to go Cathy, why don't you and I get together one day and play some of the Freddie old tunes."

"Sure" she said as she saw me off at the gate. Her kitten Dora followed us.

I don't know, but I paused at the gate and asked, "Cathy – after all these years, are you really happy?"

I don't think Cathy expected this sort of question. She took a while, gathered herself and said, "Of course I am." In the dim light of the streetlight however, I saw her eyes moisten with tears. "Oh the air pollution these days – it really makes my eyes water. I better go in."

I thought I'd check with Dora but when she did mewed for me, I couldn't understand what she meant. I then realized that it was already past 8 pm and the magical powers bestowed by the Yaksha were gone. Alas! What a pity.

In just one day, I had changed my course of life.

Many of us don't have too many options in life so we live the way others want us to. But some of us lucky ones, should live life differently and if required change the course of life.

SITTING IN THE AIRCRAFT

You can often judge a person based on his or her seat preference on an aircraft. Travelers choosing window seat may do so because they want to be aloof and private and look outside the window during take-off and landing. Some take the window seat because they want to take pictures two thousand feet above the ground and post them on Facebook. Some choose a window seat mainly to work. These are typical business executives who want to work on their laptops without any disturbance so they can finish their PowerPoint presentations before reaching their destination.

Those who choose aisle seat want to stretch their legs in the galley and are the ones who need to visit the loo more often.

Then there are always some perverts who want choose the aisle seat just so their shoulders can brush the female flight attendants who are busy walking up and down. The flight attendants do their best to avoid these aisle seat passengers but it is difficult at times, especially when the travelers consider this lugging as part of the price of the ticket. You see them, pretending to be asleep with their eyes closed and bodies leaning towards the galley, looking like crocodiles.

The passengers in the middle seats are clearly not the frequent travelers. They get stuck with these seats because they did not pre-select their seats. A lot of them don't even know that it is possible to do so. So when they check in late, they get the middle seat and are often uncomfortably squeezed in between passengers who hog the armrests on both sides. The middle seat can be a pain on long haul flights requiring an almost yogi-like mind-set that can accept and endure the situation.

There are some passengers who prefer the first row with extra leg room and the added advantage being able to exit the aircraft quickly. These passengers are served first and can dine with minimum inconvenience. Sometimes, you land up with someone insensitive in the front row who reclines the seat when you are eating, jamming the tray on your stomach. For people with big tummy like me, this is rather irritating and you have to request to the front seat passenger to move, by tapping on the shoulder.

I think the smartest passengers are those who book the emergency row. This row provides the maximum leg room. Also passengers sitting in the emergency row look like the most seasoned and professional of travelers. The only slight pain is that they have to listen to the one minute talk by the flight attendant on emergency procedures and most importantly - how to open the door during emergency! It's a pity that most of the time these passengers don't listen to the instructions.

The seats in today's modern aircrafts can be pretty sophisticated but it takes a while sometimes to figure out what happens when you press a particular button as almost always, something quite the opposite happens, especially while handling the footrest. Then feeling rather foolish, you have to ask the attendants for help - especially when you are trying to make your bed flat. You see experienced business and first class passengers who seem to know everything about the secret of maneuvering the seat into a bed.

The most exciting part of the travel is however the passenger sitting next to you. That person has the potential to make your travel interesting and sometimes even memorable.

I recall I was travelling from Bangkok to Mumbai on Air India. I got into the aircraft, took my seat and was immersed reading the reports I was to review. I didn't even look around and bother to see who was sitting next to me.

I soon realized that many passengers were queuing next to my seat and others kept peeping over to look. I wondered why especially since it was starting to get a bit annoying. I turned to the passenger sitting on the next seat and asked what was happening. The man said, "Indians love cricket." I looked at the passenger again and realized it was Sir Vivian Richards! No wonder he was drawing all that attention.

Sir Richards smiled and said, "You don't seem to be the cricket type."

As we got into a conversation, it so happened that our aircraft engine developed a snag (very typical of Air India!) and we were asked to deplane and move to a hotel. As Sir Vivian Richards and I got into the bus, all passengers stood up and gave him a standing ovation. That was really touching and heartwarming experience! Sir Richards and I were allotted a room to share for the next few hours. As we waited, he educated me on the subject of cricket and did so gladly!

Once on a flight to Delhi, I was in a window seat with an empty aisle seat next to me. Just as the aircraft was about to depart, the last passenger entered. It was Amitabh Bachhan in a white kurta and red tripunda on his forehead. He looked amazing.

He came up to the row I was in and asked in his trademark voice if I would switch seats with him, due to security reasons. I was happy to do so and we switched the seats.

We chatted all through the two hour journey. I gave him a bit of a discourse on the environment and the poor him listened to me attentively and showed a lot of interest. I would like to think that he wasn't using any of his amazing acting talent and was genuinely interested in what I had to say. He was extremely warm, polite and sophisticated.

Speaking of sophistication, I am reminded of my plane ride with Mr. Ratan Tata. I was on a flight from Zurich to Mumbai and was booked on business class. Due to some glitch in the booking procedure, I got upgraded to the first class and found myself seated next to Mr. Ratan Tata. When Mr. Tata asked me what do I do – I answered that I work as an environmental consultant. He exclaimed, "An environmental consultant flying first class? – you must be doing very well?" (Oh how I wish that was true!)

The Swiss airhostess came with a trolley full of rare wines and platters of cheese. I was about to take full advantage of my upgrade and sample some of these wines when Mr. Tata said to the airhostess, "Oh, not for us. Dr. Modak and I are really tired of the wining that goes on in flight and we would much rather have some still water." I was speechless, shocked, annoyed and frustrated but also very impressed with his kind of sophistication.

After half hour, Mr. Tata fell asleep and I promptly called the airhostess and told her that I had changed my mind about the wine! And she obliged – rather generously so.

Another time, I was in the lounge at the Bahrain airport, (headed to Mumbai from Cairo, on Gulf Air) when I saw a very handsome tall person with a lady on a wheelchair. Both were very noticeable and I wondered where they were flying to. I left the lounge early to do some shopping and when I boarded the aircraft, I saw that the man and the lady were already there. I had a window seat and the tall handsome man had a seat right next to me. The lady was sitting in the aisle seat in the middle row.

As soon as I sat down, the man held my hand and said, "Nothing like sitting next to a Doctor – I am so relieved." I was surprised and was about to inform him that I was actually a Doctor of Engineering and not the medical kind. The Man however continued, "I insisted to the Gulf Air staff that we get a seat next to a doctor and they found you in the passenger list. My sister who is sitting next to me is suffering from a brain blood clot. She fell down from a stool while drying clothes and the fall led to a head injury. She now needs an emergency operation and as the Gamma Knife facility is available at the Hinduja Hospital in Mumbai, that's where we are headed."

I understood the gravity of the situation and didn't say anything.

"Doctor, do you think my sister should raise her feet?" the Man asked. I did not know what to say!

"Let her do whatever is comfortable" I muttered and the lady obeyed and raised her feet.

The aircraft took off and we chatted for a while as the Man told me more about the accident. I was simply counting the minutes until we landed in Mumbai, praying that there would be no emergency in-flight.

I tried to sleep but the Man wouldn't let me. "Please Doctor, can you stay awake with me? for my sister?" He urged.

He then said, "I suppose you know who I am". When I said I didn't, he was surprised. "Everyone knows me." he said. "I am Captain Raju."

Captain Raju is one of the most famous and successful Malyali actors in India. I don't speak Malayalam nor do I see any Malyali movies so I had no idea who he was. I later learnt that Captain Raju saw my name on the passenger list as Dr. M. Prasad (not Dr. Prasad Modak) and thought that I was a Malyali too.

We landed in Mumbai without any incident. As I rushed out of the airport, I saw banners of welcome for Captain Raju and hundreds of his fans waiting to catch a glimpse of him.

After this episode, I gave strict instructions to my travel agent to NEVER put my name as Dr. Prasad Modak on my tickets. Prasad Modak was just enough!

07
Travelling Professors

I started working in Mauritius as a Consultant in 1998, working on the modeling of air emissions from the Valentina Industrial Estate.

In 2000, I got an opportunity to teach a few sessions on Cleaner Production to executive students at the University of Mauritius (UoM). The classes would start at 4pm in the afternoon and end by 6pm. After the sessions were done, I used to be dropped by the University car to my favorite hotel Vilas Caroline that was on the beach of flic and flac.

Vilas Caroline was a special place. Its manager, Mrs. Narain, would have an easy chair with a library shelf and a lamp, set up for me on the beach. The library shelf was for books that I had brought with me from Mumbai. I would then settle into the chair during sunset with a blend of Mauritian rum and coke and read books that ordinarily I would never have found time for.

The sound of waves in the background was so soothing that it made the book I was reading inspiring and thought-provoking. A chef would walk up to me at around 8pm to take my order for dinner. Mrs. Narain never presented me a menu – she used to say, "We will cook what you want!" What a luxury offering and understanding of the customer!

One evening as I stepped out of the class and reached the car parking area, I saw that there was an elderly couple already sitting in my car. I paused and thought that there must have been some mistake and started looking around for another car. The man from the car waved and stepped out. He said, "It's your car my friend. I am Professor Allen and this is my wife Joe. Like you, we both teach at the University. Today our car has been taken to the garage for servicing, so may we get a ride to our hotel? We live at a motel close to the Vilas Caroline." He was wearing a beach hat and had a friendly face. We shook hands and I said, "No problem!" and took the front seat next to the driver.

"So Professors Allen and Joe- what do you teach at UoM?" I asked. Joe was quick to respond. "I am French and I teach economics. Allen is British (you could make this out from his accent) and teaches applied mathematics." In a few minutes, I learnt that Allen and Joe had been regulars at UoM for the past 5 years. They would teach graduate students modules that spanned over 3 weeks. These modules fit into the academic requirements of UoM.

"Do you teach only at UoM?" I asked. Allen explained that they taught at a number of universities across the world. "We have selected 6 locations and teach when the weather is the best and there are festivities around that we can enjoy. So, in January; we teach at the Indian Institute of Management in Bangalore; in March we are at the University of Aachen in Germany; then in May in Mauritius followed by teaching at Stanford University in July. We then move to Tokyo University in October and spend November teaching is at Asian Institute of Management in Manila."

This was fascinating. "What about June-August?" I asked, very curious to know.

"We also do some teaching on a cruise. Initially we taught on the Queen Elizabeth 2 but now, we teach sessions on Alaskan Cruise liners and those cruises are in July-August." Allen explained.

"Are people interested in attending classes on a cruise?" I asked.

Joe had an interesting explanation. "We normally pick up a corporate house and teach their top teams. We use case studies to show how economics and applied mathematics could be used for better business planning and analyses. The pedagogy used in these sessions is very innovative and that is our brand. We don't overload our students and usually work in an informal setup. In company of nature, people tend to learn more effectively."

Allen added, "Our son and daughter join the cruise with their spouses. My son-in-law is a Green Chef and sometimes he cooks for our course participants (depending on his moods); our daughter is a Yoga freak and so she takes on some Yoga sessions. Our son works for a newspaper and does a travelogue. His wife is a photographer and both of them usually produce a creative at the end of the journey. Basically, we work and have fun as a family. It is like having an annual get together – and it's fully sponsored!! Also we make lots of new friends"

"Very neat!" I said feeling really envious of the life of these travelling professors. I decided that I should do something similar. Finding six universities shouldn't be too hard.

"But what about preparation of teaching materials Professors- that must be some work for you". Professor Allen smiled "Oh, don't leak this secret to others but let me tell you. The last assignment in our courses is to update our slide decks! The students work rock hard to ensure that all slides are updated with latest statistics, case studies added/ verified and a pen drive is created for us as a submission with most updated resources from the web. We move to the next destination with this output". That was something smart!

I dropped the Professors at their hotel and reached Vilas Caroline. Mrs. Narain was at the reception. "How come you're late today Dr. Modak?" She asked. "Oh nothing, met some new friends." I said. "Please could you get me two shots of rum and coke? I need to introspect about my life a bit more today."

08
Everybody should have an Angioplasty

In 2007, after I suffered a cardiac angina, my cardiologist Dr. Rajani said "Well Dr. Modak, you have a problem but you don't need an angioplasty right now as it is not an emergency. However, if you are not going to change your lifestyle, then I would recommend the angioplasty. It will cost you a day's stay at Hinduja Hospital and I will operate on you myself using this new method called "radial artery access." I agreed to the procedure as I knew I won't be changing my lifestyle just for the sake of my heart!"

The surgery was performed the very next day and I was wheeled into the Operation Theater (OT) early in the morning. There were stories floating around the surgical floor about how something went wrong with a patient's angioplasty while ballooning and how the stent did not work and how eventually, an emergency by-pass surgery had to be performed. My wife and children waited outside the OT – anxious and tensed!

On entering the OT, I realized that ultimately, I have to face the reality of life all by myself. I would have to go through these crucial moments all alone without my wife and children. As the great realization dawned on me and it changed my outlook on life.

I actually enjoyed the angioplasty procedure. It gave me terrific exposure to some cutting-edge technology and I was simply amazed! Dr. Rajani and his team had a great sense of humor and it was nice chatting with them. The anesthetist asked me some stupid questions and the needle got in from my wrist without any pain. The stent was placed 10 minutes after ballooning and the whole thing was over in just 25 minutes.

"You are all set for the next 8 years." Dr. Rajani told me. "We can put another stent in later, if required."

I got home and a number of my friends came by to see me. Then I got a call from my good friend Surya Chandak who was working with UNEP in Osaka (Japan). He had undergone two angioplasties and one by-pass surgery. Quite the seasoned veteran, he "welcomed" me to the club and ended our phone conversation with some advice, "Prasad, from now onwards listen to your body. Do exactly what your body tells you."

I decided to follow his advice but as I thought about it, I realized that I should also do what my mind tells me and not just my body.

For years now, I have been a circular face person (I recommend you read the subject of psycho-geometrics if you are interested in knowing about the shapes of the faces). I have never been outspoken and have always tried to adjust and be as friendly and considerate as possible. After the angioplasty reaffirmed the fact that I wasn't going to live forever and I decided to speak my mind more often and not waste time trying always to be proper and diplomatic.

So I started speaking my mind -- I would now honestly tell a student that their presentation was "rubbish" within the first five minutes, rather than sit through it for an hour! When chairing sessions in conferences, I would now stop the speaker bluntly and ring the bell without hesitating if he/she had overshot the allotted time, irrespective of the person's title, position or seniority. Even while negotiating projects and consultancy fees with clients (who were nasty, petty or mostly just fat headed), I would simply get up and walk out saying, "Not interested!"

I bought two large (A2 size) sheets of paper and on one sheet I wrote in bold letters, "WHAT I LIKE" and on the other sheet, I wrote "WHAT I DON'T LIKE." I made copies of both sheets and put them up on a wall at home and at my office to serve as a constant reminder to me and others. Trust me when I tell you that this was NOT easy. In fact I recommend you try it for yourself.

Through the publication of these sheets, I now stood tall -- frank and fearless! Consequently life got simplified.

So many times in our life we suppress our emotions, don't express our aspirations clearly. We don't vent our thoughts and feelings (both positive and negative). Often out of sheer politeness or some misguided notion of "being well behaved", we stay silent or don't act. We simply don't allow ourselves to live free. Then later we repent and are full of regret when we say things like, "Wish I had…" or "Wish I did…"

But by then, it is almost always, too late!

However, despite my angioplasty and the life changing realizations it brought on, I still wasn't able to reach the highest stage of free expression, courage and outspokenness.

To elaborate, some forty odd years ago, I had written a silly letter of adoration to a classmate who had charmed me immensely. But as she had chosen to marry someone else and had been living happily ever since, I always believed that she had junked my letter and forgotten all about it.

Very recently and to my great surprise, she sent me a scanned copy of this very letter asking whether I still remembered this mischief.

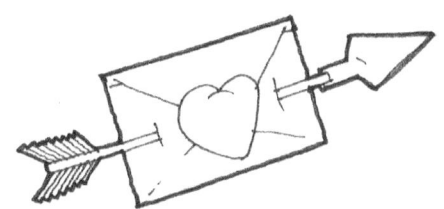

She had preserved that letter! I felt like calling to ask her why? -- Was it just something she never ended up throwing away, or did she actually treasure it as a fond memory? But I did not have courage to go through with the call and remained silent.

I told Dr. Rajani that angioplasty was not that very effective. He said jokingly that the next time he would place a new chemical stent in my heart and that (with all its chemicals) would work its magic and take me to the final stage of courage and Nirvana!

My eight years of angioplasty are just over – may be time for that stent.

I was in Stockholm a few months ago for a conference and I took a walk with an old friend of mine - a Swedish Professor. We had been friends for years. It was early morning near the port where we were walking and the sun was rising and there was a cool breeze all around. The weather was lovely and as we were walking, a Swedish girl, in her mid-twenties and wearing shorts, came jogging towards us.

"Oh hello Professor, so good to see you after such a long time." she said, stopping to greet us. She was a former PhD student of the professor's.

The professor hugged her and then holding her firmly in his arms, gave her a deep kiss. The girl was shocked! This was a long serious kiss signifying more than just a student–teacher relationship. I wished someone was around to play some music, preferably on a violin so as to complete the moment. But all I could do was stand there dazed, waiting.

When they were done, they exchanged a few words warmly in Swedish and then the girl left.

I couldn't resist but ask my friend, "When did you have your angioplasty?"

Now it was his turn to be surprised. "How did you know?" He asked, quite taken aback.

I only smilcd.

09

The National Anthem, Me and Cleaner Production

I got into the "business of Cleaner Production" in 1989 courtesy my good old friend Fritz Balkau at the UNEP, Industry and Environment office in Paris. I had just completed a short book on Low or Non Waste Technologies (LNWT) for Friedrich-Ebert-Stiftung (FES). Stephen Paulus at FES had coaxed me to take on this project to assess the penetration of LNWT in Indian industries. This book made the case for environmental protection through the practice of pollution prevention keeping in mind the business angle. It cited examples from 100 odd Indian industries where innovative approaches were used and since this was new information for many of the industries, it excited the readers.

Fritz had read my book on LNWT and he invited me to Paris for a workshop. That one invite opened new vistas for me on Cleaner Production.

Cleaner Production (CP) became a "fizz" phrase in the 1990s. A bunch of us at the office of UNEP in Paris had coined this term during one of our late evening work sessions. Don Huisingh had been the facilitator of this session and Jacqueline Aloisi de Larderel, the Director. Don is still very active, just retired as the editor of the Journal of Cleaner Production. We are in touch.

Jacqueline was a phenomenal visionary and a strong leader. She steered the era of CP and is due a lot of credit and kudos for bringing in a change in the environmental profession.

The Cleaner Production program of UNEP caused ripples all over the world. Programs like WBCSD's Eco-efficiency and APOs Green Productivity etc. followed later and tried create their own identity and niche but could not compete with the all-inclusive and ever-expanding concept of CP.

Several high-level seminars on CP were conducted on a bi-annual basis starting from Canterbury, Paris, Warsaw, Melbourne, Prague etc. I was one of the regular speakers on the CP Seminar circuit and this gave me an opportunity to make a lot of personal and professional contacts and network across the world.

Thailand, Egypt, Indonesia, Bangladesh, Mauritius and Vietnam were the few countries where I worked extensively on CP. In these countries, I had an opportunity to work at policy as well as practice levels (demonstration projects) and run training programs for capacity building. The period between 1996 and 2008 was a golden period for me – a chance to do something innovative, demonstrative and impactful in the area of CP.

The Cleaner Production Project in Thailand was at Samutprakarn, one of the highly industrialized clusters near Bangkok and was funded by the Asian Development Bank (ADB). It was captioned as 20/20 (targeting 20% water use reduction and 20% energy consumption reduction). In Egypt, I worked on a project called SEAM - Support for Environmental Assessment and Management, which was financed by the CP division of DFID, UK. The SEAM program ran over six years and resulted in several key publications. In Indonesia, I worked on a project called ProduksiH Bersih (means Cleaner Production in Bahasa) that was funded by the German Government. I would travel to all these countries at regular intervals and typically spend a week there, engaged mostly in field work.

I was also involved in most of the CP activities in India. These were led by the National Cleaner Production Centre (NCPC) of India's National Productivity Council (NPC). Operation of Waste Minimization Circles (WMC) was one of the very unique and interesting programs carried out by the NPC. I participated in the evaluation of WMCs on behalf of the World Bank who had partially financed the WMCs under their Industrial Pollution Prevention Project.

The frequent travelling was tiring but back then I had a motto — "Don't just travel for work; go a day early and stay two more days (if possible). Get a feel of the place, relax, make new friends and plan the next visit that would not involve work. Spend the money you earn and pamper yourself. After all, you only live once."

I didn't often follow this motto, at least not during my initial travel – but as I grew older and wiser, I began following it diligently… and it worked!

I love listening to live music, especially jazz. Therefore, on most (if not all) trips, I would spend my free evenings at jazz clubs. After a long and tiring day at work, spending time exploring these musical havens was exciting and very refreshing.

I never missed the opportunity to visit any of the great music pubs or jazz clubs that I had heard of. The places I used to frequent were Minh's Jazz in Hanoi, Nui's Blue Jazz in Bangkok, the Cairo Jazz Club and the Jaya Pub in Jakarta. Top of this list was the legendary jazz club Duc des Lombards in Paris. One day I would love to write at length about the experiences and encounters I have had at these great places.

But let me return to the subject of Cleaner Production.

I liked the idea of setting targets for a Cleaner Production program such as 20/20. In Egypt, we worked with Micro Small and Medium size industries and much of this work was to help protect the industries towards maintaining their exports meeting the market regulations. We helped sectors such as textiles where the exports had been impacted by international standards and requirements such as Eco labels (Oeko-Tex) from the markets in EU and Americas. The cheese making industries were also losing out in exports to Saudi Arabia due to their excessive use of salt in the cheese making process. In Indonesia, we promoted Cleaner Production in locations such as Jakarta, Bandung and Semarang and implemented demonstration projects with facilitation through Cleaner Production Counseling Clubs. This idea was very similar to the WMCs in India.

I had opportunities to revisit countries where I worked earlier and see the impact and sustainability of the various CP programs. In most cases, including India, I found that the results were dismal and very discouraging. There

55

was hardly any replication of the CP demonstration projects. Furthermore, capacity building of CP professionals was not taken up on a national scale and on a programmatic basis. The activities lasted only till the donor assistance was available and there was no local or national ownership.

I was expecting CP to get spread into practice on its own as it made a good business case. Instead, I noticed that subsidies and concessional loans were offered to make CP happen! That was strange. Economic benefits should in fact have been the principal drivers for CP – the environmental and social benefits were meant to be the icing on the cake! It is still puzzling as to why the industry does not take the path of simultaneously improving productivity and achieving environmental protection.

Few years ago, I was working on CP in Bangladesh and I visited a textile processing unit near Fatulah, on the outskirts of Dhaka. The owner of the factory showed me all the departments and explained the various water and energy efficiency measures undertaken – right from housekeeping, recycling, process and chemical change etc. These measures,

undertaken as a "system" were very impressive. I asked the owner what made him implement these projects and was I was expecting him to answer, "Because of the economic benefits."

So imagine my surprise (actually it was more of a shock) when the owner simply said, "I did this for my country!" I never expected such an answer. I was to speak on Cleaner Production at the Dhaka Chamber of Commerce the next day and I requested the owner of the textile factory to join me there and show a few slides on the CP projects that he implemented and tell the people present why he implemented the projects. He agreed to my request.

The next day I was at the Dhaka Chamber of Commerce ready to speak to some 50 participants, representing various industries. After my talk on CP, I asked the owner to give his short presentation and when he finished, I asked him, "Please tell us why you implemented these projects" and he answered in Bangla, "for my country."

The audience sat in stunned silence. Then a man sitting in the front row got up and spoke in low tone, "Amar sonar Bangla, Ami tomay bhalôbashi…"

He was singing the National Anthem of Bangladesh.

Then another man, this time from the third row got up and soon more men in the hall started standing up and joining in and within minutes, all the 50 participants were standing and proudly singing the national anthem.

This was simply a hair-raising experience for me and I was overwhelmed witnessing this outburst of emotions.

This matters for paradigm shifts in the concepts such as like CP.

There has to be something much more than material benefits that drive this change – something closer to the heart, in the interest of the country and towards the good of the world.

If more people thought and acted like the owner of the textile factory in Fatulah, the world we live today would be a very different (and an even better) place!

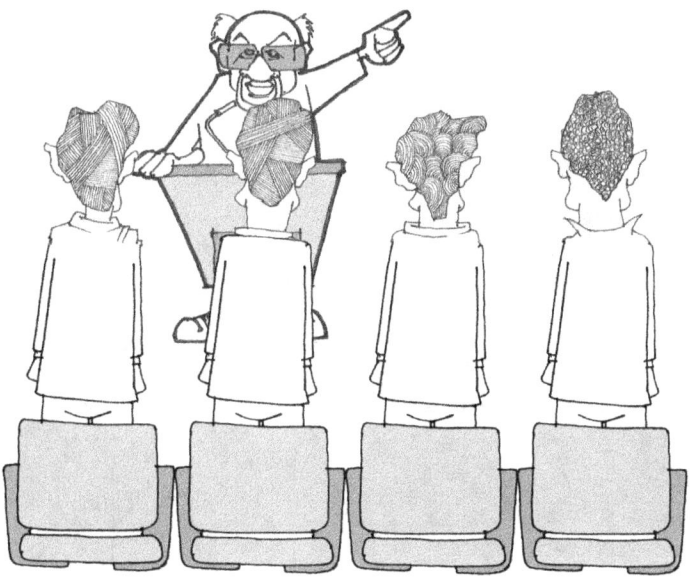

As I returned to my hotel after the meeting, I got thinking and realized that economic reasons cannot be the only drivers for bringing in the change – especially when we are aiming for changes in the behavior, practices and investments.

10

This post shares some of my experiences from the job interviews I attended at the start of my career. I hope it will be of interest to the new generation of young professionals as they embark on their own job hunt. It is a little long post, but I hope you enjoy the narration.

It was November, 1980 and I was about to complete my Master's degree in Environmental Science and Engineering at the Indian Institute of Technology (IIT), Bombay. I decided that it was time to start my job search.

Now, my father, a Public Health Engineer who had built several water and sewage treatment plants across the country, had a very low opinion of the IIT Professors. He used to say that all you end up getting there is a degree from the IIT brand and a great life lesson from the hostel experience, but no understanding related to practice and the "real" technology. He used to

have a good laugh when I used to tell him that I will design an Activated Sludge Sewage Treatment Plant with Lawrence-McCarty equations and optimize the size of the treatment plant using Dynamic Programming.

So when I went to my father for job advice, he suggested I go talk to S. P. Unwala of Candy Filters (Patterson Candy) or R. Natarajan of Dorr Oliver (Hindustan Dorr Oliver).

S. P. Unwala was one of the top experts in the field of Water Treatment and especially knowledgeable about Declining Rate Filters.

I met him at his office at Mahalaxmi Chambers.

"So, you are M. V. Modak's son and N V Modak's (NVM) nephew?" said Unawala.

N. V. Modak, my uncle was famous for building the Vaitarana Dam– now called the Modak Sagar, which supplies water to the city of Mumbai. NVM also founded the National Environmental Engineering Research Institute or NEERI.

"You have the job and I will personally coach you." Unwala continued.

I didn't like his mentioning the family connection and handed him a copy of my Masters dissertation titled "Optimal Design of Wastewater Treatment Plants under Uncertainty." I was very proud of my work and politely requested Mr. Unawala to take a look at it.

S. P. Unwala smiled at me and said, "It's not really relevant. By the way, your salary will be Rs. 750 a month. You are a special case as we usually pay Rs. 700. Let me know when you can start work?"

The interview ended but I was not very happy with the salary that was offered.

I decided to meet R. Natarajan at Hindustan Dorr Oliver (HDO) and when I asked him for an appointment, through his secretary Wilma, he said, "So you are M. V. Modak's son right? Come on Tuesday, next week and we will conduct all your interviews."

"Sir, will there be more than one interview?" I asked, getting worried.

"Of course! There will be several. At HDO, we are very selective." said Mr. Natarajan.

I liked this method better in comparison to the 5 minute chat I had with Mr. S. P. Unwala. "This company is serious about their recruitment!" I thought to myself.

R. Natarajan was busy when I went to see him on Tuesday. In fact, he had completely forgotten that he was scheduled to interview me.

Turning a few pages of my dissertation he said with a friendly grin, "Well, I don't want to get into the details but I hope you know how to size?"

Just as I was about to tell him the formulae I would use to size, he interrupted me by showing me the HDO catalogue of aerator selection.

"Modak, this is how you would size a surface aerator!" he snapped.

When I joined HDO, I learnt

that Natarajan was a well-known marketing genius. He could sell an aerator without blades and convince the client that blades are moving so fast that they could not see them!

I learnt a lot of marketing tricks from this warm, friendly and amazingly talented person who sadly is no longer with us.

"Well Modak, I am kind of busy right now so let me take you to S. R. Kotwal of the Sugar Division." said Natarajan as he ushered me to another cabin where sat a short, fair and handsome person wearing a grey suit.

"Boss Kotwal, here is the candidate I was telling you about. Will you please deal with him?" And with that brief introduction, Natarajan disappeared.

I wondered what could the Head of HDO's Sugar division possibly ask me about wastewater treatment and why was I being interviewed by a sugar specialist?

To my surprise, Mr. Kotwal began asking me a series of very detailed and technical questions. He also talked about the fundamentals of anaerobiosis; the impact of wastewater toxicity on methane generation; the typical gas yields and the economics of anaerobic digestion, etc.

After an hour of questions and detailed discussion, he seemed to be satisfied. "Your next interview is on the second floor with our Marketing Director, K. P. Mohandas (KPM) Rao. All the best!" concluded Mr. Kotwal as he asked his secretary to show me to KPM's cabin.

KPM Rao was a smart, savvy person with a vibrant personality who wore trendy half spectacles, and spoke with an American accent.

I sat in the chair in front of KPM and he started speaking about the environmental pollution control market in India. He then went on to tell me about HDO's market share and how their equipment and process technology was distinctly superior to that of their competitors. This long discourse went on for over 10 minutes.

Suddenly he stopped talking and stared at me with disappointment. Picking up the phone he buzzed Natarajan and said, "Who is this dumb guy that you sent to me? For the last 10 minutes, I have been speaking to him  and not once has he interrupted me. How will this guy be able to market HDO? Please don't send me such raw stuff again!"

As he slammed the phone down, he looked at me through his half spectacles as one would an insignificant insect and said, "You have a long way to go my friend. For now, go and meet TRK."

T. R. Krishna Rao (TRK) was the Managing Director of HDO - very smart, intelligent and a terror to everybody. I went to his office and told his secretary that Mr. K. P. Mohandas Rao has asked me to meet Mr. T. R. Krishna Rao. The secretary was eating a sandwich and she told me to push the door and go through.

TRK's cabin was really cold and there, with his feet on the table wearing shiny black shoes like the ones you would see any Prem Chopra or Ajit movie, wearing an expensive tie was the

man himself, busy on an international phone call.

"No, I am not selling my clarifloculators to Cairo and I don't like the price offered." He growled, almost shouting at the person on the other end of the line. The call continued for 5 minutes and I waited, standing in the cold, holding on to a copy of my dissertation.

When he finished, TRK slammed down the phone receiver and looking towards me said, "Who the hell are you? And how did you get into my cabin without an appointment?"

I was taken aback but told him that I had completed an interview with KPM and had been instructed me to meet him. I also told him that his secretary had asked me to go into the cabin.

TRK frowned and I watched boiling with anger "If my Secretary tells you to jump from this window, will you jump?"

Speechless once again, I didn't know what to say or how to react.

"I am the MD of HDO and I don't interview kids like you." He said sternly. "Anyway, I give you 2 minutes. Go ahead, market yourself."

In the two minutes that followed, I spoke about myself as much I could, as fast as I could but completely forgot to mention that my Master's dissertation was on Optimal Design of Wastewater Treatment Plants under Uncertainty.

TRK was listening. "Have you finished?" He said sarcastically in a tone that I did not like.

"Well, its Natarajan's business whether to hire you or not but as you stand in front of me today, you are of no value to us. I don't think HDO should pay you any salary for the first three months. In fact, we should ask you to pay us as you know nothing and will spend your time here learning and training."

"And now, my Secretary will show you the way out."

I turned to see the secretary, who had been standing behind me all this time, give me a devilish grin.

I was appointed by HDO the very next week and was to receive a salary of Rs. 800 – the extra money was so I would not accept S. P. Unwala's offer!

S. P. Unwala was extremely unhappy with my short

sightedness.

"Wearing a tie and selling equipment – is that what you want to do?" he asked.

In the years that followed, I worked closely with Unwala at the Indian Water Works Association (IWWA). Though he is with us no more, his articulate nature and great sense of (Parsi) humor will never be forgotten.

I also learnt later on that my father and TRK were close friends and that TRK was well aware that I was to meet him for an interview that day. In fact, he called my father that same night after the interview saying that he had messed with me simply break my IIT ego. He promised my father that HDO would groom me well and teach me technology, commercials and the practice of my chosen profession! And HDO indeed did do just that.

During my tenure at the HDO, I managed to sell two 50HP High Speed Floating Aerators. This was HDOs first sale in India. Getting this deal was very important in order to get pre-qualified for the bid on aerated lagoons of the Municipal Corporation of Greater Mumbai (MCGM) as the project required more than 100 such aerators. As a part of this deal, I had to put together all the skills such as aggressive marketing, using "knowledge" or technicalities judiciously, do price negotiations and finally use the "influence". After the deal was done, TRK called me to his cabin and told me how happy he was to see my transformation. My salary was doubled to Rs.1600.

Within 8 months at HDO, I was feeling restless. Marketing as a career did not interest me. Once again, I spoke to my father and he suggested a move to consulting (engineering) career. He asked me to meet S. V. Natu, Retired Chief Engineer of Irrigation at the Government of Maharashtra. Mr. Natu was working as a Consultant with

Shah Technical Consultants (STC) post his retirement. STC was the design consultant for water supply and sewerage systems project for six townships outside Mumbai city and 104 villages. The project had received loan from the World Bank and so all Bank procedures were to be followed, especially on the procurement. Mr. Natu asked me to meet the MD of STC, a Mr. Mahavir Shah (MS).

My colleague Shirish Naik, who was working with Dr. Deepak Kantawala's consulting firm at the time, was also looking for a job change. Both of us contacted Mr. Shah for an appointment to get interviewed and thanks to a good word from Mr. Natu, we were called for the interview right away.

Before the interview, Shirish and I discussed the salary package that we should be asking for. Since both our salaries were around Rs.1600, we decided to ask Rs.1800 and stay absolutely firm on it.

MS called both of us to his cabin. No technical questions were asked and we just had a general talk. We did not get a chance to show off our talent, knowledge or experience!

"The last thing left now is fixing your salaries." said MS in his typical soft and calm voice. He opened his desk drawer and took out two blank pieces of paper. Passing them on to both of us he said, "Just put down the number you will be happy with."

This was a strange move but we knew what to write and both of us "Rs.1800" and handed the papers back to MS.

We held our breath preparing for the salary negotiation as MS took a look at the numbers. He then pulled out his pen and scratched out the numbers we had written and wrote 2000 and passed the papers back to us.

 With a warm smile on his face, he said, "First learn to understand your market value. You underrated yourselves. You deserve to get more than what you are asking for."

We were sold! By offering the additional Rs. 200, Mr. Shah had won us over. We gave our best to STC during our tenure there and I will never forget the lessons learnt from MS's strategic countermove during our salary negotiations!

At STC, we were put on multiple and varied tasks. We used to be in the field for two days a week, with the Team of surveyors laying the L-sections of the sewers and scouting sites for the water reservoirs. Two days each week would then be spent with the British consultants from John Taylors, working on tender documents for the sewage treatment plants and pumping stations. For the remaining two days, we worked on the DEC-10 Main Frame computer at Tata Institute of Fundamental Research (TIFR), carrying out computer based simulations of water distribution networks (using A. G. Fowler's well-known FLOW program) and preparing bills of quantities and drawings. This required working closely with the draftsmen so turned out to be a great learning opportunity.

One day MS called me to his cabin and told me to start working on the design and tender document for the 310 MLD raw water pumping station at Shahad on the outskirts of Kalyan. While handing over a big stack of documents and a roll of ammonia print drawings, he said "Modak, you have just 3 weeks to complete all this work."

I had absolutely no idea as to how to design pumping

stations of this sort and size. While going home, I stopped by the bookshop from where I used to buy technical books and purchased the famous Pump Handbook by Karassik.

Next week, I visited the office of a Mr. Iyer, who looked after Vertical Turbine pumps at Voltas. I knew Iyer from my HDO days and thought him to be the appropriate choice. I also met some seniors of the Municipal Corporation of Greater Mumbai (MCGM) and visited some of the operating pumping stations. Everyone was very helpful. And I worked very hard on all the days including the weekends.

Exactly 3 weeks later, I walked into MS's cabin with all my outputs. One Mr. Dawyer from Jon Taylors of the UK was sitting there and MS made the introductions.

"Meet Mr. Modak, he is our Mechanical Engineer. He has just completed the first cut design, drawings and draft tender documents for the 310 MLD Shahad Raw Water Pumping Station. Please review".

I did not know what to say and as soon as Dawyer had walked out of MS's cabin with my outputs, I spoke. "Sir, you know I am not a Mechanical Engineer. I am a Civil Engineer"

There complete silence in the room and MS got out of his chair as if he gotten an electric shock!

"But after your interview I assumed you were a mechanical engineer." He said in a tone that was very unlike his usual calm manner. I could see some panic and discomfort on this face when he said, "Modak, when I asked you to do this job, you should have told me that doing a pumping station is not your cup of tea."

Looking back now, I feel that MS was absolutely right.

Next week, Dawyer returned to the STC's office and I was called to MS's cabin.

"Good work Modak!" said Dawyer. "I think we are pretty close to the final version. Looks like you have designed pumping stations such as these before."

He winked and patted me on my back. MS smiled.

As I was leaving for home that day, MS offered me a lift in his car. He was obviously very happy. "I like that you love to take on challenges Modak. Do keep it up – but cautiously." He said, presenting me with an expensive pen as a token of appreciation. I still have that pen as a treasured memento.

My third and last interview

was at IIT Bombay for the position of Lecturer at the Centre for Environmental Science and Engineering. The interview panel consisted of 8 experts who bombarded me with several questions. Most of the questions were irrelevant and were more for the panelist to show off what they knew. I was just a kid in front of these experts but I kept my cool and gave the interview my best shot.

Towards the end of the interview, one of the Professors (TK Ghosh of IIT Delhi) pointed out that I had only 2 years of experience instead of the prerequisite 3 years.

"Dr. Modak, do you have anything to say?" asked Director A. K. De.

I took a few seconds before speaking in a calm and firm voice, "Sir, are you looking for Integer number of years of experience or the Real number of years of experience? Because I can assure you that in my two integer years of experience, I have managed acquired four real years of experience. There may be applicants here with six of integer years of experience for instance but that may amount to two years of real experience."

Director De smiled and all the other panelists, including Prof TK Ghosh remained silent.

In one week, I was appointed as a Lecturer at IIT Bombay. I also received a counter offer of interest from IIT Delhi – courtesy Professor TK Ghosh. He had simply loved my response on integer and real years of experience.

After these three interviews, I never got interviewed again as I became an entrepreneur and corporate head myself. Today, each time when I take interviews, especially of the youngsters and first time jobseekers, I still recall my three interviews. And I get amused as I see some form of "Prasad Modak" in these youngsters – but of course in a different form and style!

11

For the past few years I have been organizing a Career Counseling event called Disha (means direction or guidance in Sanskrit) for the interest of students and young entrepreneurs[5].

I was very keen to have my Professor friend to speak at a Disha event but he was simply not available. Finally, due to my persistent coaxing, he agreed to join us.

In Disha, we conduct an interactive session where we ask the students the question - "What do they want to be?" I thought that getting the Professor to moderate this session would make a big difference in the interest of the students.

When we went to the auditorium, it was already packed with students. I went to the dais and introduced the Professor. His bio-data was 10 pages long and I had difficulty condensing it down to 2 minutes. But the students looked impressed.

Professor thanked me for the invitation and then spoke a few words on how important it is to decide what you want to be in the early phase of life. He then proposed that the session should be run in an interactive manner. Everyone agreed.

He asked a girl, sitting in the fourth row wearing spectacles, "So what do you want to be?" The girl stood up and said, "I want to be like Wangari Maathai or like Vandada Shiva or Kate Stohr or Safia Minney. I am really inspired with the great humanitarian work they have done and shown leadership."

---

5   See Disha at http://ekonnect.net/index.php/our-programs/eko-hub/disha for more details

Professor took a deep puff from his cigar and said, "That's not the right choice. All these women have done is essentially PR work -- they have sought publicity with no measurable impact and have in fact created obstacles in the development pathways. I suggest you rethink your life goals and dream of becoming like Kiran Shaw Muzumdar or Naina Lal Kidwai who are shining examples of women guiding India's business – with (apparent) interest in sustainability through the application of biotechnology or sustainable finance."

I had reservations on what Professor said. So I pointed out that Wangari Maathai was a woman of many firsts: not only was she the first African woman and first environmentalist to bring home a Nobel Peace Prize but she was also the front woman of the United Nations Billion Tree Campaign. Vandana Shiva too had always been an outspoken campaigner for

protecting seed biodiversity against biotech-profiteering and genetic engineering. Her grassroots approach helped to redefine food security and the green revolution as a movement that empowers local food growers, rather than big agribusiness. She was the founder of Navdanya, a NGO based in Dehradun, India which promotes organic farming and seed-saving. Kate Stohr worked hard to provide disaster relief and reconstruction services during the Hurricane Katrina and Southeast Asian tsunami crises. In 2005, her organization won the TED Prize which allowed them to develop "The Open Architecture Network", a unique open source platform for sharing sustainable and humanitarian design solutions. Safia Minney, as one of the world's foremost social entrepreneurs, established World Fair Trade Day (observed every second Saturday of May). Her work strives to change the fashion business by addressing integral issues of fair wages, gender equity, transparency, accountability, capacity building, improved working conditions and environmentally sound practices. These women were all definitely fine role models with noteworthy careers.

The Professor did not like my intervention.

He turned to the boy sitting in the last row with a full white shirt and a red tie. "How about you Sir?" He asked in all politeness.

The boy answered, "Well, I am an engineer and want to study more and complete a Doctoral degree from a reputed University in the United States. Then I want to be a Practicing Professor like Prof. S. J. Arceivala of India or Prof. W W. Eckenfelder of the United States or Professor Ryoichi Yamamoto of Japan."

"Well, let me be honest with you then," said the Professor. "All these Professors you mentioned were or are essentially undercover consultants. Indeed, they are excellent in the class rooms, or at writing books etc. but half of their energies are or were directed in grabbing consulting projects or running consulting outfits (sometimes remotely) while taking shelter at the universities or international bodies."

Not liking the Professor's caustic remarks on these outstanding academians, I said, "That's not true. Professors must get into consulting to give their students some real-world perspective. Professor Ryoichi Yamamoto is the Professor at the Institute of Industrial Science, University of Tokyo and a highly respected expert in environmentally conscious materials and design, as well as in Life-Cycle Assessment. He is currently the Science Advisor for the Ministry of Education, Culture, Sports, and Science and Technology, the President of The Institute of Life Cycle Assessment Japan, the President of The Eco-Efficient Forum of Japan, the President of International Green Procurement Network and a member of steering committee of Eco Products Exhibition. His talks in the class room are therefore laced with his rich policy experience.

Professor Eckenfelder was known internationally as a pioneer in the field of water treatment and a leading authority in industrial wastewater management.

He was an environmental engineering professor at Manhattan College, the University of Texas-Austin, and Vanderbilt University. Eckenfelder was a prolific writer and he influenced countless numbers of engineers through his many textbooks, hundreds of journal articles and of course his teaching. Among Eckenfelder's more than 30 technical books, his second book, Industrial Water Pollution Control published by McGraw-Hill, is a classic text initially intended for the classroom. Eckenfelder was the founding principal of several companies, including AWARE, Inc. in Nashville, Tennessee, which was later named Eckenfelder, Inc. in his honor. In 1998 AWARE merged with Brown and Caldwell, a California-based full-service environmental engineering firm.

Professor at Veermata Jijabai Technical Institute (VJTI) in Mumbai. He then became the Director of National Environmental Engineering Research Institute, Nagpur and finally an Advisor at the World Health Organization (WHO). He established and successfully operated the Associated Industrial Consultants (AIC) in Mumbai (the firm was later acquired by Montgomery Watson). Prof Arcievala published several classic books on wastewater treatment, water reuse and natural wastewater treatment systems where case studies have come from his practice experience."

My Professor friend did not pay much attention to my defense of these distinguished professors/consultants and continued his questioning. He now asked a student sitting in the front row who was holding an iPad in his hand. He seemed to be googling the personalities that were being mentioned. "How about you?"

After his studies at the Harvard University, Professor Soli Arceivala was

Professor asked him.

The student got up from his seat holding his iPad, put on his spectacles, took some time and said in a very thoughtful voice, "I believe that you cannot mainstream sustainability unless you sit at the top of the organization or at least hold an anchor position and shake up or inspire the system. I want to be Anand Mahindra of Mahindra & Mahindra or Jochen Zeitz of Puma."

The Professor laughed. "It's strange how you young minds don't see the chameleons in the business. All these names you mentioned are actually businessmen focusing on making profits and somehow getting to the top of the markets. Sustainability is just a clever strategy that they discovered and they were smart to project it and claim that sustainability is now in the DNA of their organizations. Go and ask folks working for them – you will see a totally different picture."

I thought that Professor was being very negative, biased and downright judgmental. The poor iPad holding student sat down in despair. I butted in immediately and said, "Friends, let me tell you a bit about Jochen Zeitz. He began

his professional career with Colgate-Palmolive in New York and Hamburg and later joined PUMA in 1990. In 1993 he was appointed Chairman and CEO of PUMA becoming the youngest CEO in German history to head a public company at the age of 30.

Zeitz managed to turn PUMA from a low priced, undesirable brand into one of the top 3 brands in the sporting goods industry. In 2008 he introduced PUMAVision, an ethical framework defined by the four key principles of being Fair, Honest, Positive and Creative as applied to all professional behavior, business procedures and relationships throughout and outside of PUMA.

Zeitz also conceived the Environmental Profit & Loss Account (E P&L) and coined the term and in May 2011 he announced PUMA's Environmental Profit & Loss Account that puts a monetary value to a businesses use of ecosystem services across the entire supply chain. In 2008 he founded the not-for-profit Zeitz Foundation of Intercultural Ecosphere Safety to support creative and innovative sustainable projects and solutions that balance conservation, community development, culture, and commerce (the "4Cs") in a quadruple bottom line approach, promoting an inclusive, holistic paradigm of conservation that enhances livelihoods and fosters intercultural dialogue while building sustainable businesses.

Zeitz has received the Strategist of the Year three times from the Financial Times Entrepreneur of the Year, Trendsetter of the Year and Best of European Business Award 2006. In 2010, the German Sustainability Foundation gave Zeitz an award for Germany's most sustainable future strategies. In 2015 Jochen Zeitz was awarded the Special Advocacy Award for Responsible Capitalism."

"Anand Mahindra is included by Fortune Magazine among the World's 50 Greatest Leaders and featured in the magazine's 2011 listing of Asia's 25 most powerful business people." I continued. "Anand is a staunch advocate of promoting girl child education and in 1996, founded Project Nanhi Kali, which provides sponsorship to underprivileged girls across India including, material support (e.g. school uniforms, school bag, shoes, socks, stationery etc.).

A student of the arts and culture, Anand believes that study of the humanities is essential in shaping leaders of the future. In November 2010, he donated $10million to support the Harvard Humanities Center in honor of his mother, Indira Mahindra. It is the largest gift for the study of humanities in Harvard's history.

Anand is co-founder of Naandi Danone, which is the largest safe drinking water provider to rural areas of India, catering to nearly 3 million customers. Founded in

1998, the Naandi Foundation works in 4 broad sectors: safe drinking water, support for urban school children, work training for unemployed youth and agricultural marketing."

The iPad student seemed to be convinced.

The Professor frowned.

The interactions continued and the students proposed several role models of India such as M. C. Mehta, the Environmental Lawyer, Dr. Deepak Apte, Director of BNHS, Sunita Narain of the Centre for Science & Environment and for each, the Professor continued finding faults and I kept pointing out the good work done by these leading personalities.

After some time, most of the students were tired of the Professor's negative and fault-finding attitude. One girl from the sixth row who was wearing a bright Tee shirt that had a slogan "We Dare", got up, faced the classroom and spoke in a tone of leadership, "Well Sirs, at least now we know what we don't want to be. We don't want to be like this Professor friend of yours. We want to be positive, like you."

My Professor Friend was shocked with this statement. There was silence in the class.

He extinguished his cigar in the tray that was placed on the table and said, "You mean you want to be like Dr. Modak? He is a shining example of a thoroughly kaleidoscoped personality, with career profile showing utmost confusion and a complete lack of clarity. He has been a Professor, a Consultant, a Corporate Honcho, an Author and Editor, an Entrepreneur and an International Adviser to Governments & Financing Institutions. He also works as an NGO for spreading awareness and conducting training on environmental management & sustainability. I could never understand what this gentleman wanted to be. He has simply been a free radical. You will waste your time and career following him."

I thought this time Professor was absolutely right. So I kept quiet.

I ended the class thanking the Professor.

12

Science, administration and politics are often difficult dots to connect. But if you do connect them well, to form a circle, then you witness sheer magic in the ripples – ripples of change!

Dr. R. D. Deshpande (RD) was the person who showed me to achieve this change.

With a very powerful, turbulent and impatient personality, RD was like a storm in my life. He was my friend and guide and even today I miss him very much.

Dr. Deshpande held a doctoral degree in Marine Biology from the UK and he spent many years as the Director of the Indian Government's Department of Science and Technology (DST). He had worked at the Indian Consulate in Washington DC over four years and even accompanied Mrs. Indira Gandhi on key diplomatic missions as the scientific attaché. He had a great understanding of politics

and of science and knew how to develop and maintain connections.

He used to be amongst the "Who's Who" in India and was close to many senior politicians such as former Maharashtra Chief Minister, Mr. Sharad Pawar. I even heard rumors that he was somehow connected to the Indian intelligence agency – RAW. But I don't think that was true.

I met Dr. Deshpande for the first time in Bangkok, where he was working with the UNEP Regional Office. I was only 26 years then and he must have been close to 55. We met while attending a meeting organized by Economic and Social Commission for Asia and the Pacific (ESCAP) and almost instantly liked each other.

He spoke very warmly to me.

After our initial meeting, we got together a few times in his office. We discussed

74

my career plans and he told me about his own career and his life experiences. He stressed on the importance of integrating science, science of administration and the politics of science in order to be effective. Mere science was not enough he used to say. I found these conversations very stimulating. This was a great learning opportunity for me.

In 1984, I started teaching at the Centre for Environmental Science and Engineering at IIT Bombay. One day in the middle of my class, I received an urgent message from the IIT Director's office instructing me to see the director (Professor B. Nag) right away. "Did I do something wrong?" I wondered as I hurriedly dismissed the class.

When I reached Professor Nag's office, sitting there chatting with the Director of IIT Mumbai, was none other than Dr. RD. I was pleasantly surprised.

"Dr. Deshpande dropped in just now and was keen to see you. He wants you to accompany him to meet the Chairman of HLL, Dr. Dutta. That is why I asked you to come right away." Professor Nag said.

Dr. RD was in a hurry and as he left to use the loo, he said to Professor Nag, "Prasad is my old friend, take good care of him!"

Professor Nag turned to me and whispered, "How the hell do you know this man? He is very influential and he seems to like you. Do stay in touch with him." And I did just that.

After retirement, Dr. RD lived in Pune and later became Senior Advisor to the Tata Group. He was heading their Environment and Natural Resources Division.

I worked with him on a project from Asian Development Bank (ADB) as a Consultant and used to shuttle between Mumbai and Pune. In the evenings we would spend time at a pub (10 Downing Street in Gera Plaza) or a restaurant (Zamus on the Dhole Patil Road) ordering garlic mushrooms and draft beers. The conversations would be on varied topics– such as diplomacy in organizations such as UN, ADB etc., scientific administration in the DST, Corporate behavior and political obligations etc. I have fond memories of these conversations, some serious and some fun stories with implicit pieces of advice. He used to say that when you take up an assignment, map the people who matter, work on them to ensure that studies or advice you would provide is

heard by the right people. "You need to network and cultivate relationship with some of the powerful personalities in the society not always for professional reasons but to understand their vision and the power they wield." He would say.

One day, when I was in the Nariman Point area of Mumbai, I got a call from Dr. RD and was told to show up right away at the Commonwealth Building opposite the Air India Tower. Saying "No" to Dr. RD was never an option and so I took a taxi and obediently arrived at the Commonwealth building. Many powerful personalities of the Tata group lived there. It was one of the most sought after addresses in Mumbai.

When I reached Commonwealth, I saw Dr RD waiting for me impatiently in the lobby. "Why so late? I am taking you to Nani." he said frowning at me.

"You mean Nani Palkhivala?" I asked, taken aback at this news.

"Who else?" Dr. RD growled.

Nani Palkhivala, one of India's most respected Jurist and Top Economist.

We reached the elevator and the liftman sitting inside got up to open the collapsible door for us. Dr. RD said, "Give this man ten rupees."

I did as I was told and as we got out of the lift on the sixth floor, Dr. RD turned to the liftman, pointing at me and said, "Ye apne Saab hai, jab dekhoge tab salaam karna mat bhulo." (He is the boss, whenever you will see him, don't forget to salute him).

When we rang the doorbell and the door was opened by a simple looking tall man with thick spectacles – this was the legendary Nani Palkhivala. He greeted us and made us sit in the drawing room where I was introduced to him.

Dr. RD and Nani must have been old and close friends. The fell into easy conversation and even included me in their discussion. The topic was India's measure of true progress – not GDP but the Gross Ecological Product. I was quite excited to chip in and voiced my thoughts and views to the best of my abilities. Both the veterans gave me a patient hearing thus over two rounds of masala tea with masca (butter) biscuits; I was party to a phenomenal conversation. Just sitting there, listening to Nani Palkhivala was a treat.

When the clock on the wall chimed to six, Nani Palkhivala stopped and told Dr. RD that it was time for him to take a walk on the Marine Drive. Dr. RD had to take flight to Nagpur and so we all got up to leave. Nani changed his clothes, told his servant to prepare the dinner and we left the apartment and pressed button for the lift. The lift arrived and with it the liftman still sitting inside on his stool. He opened the collapsible door, saw me, and saluted to me in style. Nani Palkhiwala was surprised.

"You seem to be a regular to the Commonwealth." he said.

That meant a lot!

When we reached the ground floor, Dr. RD's car was waiting to take him to the airport. I was about to hail a taxi when Nani asked me casually,

"Why don't you join me for the walk? I would like to continue our discussions. Are you in a hurry to go?"

Of course I was not in a hurry and I willingly joined him for the walk. Walking with one of India's intellectual giants along the sea was so illuminating and memorable.

We returned to the

Commonwealth after an hour's walk. Nani bade me goodbye and took the lift upstairs. "Drop in again sometime." he said. "And it need not be with Dr. RD."

When the lift came back down after dropping Nani to the 6th floor, the liftman saw me waiting and asked, "Saab, kuch chahiye?" (Sir, do you need anything?)
I gave him another ten rupee note, as an advance for the next visit and said, "Rakho!" The liftman saluted.

I now understood Dr. RD's strategy. The key was timing and when and whom to give the money to, mattered. Those ten rupees made my life that day.

13

SAYING YOU LIVE IN INDIA

Around 1993, I had received an invitation to speak at a Cleaner Production Seminar in Lisbon. My host, a Mrs. Pineda from the Department of Industry was a very enthusiastic and passionate person. Two more people – one Australian and the other Dutch were also invited. We all knew each other.

We arrived a day early as Mrs. Pineda had organized a dinner with the Minister of Industries and some select officials and industry representatives. Dinner was served on the terrace of the Ministers bungalow and began with a selection of cheese and Portuguese wines. The terrace had a terrific view of the city of Lisbon with its old mansions and thick tree foliage.

As we mingled with the invitees, talking about their interest in Cleaner Production, Mrs. Pineda approached me.

"The Minister's secretary wants to speak to you." she

said and ushered me to a room adjoining the terrace. After some pleasantries, a secretary asked me for a short CV that he could use for introducing me at the Seminar the following day.

"You are an Indian I know – currently based in New York – correct?" When I said no and that I had always lived in Bombay (now Mumbai), India; he asked me the same question again. This time he added that of course he was aware I was originally from Bombay but wasn't I based in the US for the past several years? I politely said no, emphasizing that I have always been a Bombay person!

The secretary got me a glass of Portuguese red wine and disappeared.

A few minutes later, Mrs. Pineda came in and asked me to follow her as the Minister wanted to speak to me.

The Minister, a very impressive personality,

welcomed me and following the customary greetings said, "Is this your first visit to Portugal? Stay over for couple of more days and tour the country. There is so much to see here. Also don't miss attending a Fado. We have in fact organized a Fado tomorrow night, in one of the antique cellars."

Although the origins are difficult to trace, Fado is commonly regarded as a form of song that follows a certain traditional structure. In popular belief, Fado is a form of music characterized by mournful tunes and lyrics, often about the sea or the life of the poor, and infused with a sentiment of resignation, fatefulness and melancholia. This is loosely captured by the Portuguese word saudade, or "longing", symbolizing a feeling of loss.

I was, of course very keen to attend the Fado.

Then the Minister said, "I just was told that you live in Bombay. I always thought that you resided in New York."

After I explained that I lived in Bombay and not New

York, the Minister came a bit closer to me and spoke in a concerned whisper, "Dr. Modak, I know about your international work and that's why we invited you here. However, the industry in Portugal is still kind of biased. They don't mind receiving inputs and advice from the Dutch and the Australian experts or even someone from the United States. But they won't listen to an Indian living in Bombay." He paused and I could see he was embarrassed by what he had just told me.

He continued, "Will it be OK Dr. Modak, if tomorrow, we introduce you as an Indian, born in Bombay but currently residing and working in New York? It is a small change, but if you accept my request, it will really help."

At first I didn't know what to say but then I politely and respectfully told the Minister that I prefer to be introduced correctly, as born, living and working in Bombay!

When Mrs. Pineda came to drop me to the hotel post dinner, she brought up the conversation I had with the Minister.

"I am sorry about what he said – but he really has a point. You may find the response from the industries tomorrow to be rather lukewarm after the introduction."

"Well Mrs. Pineda. I would rather be who I am." I said firmly.

The next day, the Seminar was inaugurated by the Minister and all three of us as experts were formally introduced. I was the last speaker. We did pretty well and the Minister stayed throughout the session.

Contrary to the Minister's concerns, my presentation was well received by the industry participants. There were number of questions asked and specific advice was requested. The translator had a tough time as the discussions became rather animated after a while but the Minister was very pleased.

After the Seminar, we were scheduled to make field visits to some of the industries. Mrs. Pineda met with us to coordinate our field visits. She told my Australian colleague that he was going to visit the food packaging industries that were an hour away. Our Dutch friend was going to be spending all of the next day visiting some electroplating industries. He had a two hour drive to look forward to. Then

Mrs. Pineda turned to me and said, "Prasad, you will need to spend three days in the field. We are sending you to Covilha. You will have to start right away."

"Why don't you like me Mrs. Pineda?" I asked. "Why are you torturing me?"

Mrs. Pineda took me aside to explain, "Dude, you don't realize how lucky you are? Representatives of the Textile Industries in Covilha were present today and they were really impressed with your work. They would like you to personally carry out the in-plant visits." "Also," she continued, "Covilha is great tourist destination, up in the mountains. My colleague Paulo will drive you there. A century old Vila has been reserved for you to stay in. The Minister saw to it personally."

I was delighted and looking forward to my excursion outside Lisbon.

Paulo drove me to Covilha which was approximately 280 km from Lisbon. We travelled to the mountains through the vineyards and that evening, we stopped at a Fado cellar in the evening to sample the famous Adega wine.

Paulo turned out to be very talkative person. He told me about his life and his family, especially his elder sister Maria. He simply adored his sister. On our journey to and fro Covilha, I learned everything there was to know about Maria – her moods, her dress sense, her fancies, her career interests etc. Maria, it seems was specializing in Environmental Impact Assessment (EIA).

"One day I will introduce you to Maria." Paulo told me proudly.

Of course in the process of our non-stop dialogue, Paulo extracted every detail about me – my wife Kiran, kids Devika and Pranav and our life in Mumbai. I also told him my "Minister story".

I returned from Lisbon happy to have experienced Covilha. The travel there, the stay and the interactions with industries was all very memorable.

The very next month I was in Shanghai attending the annual convention of the International Association of Impact Assessment (IAIA). As I stood in the registration queue, there were two women chatting animatedly in the front of me. One of them was especially chatty and she was telling her friend, "My brother Paulo drove an Indian to Covilho last month. He said that this Indian guy was very interesting and they both had long conversations. Paulo was enamored by him that he now wants to holiday in India and visit Bombay. Also he wants me to join."

I immediately realized that I was standing right next to Paulo's dear sister – the famous Maria. What an unbelievable coincidence!

I politely interrupted them and introduced myself without mentioning Paulo.

The queue was long enough for some more conversation. Amongst other topics, I spoke about face reading, science of phrenology and works reported in the Purushsuktam of ancient Indian scripts on how to read minds.

"This is a very interesting piece of information about India that my brother Paulo should know", said Maria.

Then concentrating on Maria's face, I offered to tell her life's story.

"Maria -you like green color, you are allergic to milk products, and you like to travel, especially on the sea coasts. You tend to spend a lot. You are a professor at the Lisbon University...." I went on and on and told her everything that Paulo had told me about her.

Maria was amazed. She told her friend that everything I had said was absolutely true. "Now I really want to visit India. How could you know so much about me by simply looking at my face? Only my brother knows me this well. You must teach me."

I just smiled – deciding not to tell her my secret – but eventually I did.

Maria and I met couple of times during the IAIA meetings and I saw her last at a meeting organized by UNEP in Geneva. Today, Maria is a well-respected EIA expert with several publications including a really good book on the subject of Strategic Environmental Impact Assessment. I really respect her work.

This is a pretty old story – some 20 years ago and I don't know whether the bias still remains.

I never met Paulo or Mrs. Pineda again. I plan to visit Covilha once again, listen to Fado and sip Adega wine.

14

When we were completing our Masters in Environmental Science and Engineering at IIT Bombay, we all wanted to become "Environmental Consultants." It was the 1980s and the environmental consulting market wasn't much established in India.

The year was 1976 and I was an intern at Hindustan Dorr Oliver (HDO) in Mumbai. I was in the laboratory conducting some wastewater treatability studies when I overheard my seniors A. D. Kini and S. L. Nayak discussing how they could translate the results of the treatability studies to the plant design. "We will have to ask the Doctor." said A. D. Kini.

"Who is the Doctor?" I asked (a dumb question).

"Dr. Deepak Kantawala, our Consultant." Kini answered. "He is an authority on the treatment of industrial wastewaters. He completed his doctoral studies at Washington University, St Louis in the United States."

Next week, I saw the famous Dr. Deepak Kantawala at HDO. Dressed in his trademark Quadra jeans, a white shirt with cufflinks and a red tie and sporting long whiskers, was walking around the place smoking a pipe that had a unique aroma of tobacco. I learnt that he ran a company called Environmental Engineering Consultants (EEC) at the Nariman Point.

Dr. Deepak Kantawala (or Doctor) became our hero.

We all wanted to follow his example in shaping our careers. One of my colleague and a close friend, Shirish Naik who joined EEC after completing of his Masters used to say that the Doctor's library was a real treasure trove. It had all the consulting reports that he had completed for the industries (many of them, multinationals) he had worked with. The library also housed a complete collection of Purdue University's Annual Industrial Waste Conferences. One could spend hours browsing through these reports and conference volumes.

One day, Shirish and I decided that the best way to become a Consultant was to steal the Doctor's treasures. We thought that if we photocopied all the Doctor's important consulting reports, we would be armed with enough "knowledge" to not only compete with Dr. Kantawala but even surpass him and become the most sought after Consultants in India.

But the problem we faced was of photocopying the consulting reports discretely. It had to be done after office hours and without the Doctor or other seniors in the office finding out. The only way was to get access to the Doctor's office on the weekend.

I had the idea of approaching the Doctor as IIT MTech students, requesting use of his library over a weekend. We were sure that given Dr. Kantawala's love for students, (he had been a Professor at MS University in Vadodara before becoming a Consultant) he would not object and allow us to use the office/library over the weekend.

We met him in his office and made our request. He was very pleased to know that we were interested in spending our "precious" weekends in his library with his reports and the books. He took a deep puff from his pipe and thought about how he could get us access to his office for the weekend.

"Where do you stay Prasad?" He asked.

"Shivaji Park." I replied.

"Oh, then it is pretty straight forward. Stand outside the Sanman restaurant on the Cadel Road around 7pm this Friday evening. I live in Juhu and will be passing over Cadel Road so I can give you my office key at the Sanman spot. You and Shirish can use my office and library over the weekend to your hearts' content. On Monday morning, wait opposite Sanman at 8am sharp and I will pick up the keys from you on my way to the office."

We were shocked with the ease in which he made this proposition. Clearly, the poor Professor/ Consultant didn't suspect our devilish motive. We readily agreed to Doctor's proposal.

We then went to a photocopying shop at Nariman Point (next to Dr. Kantawala's office) and negotiated and booked photocopying services that would get us good quality prints in the shortest time possible. We estimated on photocopying of some 1000 pages each day and the proposed cost of Rs.1000/- was well worth the resultant "knowledge acquisition."

As agreed, I picked up the office key from the Doctor on the following Friday evening and on Saturday morning, Shirish and I arrived at the EEC office on the 9th floor of Mittal Chambers at Nariman Point. We opened the office and excitedly rushed into the library of treasures.

We first picked up the report prepared for Ciba-Geigy, then Park Davis and then Pfizer and so on. Ensuring that we had both the treatability studies as well as the design reports, we also included (in our stash), the structural designs of the treatment plants prepared

by Dr. Kantawala's cousin Mahendra Shah, a wizard in this subject.

After two hours of hard work, we had amassed an impressive heap of "knowledge" on the desk of the library. The next task was to move this pile of wisdom to the photocopying shop and then go off for lunch at the Woodlands (a famous south Indian restaurant located on the ground floor of Mittal Chambers and that served a great grape juice). Once the photocopying was done, all we had to do was take the original reports/books back to the EEC office and put them back in their designated place. We were about to begin our secret mission when something made us stop and look at each other. Suddenly we felt that what we were about to do was something very wrong indeed. Not only was it completely unethical and unprofessional but it was shameful, not only to us but to our families as well.

Dr. Kantawala had trusted us without hesitation when he had handed over the office keys so that we use this library to read and learn. Therefore it would be very wrong on our part to cheat and steal his consulting reports. We were clearly misusing his kindness and generosity. We paused and decided not to go through with our devious scheme.

We put back all the reports -- the Ciba Giegy, Park Davis, etc in complete silence, skipped our lunch at the Woodlands and went home.

On Monday morning, I met Dr. Kantawala as planned at the Sanman spot. As I handed over the keys, I asked, "Doctor, may I get a ride till Worli Naka?" "Sure!" said Dr. Kantawala.

During the journey from Shivaji Park to Worli, I told the Doctor everything. I confessed about our ulterior motives, the plan and the failure/abortion of the plan. He heard me out patiently, puffing on his pipe with the unique tobacco scent.

He then smiled and said, "I knew you and your friend were up to something – but what, I wasn't sure. I had however confidence that both of you won't do anything unethical that would tarnish your souls and damage your reputations or that of your families'." He then patted on my back and said, "Prasad, if knowledge was so simple to acquire then universities and such halls of knowledge would be have been long replaced by photocopying machines!"

I understood what he meant. There was a difference between possessing documents and possessing knowledge. Most think of the former and keep stocking the documents.

This became clearer to me years later, during my tenure at IIT Bombay; I was developing water quality modeling software for application on the river Ganga, for a project funded by the Ministry of Environment and Forests (MoEF). The models we were developing were unique, Ganga relevant and complex and meant for optimizing investments on the wastewater treatment plants along the river. At the time there was a "rival" research group at an institution of national importance also working on water quality modeling.

One evening, a close friend at the MoEF called to alert me that one of my team members was quitting and he intended to "steal" the source code of our models on a Mag Tape before he joined the rival research group.

"Stop this guy, Dr. Modak and don't let him take away the source code!" my friend said earnestly with my best interest in mind.

I thought for a while as I recalled the story of the keys to the office of Dr. Deepak Kantawala.

"Won't harm me at all!" I told my well-meaning friend and let the team member quit without any questions. As expected, our modeling software was indeed "stolen".

Soon after, however, I was able to build far superior water quality models by working with two brilliant masters' students – Rakesh Kumar Gelda and C. Clement Prabhakar. Our models solved coupled DO-BOD equations in two dimensional space, factoring the transverse dispersion using (for the first time) the Crank-Nicholson algorithm. The model calibration used advanced techniques of non-linear optimization with heuristics. The MoEF topped up our funding as we were found to be way ahead of the competing institution!

Rakesh Kumar Gelda

Clement Prabhakar

You cannot steal knowledge. In fact, knowledge sharing helps one to grow.

Only those who are insecure try to hide and lock away the knowledge.

Today, the concept of Intellectual Property Rights (IPR) and the consequent regulations have brought in the barriers, and given great business to the lawyers.

Sometimes, the need and quest for personal recognition affects the free flow of knowledge. The desire for fame and recognition and credit (whether deserved or undeserved) is, I believe, the most difficult thing to conquer and greatest hindrance to free knowledge sharing and growth.

You may recall that Jagadish Chandra Bose was the first to invent a wireless coherer and an instrument for indicating the refraction of electric waves. However, instead of trying to gain any commercial benefit from this invention, Bose made his inventions freely available to the public in order to allow others to further develop his research. He later turned his attention from the inorganic to the organic world where his

revolutionary discoveries as a plant physiologist outpaced even his radical achievements as a physicist. Although Bose filed for a patent for one of his inventions due to peer pressure, his reluctance to any form of patenting was well known[6].

I applaud and salute his ability to go beyond the quest of personal recognition and benefit and enjoy his scientific discoveries/inventions and even be generous enough to share his knowledge freely for society's advancement and wellbeing.

So you don't have to look for or work towards recognition. Recognition comes to you.

Every day I take a walk around Shivaji Park and pass the restaurant Sanman on Cadel Road. I remember Dr. Deepak Kantawala and the keys that opened my mind making me the person I am today and hope to always be.

---

6   Bose's place in history has now been re-evaluated. He is now officially credited with inventing the first wireless detection device, discovering millimetre length electromagnetic waves, and being a pioneer in the field of biophysics

15

My Workshop Memoirs

It is often hard to distinguish the terms workshop, seminar, symposium etc. While there are definitions available, generally these events create opportunities to bring the stakeholders together. With the advent of internet based communication technologies, we don't have to physically bring together the stakeholders anymore. Webinars instead of seminars can be easily conducted but there is no substitute for the face to face meets.

Workshops are platforms for more active engagement. While both "open" and "closed" formats are possible, the latter format is generally preferred. Workshops often entail group based activities and tasks and involves important brainstorming (a term popularized by Alex Faickney Osborn in 1953. You should not miss reading his book Applied Imagination). During these brainstorming sessions, there is no discussion or criticism and evaluation of ideas takes place later. Osborn credited the origin of the process to Hindu teachers in India, who used the method of Prai (outside yourself) Barshana (question) for over 400 years.

I remember the first international workshop that I organized. The subject was Water Quality Management. At that time, I was inducted as a Consultant to the Ganga Action Plan and was closely working with Dr. Niloy Choudhari, Chairman of the Central Pollution Control Board (CPCB) and K. C. Sivaramakrishnan, Project Director at the Ganga Project Directorate (GPD). At that time, there was a beeline of international consultants queuing up at the GPD, selling their skills and experience. I used to attend presentations from agencies like Thames Water, Seven Trent from the UK, US Environmental Protection Agency, Lyonnaise des Eaux France S.A., Ruhrverband, Germany etc.

I came up with an idea of holding an international workshop at IIT Bombay that brought together the vendors and the academia for an exposition with discussions. The workshop was conceived as a 5 day residential event with 50 participants.

This workshop was an amazing experience for me. It provided me with an amazing opportunity to learn event coordination & logistics; to better understand science based politics; and of course to get a deeper understanding of the subjects - water quality modelling, wastewater treatment, policies, regulation and standards and most importantly the economics of water quality management. The workshop was attended by some of the great personalities across the world – many of them were inspiring and were like lighthouses.

I gave the opening speech at the Workshop.

All the participants were accommodated at IIT Guest house next to the scenic Powai Lake.

I recall that one of the evenings K. C. Shivaramakrishnan (KC) asked me to organize a car to take him to meet L. C. Gupta (LC), the then Chairman of CIDCO on Marine Drive. The car dropped him at LC's house in the evening where he was to have dinner. After the dinner, KC came down and did not find the car. He called me and angrily growled, "Send me another car Dr. Modak– your driver has simply vanished!"

In reality, the poor driver was right there –only few meters away, but KC was expecting him to be parked right outside the gate with door open waiting for him. So typical of a senior IAS officer!! I took another car and we drove from Powai to i at 10pm. I went up to LC's house and found that KC was still fuming.

We drove back to Powai and KC cooled down especially when I explained that my driver was right there waiting for him. As we reached the campus, KC said, "Dr. Modak, if you are OK, let us go to your office and discuss the Ganga Action Plan. I don't think I am in a mood to sleep." It was 11pm then.

We went to my office at the Centre for Environmental Science and Engineering. Some students were working in the laboratory and my colleague Radha Gopalan was conducting her experiments. I asked Radha to make some coffee on a bunsen burner using a corning glass beaker. KC started talking and he

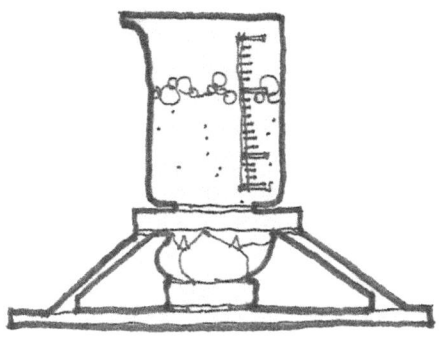

gave us amazing insights into the Ganga Action Plan. He spoke not just about the politics but the challenges of urban infrastructure, administration and finance (which essentially were his areas of specialization). We asked him questions and the discussions went on till 1am. As I dropped him at the Guest House, KC said, "Thank you Dr. Modak, you let me vent today. And I am really sorry for all the trouble."

"Sir," I said, "to me this session was the best part of our Workshop! It is I who must thank you."

My interest of holding strategic workshops continued. In 1990, I approached the Asia Pacific Centre for Transfer of Technology (APCTT) with my proposal to hold a 5 day regional workshop on Waste Management & Recycling. The idea was to bring together senior management of the Government and top notch Academia in the Asia-Pacific region and expose them to the paradigm shift of waste to resource management. I booked the entire Valvan Village Resort at Lonavala, a hill station between Mumbai and Pune. We were 50 participants representing counties like Sri Lanka, Nepal, Bangladesh, Pakistan, Thailand, Philippines, Indonesia and of course India.

The workshop had several features – group work, field visits, software demonstrations, videos. We had cultural events too that included a violin recital and a Bharatanatyam performance.

There were four participants from Pakistan and all four were worried and tensed to be in India. When they arrived in Mumbai, we organized two cars for them to travel to Lonavala. I proposed two Pakistanis would sit with two of my colleagues in each car. They refused and said that all four of them must stay together and our second car with my colleagues could lead the way. I was not happy with this arrangement but finally I gave up and agreed. The cars took off in the morning.

The driver of the car with the 4 Pakistani colleagues jumped the traffic signal in Chembur near the Bhabha Atomic Research Center (BARC) and a

traffic policeman stopped the car and asked the driver for his license. Then very casually, the policeman asked the travelers, "Sir, where are you from?" One of the Pakistanis answered, "From Islamabad!" There was a grave silence -- People from Pakistan next to BARC? This was just not acceptable.

I was immediately summoned to the Police Headquarters in Mumbai for an explanation. Fortunately, the then Inspector General of Police, Mr. Vasant Saraf was a friend (He was Counselor at the Indian Embassy in Bangkok when I used to live there). I was told to take the Pakistanis to the police station in Lonavala to register them every evening during their entire stay. This added a new dimension to the Workshop and a new lesson learnt!

In 1992, I was invited by

the USAID to participate in a 3 day workshop on a Nile Cruise in Egypt. The workshop theme focused on the Business in the Environment Sector in the next 25 years. The participants included CEOs of companies like Metcalf & Eddy, Bi-Water and CH2M Hill etc. There was so much to learn, especially for me! We don't see such workshops in India. We should definitely host such events.

In 2002, the World Bank asked me to prepare the Strategic Environment Assessment (SEA) for the Palar River Basin in Tamil Nadu. For this work, I proposed a 3 day residential workshop at Kanchipuram, the city of the Shankaracharyas. The workshop had 40 participants and we booked the entire hotel. Three Ministers of the State participated as did the farmers who were impacted due to pollution. They came in the traditional veshty.

There were rules of conduct for the workshop. One of them was not to argue based on emotions. All arguments were to be evidence based. For this I had set up a Knowledge Room in the hotel. The room had the maps, reports, data etc. along with access to the Internet. All the participants were encouraged to bring the information they had and place it in the Knowledge Room. This rule actually worked and the workshop outcomes had the consensus and all the information necessary for taking actions. Thus, Asia's first river basin board was formed.

In 2004, I conducted a workshop on Cleaner Production in Tagaytay in the Philippines. Tagaytay is one of the most popular tourist destinations because of its outstanding scenery and cooler climate provided by its high altitude. Tagaytay overlooks the Taal Lake in Batangas and provides one of the iconic views. I was the workshop organizer and there was no pre-fixed agenda. There were only 20 participants – a selected group of internationally known experts on Cleaner Production. On the first day, we worked

on the agenda, deciding "what to do" over the next 3 days. We decided the workshop structure, topics to be dealt with and the lead speakers. A consensus was reached at the end of first day. The agenda ensured that we achieve the outcomes we were looking for. I enjoyed this style of workshop design and conduct. Instead of pre-fixing the agenda apriori, it is often more effective to develop the agenda as a group and then work together. Such workshops rarely happen since you need a really mature or experienced group of participants!

During one of my trips to Southampton in the UK, I met a Professor who used to run workshops on the Finite Element Methods on the Queen Elizabeth II (ocean liner) that plied between London and New York. The workshops were run by the Professor and his family and were on a micro-scale - only 15 select participants. His wife was a travel agent who would do the bookings and handle logistics. The daughter was a Yoga and Health food freak and so she would conduct Yoga sessions on the deck and design the food menus. The son was into photo-journalism and publishing and he would produce a book of the Professor's lectures at

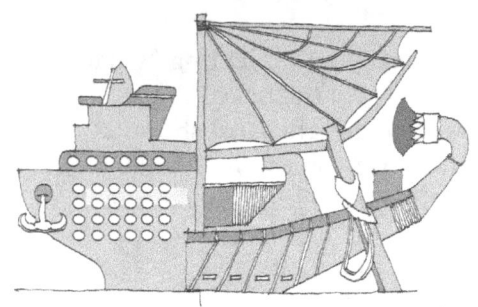

when the weather is good."

Friends – I am very serious!! Anyone interested to join? Write to me. THERE ARE ONLY LIMITED SEATS

end of the cruise. Wow!! The family used to have great time being together every year. It was a paid holiday with ample opportunity to garner business through the connection with the participants. I liked this model.

I told my Professor friend about the idea of workshop on the cruise.

He was excited.

"Let us do this Dr. Modak." He said. "We will book Ocean World, the luxury liner that plies between Pattaya, Ko Samui and Cambodia over 3 nights and 4 days. I will join you and we will teach sustainability to the top business leaders of Asia. The theme could be Strategizing Business of Tomorrow. Your son-in-law is a sustainability chef of repute, your daughter is a Yoga and Health Freak and your son is a renewable energy nerd. So it will all work perfectly!"

"True." I responded "Let us run the workshop on the Ocean World. Let us do it during November-December

16

Never Jump the Queue

This blog post is one of my real travel experiences.

I received an invitation to speak at an International Conference at Alexandria in Egypt. This conference had been organized by Professor Ahmed Hamza and his wife Samia Saad. My friend Jim Gallup from US AID had arranged the funding. Jim ran the Environmental Pollution Prevention Project (EP3) that focused on Industrial Pollution Prevention.

I was thrilled as I had never traveled to Egypt before. Also I would be able to catch up with Ahmed and Samia, both of whom I knew very well and as well as Jim.

I was teaching at IIT Bombay at that time and we had a PhD Student from Alexandria who's name was Hamdi Saif. When I told Hamdi that I have an invite from Alexandria, he was excited and said, "Sir, I will accompany you to the Egyptian Consulate and help you get the visa on priority basis."

Are you flying our national airline Egypt Air?" he asked eagerly.

Next week, Hamdi took me to the Egyptian Consulate in Mumbai and we met with the Counselor in his office. The Counselor and Hamdi spoke in Arabic but I could sense that Hamdi was telling him of the importance of this meeting and how I was an internationally sought expert (essentially marketing me!).

The Counselor got me a strong Egyptian coffee and in a loud, friendly voice spoke of how Egypt and India have great ties of friendship. He told me that I would enjoy visiting Egypt and that I should not miss seeing the pyramids and definitely take a cruise on the river Nile. I assured him that

95

both these items were top of my "to do" list.

Then with a friendly smile, the Counselor personally stamped the visa sticker on to my passport. After this was done, he pulled out a Mont Blanc pen from his shirt pocket and started writing in Arabic on the stamped page.

"Sir, May I know what you are writing on that page?" I asked, thinking it was best to know as it was my document!

"Oh, don't worry – it's for your own good." The Counselor laughed and handing over my passport.

The following week, I boarded an Egypt Air flight to Cairo.

On the aircraft, I saw the wife of one of another Egyptian student who studied at IIT. "Sir, what a pleasant surprise" she said "Where are you heading to?"

"Alexandria." I said and told her that I planned to take the Desert Bus from the airport.

Shaheen, that was her

name, said that queues at Immigration in Cairo were often very long. As she found it simply exasperating, she was getting a friend, a senior official (of the rank of Major) from Egyptian Army, to whisk her out.

"Just walk with me and we will breeze through immigration and customs." she told me.

"Oh this is just like in India." I said. I had seen many VIPs zipping through immigration and customs at Mumbai airport.

Just as Shaheen had said, the queue for immigration at Cairo was looong. She smiled and said, "Follow me!"

We were greeted by a tall handsome man wearing an Egyptian Army uniform complete with a lot of flashing medals/ decorations. Shaheen spoke to him in Arabic and explained "my case". The Man from Egyptian Army asked for my passport and disappeared.

In just five minutes, he had returned with our passports duly stamped. "Here you are Sir." he said. "All done and you are ready to go." We exited the airport and Shaheen was kind enough to drop me to the bus station for the Desert Bus.

Three hours later, I reached Ramada Hotel in Alexandria – the Venue of the Conference. Ahmed and Samia were there to greet me and Jim was around too. The Conference was the same as always. We had more fun outside the conference room spending out free evenings going to nice places to eat and relaxing on the chairs by the Mediterranean Sea.

After the conference, we moved to Cairo and stayed at Hotel Pyramids. After a day's stay in Cairo, we flew to Aswan and boarded a river cruise on the Nile. The cruise ship was luxurious complete with its own golf course, swimming pool, a bar and even a bus. There also was an in-house belly dancer!

We sailed along the Nile making various stops for sightseeing during which we would leave the boat on the in-house bus. While on the board, Jim kept us busy in brainstorming sessions where we discussed the future of the environmental business over the next 20 years. I thought that was a great idea. Our discussions gave me a good insight about the future as we took a stock of what was happening now - the challenges faced and the opportunities ahead. I had never come across such discussions or forums in India and felt that we really needed such meetings.

We reached Luxor where the cruise ended. Like most others, I was to take a flight Luxor to Cairo and then connect to Mumbai.

Before departing, Prof. Hamza hugged me goodbye and said, "Come again my friend!"

Then as a matter of routine, he asked, "Prasad, I hope you have notified the police station about your entry into Egypt?"

I told him I hadn't and asked if it was required?

"Yes it is and you should have done so." said Prof. Hamza. "I suppose you are carrying the customs clearance certificate regarding the foreign exchange you brought in to the country"

"No. I don't have that either." I told him.

"How come?" Hamza said in a voice full of concern. "You must have been informed by the office of Immigration and Customs when you entered Egypt."

I told him about my VIP entry at Cairo.

Then Hamza asked me a final question. "Do you have the telephone numbers of the Indian Embassy in Cairo? You need to contact your Embassy I see now a great difficulty for you to leave Egypt. Inshallah!"

Realizing the gravity of the situation, I went to the post office at Luxor airport, found a phone, called my wife. "I may be a bit delayed. Perhaps by a couple of days." I told her.

Apparently, Egyptian laws were very strict when it came to notifying police and declaring foreign exchange. I reached Cairo from Luxor and that was just fine. But the problem was immigrating out of Cairo to Mumbai. I was to fly Emirates via Dubai.

I stood in the queue with my heart beating heavily.

"Sir!" said a stern looking immigration officer "Where is the stamp from the local police station."

Apparently, if you stayed less than 7 days in Egypt, then you didn't require a stamp but I was exiting on the 8th day. I requested the officer to excuse me, "I just missed by a day Sir. I could not get earlier flight." I said most apologetically. The Officer did not like my defense.

"Where is your Customs Clearance Certificate?" He asked, not addressing me as "Sir" this time.

"I don't have one as I did not bring in any foreign exchange." I said.

Apparently, if you don't bring in foreign exchange then such a certificate is not necessary. (I was actually carrying a few hundred dollars in my wallet and a body search would have shown that I was blatantly lying.)

The Immigration Officer did not like this answer either. He browsed through the pages of my passport and saw all the stamps from some of the places we had visited on the cruise.

"Carrying no money and travelling on the Nile Cruise eh?" He asked eyeing me suspiciously.

"Well", I said "I was sponsored by US AID."

Now the Immigration Officer's face became serious and grim.

"Please step out of the line; we need to talk to you. You cannot

board this flight." He said in an icy tone.

He then got up and shouted in Arabic.

I moved out of the line.

A huge Egyptian Immigration Officer then walked in. He took my passport from the Immigration Officer who was interrogating me. His face was even sterner. He reached page of the visa stamp, looked at it and then at me. He looked at it again and almost seemed to melt!

He shouted at the desk officer in Arabic and then turning towards me, he spoke in a most apologetic tone.

"Extremely sorry Sir, there has been some mistake. It says here that you are the Government of Egypt's Very Important Guest."

So that's what the Counselor in Mumbai wrote on my visa page. I realized the power of that Monte Blanc pen. Wow!!!

The Immigration Officer immediately asked one of his colleagues to escort me to Egypt Airs business class lounge and told him,

"Sir is an important guest but has no money (as that's what I had said!). Please serve him some sandwiches and juice – complements of the airport."

I was relieved but also very embarrassed.

When I reached Mumbai, I met Hamdi and narrated the whole episode to him. He spoke to the Counselor and learnt that it's very rare that Counselor has written such words on the visa page. The Counselor told Hamdi "Tell your Professor to never jump the queue again. He was lucky. I would have expected a detainment of at least a couple of days while things were checked and sorted out!"

That was 1992 and since then I have visited Egypt at least two dozen times. The Immigration rules have changed and are not so rigid any more. In each of my visits, I have never jumped the queue – not just in Egypt but all over the world!

I have always patiently stood in long queues.

You don't get to see or meet such friendly Counselors very often!! Do you?

17

Still Looking for the Three

I remember the conversation I had with the Task Manager from the time I was first contracted by the World Bank. After discussing the scope of work, he asked me, "Can you estimate, in number of days, the effort you would have to put in to complete the tasks? Also send me your CV (in the World Bank prescribed format) so that I will get your daily rate fixed by HR (Human Resources)."

I didn't understand the concept a daily rate and it took a while to get my CV cast in the World Bank format. It was quite a self-revelation. Estimating the number of days of effort was not easy. I worked on a few iterations of this estimate in order to propose something reasonable and acceptable.

A few weeks after the CV was forwarded, I received my contract which stated that I will be paid at the rate of US 500/day for over 20 days to deliver the tasks outlined in the Terms of Reference attached. Thus I was commissioned!

After that I was contracted for many such assignments. Each year, the daily billing rate was enhanced by approximately 5-10%. I also discovered that the daily rates for the most senior consultants hovered around USD 600 to 1000/day across such institutions.

I always wondered how HR fixed the daily rates just based on CVs. Of course the qualifications and experience mentioned in the CV were important factors for consideration but honestly how could the CV alone reflect a person's competency for a task? For example, REAL number of years of experience differs from the INTEGER number! I therefore had some reservations on the logic used in calculating the daily rate and continue to do so even today.

I was working with a senior Dutch colleague on a project

where we were contracted by the Royal Netherlands Embassy. During one of the dinners, he asked me whether I work on the daily rate basis. When I said yes, he strongly advised me not to follow this practice. "Getting paid by the daily (or nightly!) rate is just like prostitution." he said. "You should be charging them based on the outcomes. Charge low if outcomes intended don't materialize and charge a premium if the outcomes do - thereby having nothing to do with the daily rates and the number of days."

Seeing that I was a bit dumb founded, he further explained,

"I was recently contracted by the Vice President (VP) of SAS Airlines. He had developed a Sustainability Awareness Program (SAP) for SAS and its customers but did not have the CEO's buy in/ support. He asked me to make a presentation to the CEO, expounding his ideas with the objective of getting funds (to the tune of more than 800,000 USD) sanctioned for the SAP.

The VP said, "I will pay you a fee of 50,000 USD if you get my budget sanctioned and only 8000 USD if you don't." If I had worked according to the daily rate, then the presentation would have taken 10 days

of my time (for research and improvisation) and I would have been paid a flat fee of 10,000 USD. So I accepted the CEO's offer and fortunately, I was able to get the VP's budget sanctioned. I ended up making good money."

"This is just like our Indian jugad." I thought. But my Dutch friend had made a very valid point.

I told him that organizations like the World Bank don't think that way. Whether you achieve the desired outcome or not, you get paid for the time you spent! Few really cared for the outcomes.

My Dutch friend then said, "Don't work for the World Bank then. Seek out the clients who actually are interested in the outcomes, and who are willing to form partnerships or make deals with you based on the risks and opportunities. Through this you will understand your value better. Also, if you follow my advice, then you won't need to work for 200 days in the year – as you will be making the same money over a period of just 60 days. You can live your life better, feel good and do something else that is useful for society. This way you won't just be living and working for yourself."

This conversation made quite

an impact on my mind and I wished I could follow his advice.

I started working in Indonesia, for an Asian Development Bank (ADB) project on the development of a computer based EIA using Expert System. My work involved frequent trips to Jakarta to conduct knowledge engineering workshops with the Indonesian EIA experts. Dr. Emil Salim a well-known conservation economist with a towering personality was the Minister of Environment at the time. One day, Dr Salim asked me to accompany him to Bogor where he was scheduled to address a meeting on Biodiversity Conservation. He wanted me to visit some of the botanical gardens in Bogor with him. Bogor, a city near Jakarta, had thick forests and drizzling rains throughout the year. It was also a place with the maximum frequency of lightening.

We reached Bogor at lunch time and Dr. Salim took me to a place where you could get some of the best beef pepper steaks around. Lunch was indeed a gastronomical treat and it was more enjoyable coupled with some very enlightening conversation with Dr. Salim. Our conversation shifted along various topics – crosscutting professional and personal interests. I then told Dr. Salim about my dilemma on consulting in general, also mentioning the illogical concept of daily rates. I spoke about feeling trapped by the ever increasing number of days that I was working over the year because of this method of contracting services and he smiled as he heard me out.

"I must introduce you to the four Canadian consultants who work in Bogor." He said. "I will drop you to their office, then go to my meetings and fetch you later for a tour of the botanical gardens. I think you will enjoy meeting them."

After a few detours, we reached a complex of 5 villas tucked in a thick cluster of trees on the outskirts of the city. There was a large Vila at the center and the 4 other villas were around placed like quadrants. We reached the central Villa through a winding road dotted with tall trees on either side. I learned later that the central Villa was the main office or headquarters of the "company."

The company was founded and run by four Canadians. All four founding members -- three men and one woman, were working in the environment, natural resources and social sectors focusing primarily on biodiversity conservation and impact assessment. They had actually followed my Dutch friend's model and were doing top of the line work, successfully delivering outcomes to the clients and consequently being paid a premium in "success fees." They planned their work so that they were busy for a total of only three months each year. I also learned that they were much sought after and "booked" in advance.

"What about when you aren't working?" I asked John, one

of the senior Principals of the Company.

"Well, we have a well-stocked library in the Villa." He said. "So we read. We also write and publish monographs/

working papers regularly. We trek. Our wives are interested in cooking and so we have done a large kitchen space here where we cook health organic food. Every week there are innovations and experiments. Peter paints and Laura sings with and plays the box guitar. We also have a great stock of wines and house a well-stocked bar."

Peter told us that they love to receive creatively minded guests and they generally spent their weekends with these visitors. These sessions have always been refreshing.

The four principals and their families lived in the villas around the Central office allowing them a lot of privacy. Being old friends however, there was a continuous mingling amongst the residents of the villas, especially the children. Jim the biodiversity specialist did not have any children and so he volunteered to mentor all the kids and it seems he was a great teacher.

"Our children are raised differently." said Laura. (I soon learnt that the four families were doing a commendable work on the social front, especially with regards to education for the poor) I wanted to chat with Jim but he was immersed in a large bath tub with his cigar on the first floor of the office complex which I was told, his "thinking den."

Laura told me that this model of living and working gave all of them a sense of balance. "When you possess a certain degree of expertise then why put it on sale at the cheap daily rates with no challenges on the outcomes?" she said. "Here we set our own pace and enjoy the work we do. We complement each other on professional front and on the personal front, we will find ways to take care of each other so, dare I say it, we may not have to move to an old peoples' home when our children leave us. "

I was very impressed by the manner in which business and the art of living were beautifully blended together to form a successful collaborative and sustainable collective – almost like the perfect ecosystem. The key however was to reach the status of top of the line consultant in the early stage of life, and demonstrate outcomes working with the client not as a contractor but more as a partner. Then share risks and ride on the opportunities.

On our way back I told Dr Salim that the meeting with the four Canadians had been very inspirational and an eye opener.

On my return to Mumbai, I asked one of my real estate friends to look for 5 villas near the Mulshi dam (close to Pune). Mulshi is a wonderful place with a sprawling lake and in a week, my friend had found one such 5 villa complex.

That was the easy part; the challenge now was to find

three friends who were open to experience the Bogor philosophy. I spoke to many people – but it was either "too late" for them or they were simply not interested.

I kept looking for the other three but even after several years, I wasn't even able to find one!

And so I continue consulting on a daily rate basis for clients who only want outputs and are not interested in involving me in the outcomes.

In closing, the message or more appropriately the words of wisdom I would like to impart are as follows -- Plan early and take timely action if you want to live a different kind life.

18

I have worked in Egypt intermittently for over 12 years (between 2000 and 2012) visiting the country every four to five months (my trips there were typically a week long). I must have made more than 30 sorties to this great city. I really miss Cairo today!

My work in Egypt was focused on Cleaner Production (CP) across various industry sectors that covered dairy, textile, leather tanning, cheese making, pulp and paper and several more. The priority industry size was Small and Medium Enterprise (SME) but we often landed working with medium to large industries.

The project I worked on was called SEAM (Support on Environmental Assessment & Management). I worked as a Consultant for two cycles of SEAM – viz. SEAM-I and SEAM-II. Later, I worked for the Egyptian Pollution Abatement Project (EPAP-II). I designed the CP demonstration projects at

industries, helped in the assessment of loans, provided policy advice and trained professionals, government officials and academia on CP Opportunity Assessments.

During these 12 years, I worked closely with the Egyptian Environmental Affairs Agency (EEAA), the National Bank of Egypt (NBE), Ministry of Trade & Industry (MTI), Federation of Egyptian Industries (FEI), National Research Center (NRC), the World Bank and the European Investment Bank (EIB). I was thus intimately involved with the Egyptian "ecosystem" around industrial environmental management.

My work took me to various locations in the country like the cities of Alexandria, Mansoura, El-Mahalla El-Kubra, Sohag, etc. These were the Governorates with industrial clusters where SEAM's CP Demonstration projects were implemented. My home base however was always Cairo.

I loved the city of Mansoura as Nile moved here like a chute, winds gushing especially at the night times. We used to have late dinners on the river bank (with Shish taouk or chicken tikka) in the company of Professor Samia Massoud, Executive & Technical Director of Environmental & Water Engineering Consultants (EWATEC), her pretty daughters and the EWATECs women staff (Prof. Samia had a policy only to employ women!)

The first Egyptian I met outside Egypt and who extended me an invitation was Professor Osama El-Kholy (Sam Kholy as we used to call him). We met in Canterbury in the UK for the first High Level Cleaner Production Conference organized by UNEP's Division of Technology, Industry and Economics (DTIE). Sam was a short man unlike the average Egyptian with a large egg shaped head (that was half bald). He was the Chancellor

of Cairo University and advisor to Mostafa Tolba, the then Executive Director of UNEP

HQ at Nairobi. A great orator and philosopher, I still cherish conversations with him at the Club in Maadi (Sports and Yacht Club) next to river Nile. We used to discuss Cleaner Production and its relevance to countries like Egypt and India. I believe that today, Sam is no more.

Another interesting person I met in Egypt was Philip Jago (Phil). Phil was an Australian and my contract manager in SEAM. He managed both SEAM-I and SEAM-II that were financed by DFID and was also the Manager of EPAP-II. I learned a lot from working with Phil, especially in managing projects, the consultants and the Government. He maintained excellent records, did diligent follow ups and tracked the projects extremely well. He had a knack of getting best from the Consultants. In 2003, Phil was decorated as MBE by the Government of UK for his outstanding contribution to SEAM. He still continues working in Cairo and is now preparing for EPAP-III.

During my years working in Egypt, I could "experiment", "apply" and "learn" all my ideas on CP. With the support of Phil and the colleagues at EEAA, we could come up with projects that were innovative and led to some high quality

107

outputs[7]. I feel that this is one of the great advantages of international consulting. In India, I couldn't have done the kind of work on CP that I was able to do in Egypt. Though I was quite proximal to the Ministry of Environment & Forests in India, the Central Pollution Control Board and agencies like National Productivity Council (NPC) and the Confederation of Indian Industry (CII) – but the shear inertia, absence of vision and inter-institution rivalry did not let me replicate what I could achieve in Egypt.

I remember that the textile exports from Egypt to EU & US were hit by requirement of eco-labels and we showed on the field scale how to achieve eco-label certification to a cost-advantage and wrote a manual[8]. This manual was translated in Arabic and seminars and training programs were conducted with a backing of the Ministries of Environment, Textile and Trade. This intervention had a very positive impact in the terms of both economics and the environment and became a success story.

My work at EEAA would typically start by 9:30 am. The lunch was generally late and quick. It used to be at the Creperie des Arts Maadi (simply called the Crêperie), downstairs from the EEAA office. The walls of the restaurant were decorated with black and white pictures of Hollywood stars and currency notes from different countries. The Crêperie was run by a father and his two sons. In my 12 years and numerous visits, we only smiled and hardly spoke. All I used to do was to point at the option in the Menu.

Most evenings, Phil and I would go out to an Italian restaurant, a Thai or sometimes an Indian restaurant nearby. Thai was the favorite. We used to order glasses of sweet and mediocre local Egyptian wine, with a large bowl of peanuts followed by the main course. The idea was to talk rather than eat. When alone, I used to go to the Italian restaurant located at the ground floor of the Sofitel, where an Egyptian guitarist

---

7   Visit http://www.eeaa.gov.eg/seam/ to download the outputs we produced.The EPAP Website gives additional details. The eco-labeling manual on this website that I wrote is perhaps one of the few manuals available today that describes a real industry application with costs and benefits.

8   http://www.eeaa.gov.eg/seam/Manuals/ecolabell/Cover.PDF

used to play some nice old numbers – but used to repeat them most of the times.

I always stayed at the Sofitel in Cairo. The hotel was on the bank of the Nile and had a view of the Pyramids. The EEAA office, where I used to work, was just a 2 minute walk from Sofitel. Sometimes I used to prefer to stay at the Marriot at Zamalek in the city and take a taxi on the Corniche. The Marriot had all the vibrancy and proximity to the shopping areas but more importantly it was close to the famous La Bodega restaurant. La Bodega was a perfect place for playing the high-society game of "seen and be seen" without spending too much money. I loved the ambience, style and of course the food at La Bodega.

Amongst the numerous dinners I had at this restaurant, one of the dinners was with Laila Iskander and Phil. Phil knew her well because of SEAM-I and I was also independently in touch with her. Laila studied Economics, Political Science and Business at Cairo University. She later acquired a Doctorate of Education from the Teacher's College at Columbia University in New York. Laila is well known today for her notable work with the zabbaleen[9] or garbage collectors where she established an informal recycling school way back in 1982 to teach children basic literacy, health and hygiene – a project for which she received the Goldman Environmental Prize[10] in 1994.

Laila was (and is) a very vocal and high energy person. During the dinner we had, she criticized Hosni Mubarak – and loudly too. This was something not acceptable or not generally done as Mubarak was the President of Egypt and was very powerful. I told Laila to cool down but instead she started speaking even louder, "I don't care if Mubarak and his cronies send me to a prison" – she yelled. I thought that I will also be sent to an Egyptian prison along with Laila. So I behaved as if I did not know her at all and it was just a chance that we were sitting on the same dining table!

After Mubarak's departure, Egypt went into turmoil and I stopped my missions to

---

9   https://en.wikipedia.org/wiki/Zabbaleen
10   https://en.wikipedia.org/wiki/Goldman_Environmental_Prize

Cairo. I checked with Phil about Laila Iskander and I learnt that she had become the Minister of Environment (i.e. boss of EEAA). She did an excellent job there and increased proximity of the agency with the civil society. She took a strong stand to oppose the import of coal on environmental grounds and this was not accepted by the politicians and the industry. She was obviously moved out and transferred to the Ministry of Cultural Affairs (Urban Development)[11].

One of the other places I used to frequent was the Cairo Opera House. This was the place for music and opera. We used to book the tickets, go early to have coffee in the lounge and then take the seats. I could watch several famous operas in this great opera house with artists from Europe and enjoy some of the intimate solo music shows. I remember attending piano recitals by legendary Omar Khairat. Omar studied piano with Italian Maestro Vincenzo Carro and followed correspondence courses in music theory and composition with the Trinity College in England. According to music experts and critics, Omar Khairat's music bridges

contemporary Arab music and Western music reflecting genuine maturity.

But the greatest attraction to me was the Cairo Jazz Club, a place to be and in my opinion just as important as visiting the Pyramids! For well over a decade, the Cairo Jazz Club LLC has stood the test of time as Cairo's ultimate live music hub. The Cairo Jazz Club (or simply CJC) functioned as a portal for manifesting art and expression through music. It has stood witness to the rise of many fresh talents, regularly hosting the finest live acts in town, as well as international artists. The club's motto is "We serve good moods" and that is precisely what is on the menu every day of the week.

On one of the Friday evenings, I and my Dutch consultant friend on EPAP-II visited the CJC. We arrived by 10 pm as we knew that the real talented performers start warming up only by 11pm. On that day there was a performance from a group from Lebanon. The group specialized in refreshing and groovy retelling of songs from the Balkans and the Middle East. When the band started performing, we could feel their warmth and energy, weaving a tapestry of

---

11 See http://www.madamasr.com/sections/environment/new-minister-different-environment

delicate melodies, vocal harmonies, mesmeric percussion, punchy brass and wild floor (and hip) shaking bass-lines. This "music experience" was simply enthralling. The CJC was packed and full with smoke, coming from expensive cigarettes.

When I feel happy about the music, I have a habit to send an offer to the lead performer on a chit telling how I adored the performance – and saying that there is one free drink waiting for each member of the band – at the bar – courtesy me. So I sent across such a chit to the lead singer who was a short Lebanese woman with curly wild hair, wearing traditional Gambaz dress. I went across to tell the bartender that the bill would be on me. I lost my seat in this process and decided to stick on to the bar stool and continue listening to the Band.

The show was over by 12:30am and the Band with the lead lady reached the Bar. The support staff was "packing" the drums, a Korg Keyboard, guitars and all the "electronics". The lady got my chit from the bartender. As her colleagues were picking

a drink of their choice, she lit a cigarette and asked the bartender who the sponsor was. When he pointed at me, she strode across to me like a graceful lioness.

"Hey, thank you so much for your appreciation!" She said in a perfect American accent. Then dragging a deep puff from her cigarette, she sat crossed legged on the bar stool, winked at me and said, "We are going now to my house on the Corniche and are absolutely "hot" to continue singing and playing music. We cannot stop now. Would you like to join? Hop in if you want to – we are moving out in next 20 min."

I asked my Dutch colleague and he was game. The lady spoke to her colleagues in Arabic.

In the next forty minutes we were at her bungalow. As soon as we reached, all members of the team unpacked the boxes. The drums, the guitars were back in position and the "electronics" with Korg keyboard was set up. And wow, they started singing and playing again!

This time the music came from the heart and perhaps

was a treasure that the band wouldn't otherwise share with any outsider! Some of the songs that they performed at CJC were now played differently with subtle impromptu! The session went on till 4 am with short breaks for shots of Egyptian coffee. I don't know why they stopped at all!

They got us a taxi at 4:30am so that we could get back to the Sofitel. The lady, the lead singer, saw us off till the gate of her bungalow. While bidding good bye, she said, "Thanks for buying us the drinks and for coming here to continue appreciating us." I said on the contrary …!!

She opened the door of the taxi for us, spoke to the driver in Arabic and said, "Your taxi bill to go back to the hotel and it's on us. You don't pay."

On Sunday morning when I was in the office, I told this incident to the secretary Nelly. Nelly was shocked, "This is something crazy" she said and then dialed the CJC. There was some animated conversation in Arabic. After she put the phone down, she shouted in Arabic and got all the colleagues to her desk. Then another round of high pitched

conversation took place in Arabic. I stood there looking absolutely dumbfounded and not understanding what was happening.

Then Nelly turned to me and said, "Do you know who that woman was? You are the luckiest guy in the town. We simply envy you."

Apparently that lead lady Lebanese singer was one of the most sought after in the Arab world. I don't remember her name today but when I departed at the Cairo International Airport, I saw a number of Compact Disks in the music shop with covers featuring her face.

"Dr. Modak, You should have taken a photo standing next to her or at least taken her autograph." said Nelly with a frustrated look.

"Next time – I certainly will!" I said to Nelly in a reassuring tone.

But the next time never happened!

Blues rarely repeat. Do they?

19

It was a typical morning rush hour and as usual, I was driving to my office weeding through the traffic. When I stopped at the signal near the SiddhiVinayak temple in Prabhadevi, a tall man standing at the signal opened the front door and took seat next to me. I was surprised – how did this guy get into my car when the doors were latched?

As I sat there stunned and unable to speak, the Man smiled and said "Don't panic Dr. Modak. I am not terrorist or an extremist. I am – as many call me –God!"

Now I actually happened to know many psychopaths who think them-selves to be divine and I thought pulling over to the side of the road and somehow getting this crazy guy out of my car. But there were still 75 seconds left for the signal to turn green.

The Man continued, "Dr. Modak, I am not a psychic. I am the God – as many call me

so."

"Well then Mr. God, why are you here?" I asked.

The Man spoke calmly but again with a smile (that now looked a bit divine), "Dr. Modak, I came here to tell you that you have only 30 minutes to live. You will drive straight from Prabhadevi to the Babulnath Temple, then take a right turn and stop the car under a Banyan tree. You will switch off the ignition and rest your head on the steering wheel. It will be a massive cardiac arrest. I will join you there to free your soul and take you with me. It will be a painless death – so natural – just like a leaf falling from the Banyan tree. So don't worry."

The Man said all this so seriously that I almost believed him. I took a second look at him and saw that he did indeed have a "Godly" face and a divine aura. His eyes were full of compassion and kindness.

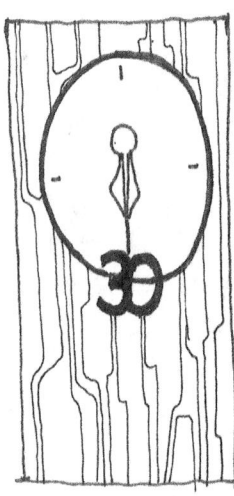

"Well, see you at Babulnath in the next 30 minutes Dr. Modak", said the Man – (or God) and simply disappeared.

The traffic signal turned green and as I drove ahead, I started thinking.

Assuming the Man was really the God and that I had only 30 minutes of life left, I didn't know what to do. There was so much of unfinished business and thirty minutes was just not enough. "That's too short a notice to give someone who is going to die", I muttered to myself and shifted the gears to move towards the Babulnath Temple. I was now heading towards the Worli sea face.

I first thought of my family - my wife, my daughter and son. My sudden death will be quite a shock to them. I felt bad. Not fair Mr. God!

I had always been too shy to tell my wife that I love her and that I love her deeply. I wish I had said so now. May be she already knows and I don't have to say it – I convinced myself.

My son and daughter stay in the United States. This Christmas I wanted to have a family get-together for old times' sake. I wanted us all to sleep on the same bed – with me telling them the same stupid stories I used to when they were kids. They would laugh at my silliest pranks and jokes. What a great stress buster it was. But I now knew that was not going to happen.

I thought of calling all of them just listen to their voices. But I stopped myself as I thought I will be choked with emotions. "Come on – Let's be practical." I told myself.

Then thought about my three elder sisters and that I won't be seeing them again. This hit me hard and I felt wounded as I had not seen them lately – despite their repeated invites. Work had kept me busy. "Was that worth it? I asked myself.

My car was now at Haji Ali.

I looked at the watch. There were only 10 minutes left before I reached the Babulnath Temple. "That's where my story ends." I said with a sigh.

I thought of my friends and colleagues, the good times we had and all the good work we did. I remembered all the men and women I have worked with – in my office and across the world. Some interesting faces flashed with bitter sweet memories. I won't be seeing these faces again.

I thought of my Roland keyboard and my collection of music. I realized that I hardly had time to play or listen to music anymore.

I then thought about this book on Environmental Management that I have been meaning to write. "It will remain incomplete" I said.

My heart longed for the lectures I used to give and the pleasure I used to get from working with my research students. There were so many intellectually rewarding and inspirational discussions.

I recalled my ambitions. I always wanted to bring change in environmental governance, reform environmental education and build more environmental entrepreneurs that practice ethically. These dreams had not yet been realized.

I had always assumed that I had enough time to do what I wanted to! But that was the mistake. We often don't realize how limited our time is.

I reached the Babulnath Temple and entered the alley as instructed by God. I found that large Banyan tree. I parked and switched off the ignition.

I was calm now as the reality of death had sunk in.

God was waiting.

He opened the door and took a seat. There was silence for a while and then He said, "Dr. Modak, You arrived on time – but my apologies. There has been a mistake. The thirty minute warning was for someone else. You still have more time – a few years perhaps. But I will have to check the records." He smiled – a bit naughtily – "Generally, my staff does not make such mistakes. My apologies again!"

I was speechless. That 30 minute drive from SiddhiVinayak to Babulnath Temple was the hardest of my life. This drive had made me review my life of 60 years in just 30 minutes – and rather brutally to realize what I ought to have done and what not! There was so much in my chest. I was pretentious and perhaps hiding my emotions all these years. I never realized that there was so much unfinished business in my professional life.

I thought of two options. The first being getting on with my life, doing exactly what I wanted to do, talking to my wife, meeting my children and sisters, spending time with my friends and colleagues and working hard to make my professional dreams come true. But I thought that this option was not very exciting!

The second option was to convince God that there could not have been such a mistake and the 30 minutes warning was indeed for me. That seemed to make more sense as I was now ready to die.

I looked up to God to argue my case for the second option, but by then he had simply disappeared!

The next time you stop at the traffic signal next to the SiddhiVinayak temple, look for a tall Man. He will make your 30 minute ride from Prabhadevi to Babulnath – a journey to remember.

20

THE MERLION OF SINGAPORE

This story is real, but I have changed the setting, names and characters in the interest of privacy. I have also blended a few instances. A little lengthy post but I do hope you enjoy the coincidences and experiences. Personally, I learnt a lot and understood myself better in the process.

In 1995, I joined a mission on a project for the Development of an Expert System for Environmental Impact Assessment (EIA). The project was very interesting and technically challenging. It was also perhaps way ahead of the times.

The idea was to develop a Computer based Expert system that would help Staff at the Environmental Regulators at the National Governments to identify significant environmental and social issues for a project and come up with mitigation measures to prepare an Environmental Management Plan (EMP). The system would also come up with a Terms of Reference for the collection of the baseline data that would help in assessing the significance of issues and the effectiveness of the EMP. This system would have a GIS interface.

The Expert System was to be cast in the form of a rule base. Rules had to be developed by mining data, information and knowledge and later by extracting "the experience" and "ability to assess" from the national experts.

A typical impact assessment rule was structured as follows... If an ACTIVITY takes place in a PROJECT (with certain timing, at a certain scale and following a particular method or methodology) and if the ENVIRONMENTAL COMPONENT exists in the AREA OF INFLUENCE (with certain sensitivity, abundance and economic & ecological importance) and certain conditions prevail at the SITE (e.g. low mixing heights), THEN the impact (or CHANGE IN ENVIRONMENTAL COMPONENTS/S) could be SIGNIFICANT. This inference is drawn based on data, documents and experience of experts (all details listed or tagged to the RULE) at 80% of CERTAINTY or CONFIDENCE.

My job was "knowledge engineering" or the creation of the RULES. The target countries were Philippines, Malaysia, Thailand and Indonesia. The sectors for which these RULES were to be developed were Thermal Power (Thailand), Irrigation (Indonesia), Water Supply (Philippines) and Highways (Malaysia). The idea was to hold knowledge engineering workshops in each of these countries over one week, inviting subject matter experts and using a RULE CAPTURING SOFTWARE to extract knowledge on impact assessment from the experts. Through these workshops, I could build approximately 1000 RULES on impact assessment. These RULES formed the core of the Expert System and represented the "minds" and associated "evidence" from more than 100 Environmental Impact Assessment (EIA) experts from these four countries addressing the four key

sectors.

I wish I could do such work in India. My repeated requests to Indian Ministry of Environment & Forests have been in vain, thanks to the Indian bureaucracy and a complete lack of "vision". It's a real pity that I could never get the Ministry of Environment and Forests, Government of India on board.

The team for this four week mission consisted of four members -- our team leader Jim, two others called Mike and Shona and I was the fourth member. Jim and Mike hailed from Canada and Shona was from Aberdeen in Scotland.

We set out on our mission by meeting in Manila. We were to spend a week in the Philippines followed by visits to Bangkok, Kuala Lumpur and Jakarta and finally exit from Singapore. We were to meet with the environmental regulators and conduct knowledge engineering workshops in each of the four project countries. In those days, the internet was still in its infancy and so were laptop computers. Each of my fellow team members had their own laptops along with subscriptions to dial up Internet services the four cities we were scheduled to work out of. Their internet service provider had also provided them with local telephone numbers through which they could access the internet using the modems that were attached to the laptops. These modems used to make a beep beep sound and then a gurrr at the end when the laptops connected to the local server!!

I was desperate to stay connected on the internet. The mission was rather long and I was wondering how to access my email box. I did not have a laptop either! Those were the days when emails trickled in, unlike now when I am constantly being flooded with mail. However, I was keen to receive and read the few messages that did coming.

During our first dinner in Manila, I expressed my worries on internet connectivity. Shona a very warm and friendly person in her mid-thirties understood my concerns. She proposed a solution.

"I don't work late at night so I can pass my laptop to you, post dinner." She said. "I will teach you how to dial up on the modem and access the local city server. Ask your colleagues in Mumbai to access your email box and forward your emails to my email id. Once connected, your emails will get downloaded along with my stuff. You can then read and respond. Bring the laptop when we meet in the morning for breakfast. OK?"

I was really touched by Shona's offer. Giving me access to her personal email was extremely generous. May be she trusted me or she was a good face reader or maybe she was a genuinely nice person, kind and helpful to everyone. Thinking back now, she may have been all those things.

Shona further added, "Do me a favor however, I don't know how much your email traffic is. Assuming it is high enough, just clean up the junk so there isn't any clutter in my mail box. But make sure you don't delete my emails in the process!!" She smiled as she said this and I noticed the dimples.

"Done!" I said

So began our daily laptop share. My very first access worked and I could read and respond to my emails. I had given a trusted student at IIT Bombay, access to my email and he would check my inbox and forward my emails to Shona's email account. As per our agreement, I would keep Shona's inbox clutter free religiously deleting my personal stuff and junk emails.

When I downloaded emails I found a large chunk of the emails belonged to Shona.

To weed out my emails, I would read the subject lines. Many of Shona's emails were from her husband George. I was often tempted to read these but refrained doing so on ethical grounds and because I did not want to betray the trust she showed me.

Shona was an amazing person to work with. We developed a process of developing the EMP based on ACTIVITIES and ENVIRONMENTAL COMPONENTS and I thought that it was very unique and added a lot of value to our project. Our approach essentially consisted of a combinatorial framework where alternatives were developed both around PROJECT ACTIVITIES and the impacted ENVIRONMENTAL COMPONENTS to achieve cost-effectiveness as well as sustainability. ACTIVITIES were either dropped, modified or "appended" with CONTROLS or MITIGATIONS and COMPONENTS were shielded, relocated or enhanced. I still use this approach in the development of project EMPs.

In the course of developing our approach, Shona and I had several brainstorming

sessions and discussion in the coffee shops of the hotels we stayed at during the mission. We also had several (friendly) arguments. The discussions were often "recorded" on the paper napkins that we used to carry to our rooms. We became good friends and started socializing after the days' work got done.

One night, as I was downloading my emails on Shona's laptop, I saw an email with the subject line "Re: This Guy Prasad Modak" from George. Obviously, Shona had written to her husband George about me and he had responded. I was extremely curious and wanted to know what Shona thought of me... as a colleague and now as a friend.

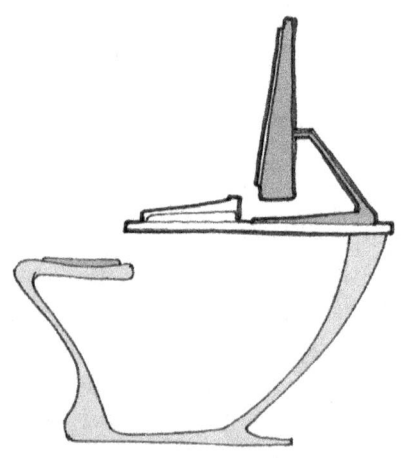

I debated with myself as to whether I should open the email and intrude on Shona's privacy. The more important issue was that of trust. Opening the email would be completely unethical and a betrayal of Shona's trust in me. I saw myself to be so "small" even with this thought. I got up and walked to the window overlooking the now deserted streets of Makati. I tried my best to divert my mind but I couldn't curb my curiosity.

The resistance to doing something unethical was melting away and finally I gave in to temptation.

"OK, let me do this ONLY one time." I told myself as I opened the email.

[When I think back to the incident now, I still feel ashamed. It was not right for me to open Shona's email. I have to chalk my actions to human weakness!]

In the email, Shona had introduced me to George. She had found me professionally good; was happy that I did not intrude her privacy and she liked working with me as I did not dominate conversations like most Indians do. To this George had responded, "tell me more about Prasad Modak." He ended his email suggesting she visit a coffee shop that was actually a library in Manila.

The next day was Saturday and all of us were having a lazy breakfast at the Edsa Plaza hotel. Jim and Mike wanted to go for shopping. Shona said that she was not interested in shopping but was looking for a place to relax and read a book in peace. I came up with a suggestion to go to Cool Beans. Cool Beans is the first and only library cafe in the Philippines to serve Philippine Highland Coffee (PHC). Cool Beans also had a large collection of over 500 pieces of reading material! This library cafe also has a very homey, cozy environment. It has couches so that customers could lounge comfortable while reading and having coffee. Today Cool Beans is located at 67 Maginhawa St., Brgy. UP Village, Diliman, Quezon City.

Shona was quite excited when we reached Cool Beans. She ordered a large cup of PHC, inhaled its unique aroma and took a deep sip. She said, "My husband George probably wanted me to visit this very place. Thanks so much Prasad for bringing me here."

"My pleasure!" I said. Shona picked up a copy of a book by Scot Fitzgerald and I chose to read Thurber's Carnival. We sank into the couches and read our books for an hour. Then after a second round of PHC, we left Cool Beans.

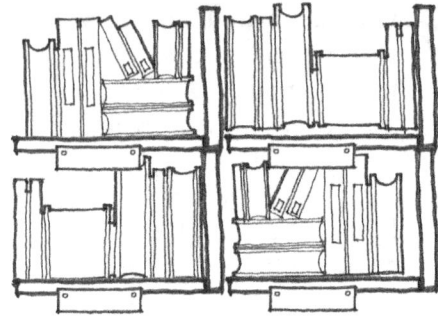

The next night, I accessed the emails once again. George had responded. This time I opened the email right away without a second thought. I was shamelessly addicted.... Shona had written about her enjoyable visit to Cool Beans, her conversations with me and especially my choice of the book at the café.

Soon we moved to Bangkok and my regular reading of her emails continued. Each night I used to be eagerly waiting for Shona to walk up to my room with her laptop. I became part of the world of George and Shona. Many times in our conversations, I used to see traces of views and thoughts expresses in the emails I had read – I then scuttled around making subtle remarks that were aligned to Shona's point of view. Shona used to show surprise at the apparent similarity of our thoughts. Mike and Jim often said that although we lived thousands of kilometers apart, we shared very similar views and

interests in life! To ensure that my secret would not come out, I used to sometimes disagree or voice another point of view – but only occasionally.

In Jakarta, George was keen that Shona visits the Jaya Pub. I suggested we go to this famous pub on a Friday evening. Shona was delighted at my suggestion. Mike joined us as we listened to some great jazz music on Indonesian flutes. Shona wrote George a long email telling him what a great time she had.

We moved on to Kuala Lumpur and on the very first evening there, we went to eat authentic idli-dosa (as per George's suggestion) at the Saravana Bhavan. The spice in the food brought tears to Shona's eyes but when she wrote to George she said that she has been well taken care of by her new Indian friend!

"This guy knows my mind – you don't worry." she wrote.

Working with Shona was a pleasure and extremely rewarding. I think our four weeks mission made us mature on the science behind EIA and its application in practice. We could understand the unevenness of EIA related governance in the four rising economies of Asia and across the four key sectors. Interactions with EIA specialists in the knowledge engineering workshops also greatly helped us in improving our own understanding. We made several new friends in this process. Shona was a very open personality and so we would gel well and synergize our thought processes and experience.

We reached Singapore -- the last stop on our four country journey. George had asked Shona to bring home a large statue (12" height) of the famous Merlion.

The Merlion is the national personification of Singapore. Its name combines "mer" meaning the sea and "lion". The fish body represents Singapore's origin as a fishing village -- it was called Temasek then, which means "sea town" in Javanese. The lion head represents Singapore's original name— Singapura —meaning "lion city" or "kota singa". It is truly a unique Singapore souvenir.

George was hosting a dinner for friends on the very next day after Shona's return and he wanted to place this large Merlion statue on the bar counter.

"It will look so majestic" he wrote. "And Shona please don't forget!"

Shona – as I knew now – was a very forgetful and absent minded person.

We reached Changi airport on the last day of our mission. My flight from Singapore to Mumbai, was an hour earlier than Shona's flight to take off to London. We were busy wrapping up on that last day and so I realize that Shona had no time to go to a shop and buy the Merlion statue that George had asked for. But I

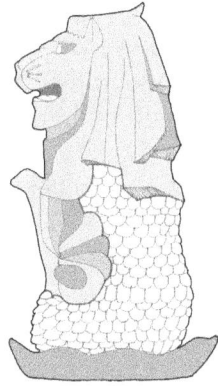

thought she could easily pick one up from the handicraft shops in the duty free area of the airport.

As we were strolling around the duty free area of Changi, I realized that Shona had completely forgotten about the Merlion. She bought some perfumes, a scarf, and a silk shirt for George. She actually walked by the handicraft shop that sold Merlion statues but missed picking the 12" piece that George wanted.

I was worried.

Soon there wasn't much time left for my flight. "Let me walk with you to the train to your Terminal Prasad.", Shona said. She wrapped her new silk scarf around her neck and looked stunning.

"We must keep in touch" she said.

I continued to be tensed as I was thinking of the Merlion. Getting the Merlion to George was very important. It was to be placed on the Bar stool at the party he was hosting to celebrate Shona's return. I could imagine how disappointed George would be if Shona missed getting the Merlion. I did not want this to happen.

I got into the train and as Shona stood outside waving good bye to me, I shouted, "Shona – Please don't forget the Singapore Merlion – George wants it….."

Just then the doors shut but I could see from the glass that Shona was shell shocked. She probably could not believe what I had said. But she was very intelligent and she quickly understood what was happening… The secret of our congruence was out.

She smiled her dimples and said something that I could not hear but from the way her lips moved I could guess that she was saying, "You RASCAL!"

I waved Goodbye!

Did I meet with Shona again? I was to do a mission over 2 weeks with her in Ho Chi Minh City on EIA, five years later. She opted not to join due to other reasons.

21

Coffee that was so hard to refuse

I was in Montreal to attend an international meeting on Ecocities. I arrived there a day early as I was keen to listen to the Jazz played at Modavie – a famous bistro in old Montreal. A place I will highly recommend.

Seven nights a week, local bands take the stage at Modavie. Modavie's spirited setting encompasses two floors and sets the scene for a night of great tunes and top dining. Even the bistro's wine menu hits the right notes.

I booked the table closest to the artists' performing area. The artist for that evening was one of the "golden oldies" originally from Chicago.

Jazz/Adult contemporary singer Sara Latendresse performing at Modavie When I arrived at the Modavie, few guests were around but most tables were not occupied. Soon people started pouring in. I asked for a glass of Brut blanc de blancs – pretty standard stuff and sat sipping my wine and reading the flyer placed on the table about the artist performing that night. Someone passed by me and a whiff of their perfume immediately caught my attention.

"Wow! That smells amazing." I thought to myself and looked for the source of this superb fragrance.

It was an elegant woman, perhaps 40-45 years old. She was beautiful with blonde hair and blue eyes and had taken a seat at the table adjoining mine. Like me, she was alone.

The Lady asked for the wine menu and after some discussion with the bar tender, ordered the Michel Jodoin – a sparkling wine. "Good choice!" I said to myself.

The jazz performance began and the sound of the strings on the box guitar was great, as were the voices of the two singers (a father and daughter singing duo - I learnt later). The choice of the jazz numbers was amazing too. It unfolded my memories.

In the short break that followed, the Lady and I happened to look at each other and I gave her a "thumbs up" to express my appreciation of the music being played. She responded with a warm smile and the twinkle in her eyes seemed to say, "I totally agree."

When the performance resumes, the male artist (the father), asked for requests and I wrote down mine. It was for Autumn Leaves by Tal Farlow I always liked listening to this great song.

The Great Tal Farlow Many from the audience handed in their requests as did the Lady next to me. The Artist skimmed through all the requests deciding what songs he could play and the order in which he would play them.

After he completed his "inspection", he spoke into the mike and said softly. "All very inspiring and challenging requests – but in the limited time we have, let me see what we can do."

"But I see something very interesting here." he said after a short pause. "I have received two requests for the same song. This is a song by Tal Farlow – a brilliant request. Haven't played Tal for quite a while and would love to. May I however ask the two Tal fan in the audience to raise their hand? I am just curious."

I raised my hand and was pleasantly surprised to see that my fellow Tal fan was the Lady at the next table.

"Oh, you two are sitting alone on separate tables but seem to share a similar taste!" said the artist. "Why don't you take the same table? You may enjoy my rendition of Tal Farlow better together."

"That is a rather outrageous suggestion." I thought, but before I could do or say

anything, the Lady got up and holding the empty chair at my table said, "May I?"

"Of course" I said, adjusting my chair so that she could be more comfortable. The cloud of that extraordinary perfume now got closer to me.

We listened to the Autumn Leaves together. The Artists did pretty well and it was an enjoyable experience. After the song ended, we clapped the longest.

We stayed for coffee after the performance and got talking. The Lady - Kenza, was originally from Egypt. She had an Egyptian mother and a French father and was now a Canadian citizen living in Calgary. We spoke about other works of Tal and other Jazz Guitar performers.

Coincidently, Kenza had also come to Montreal for the Ecocity conference. "What a small world!" she exclaimed and we decided to catch up the next day at the conference.

The next day was busy. The conference had around 800 participants and several parallel sessions. I bumped into Kenza at one of these parallel sessions. She was so noticeable in the crowd.

"Where were you during lunch?" she asked. "I was looking for some company!"

"Well it will cost you a coffee." I said. "That's my fee."

(Many who know me, are aware that this is my style of saying – "you are most welcome" – or "it's on the house or don't worry– I will be glad to help")"Done!" Kenza said and then continued in an excited tone. "By the way, there is a great performance at the Modavie tonight. It's a solo by Greg Clayton (Greg was nominated for the 2008 Canadian national jazz awards in the Acoustic Band of the Year category). Should we book the table?"

I told her I would and then booked the best table possible.

We met at Modavie that evening and this time I ordered the sparkling wine that Kenza had chosen when I first met her. The bar tender smiled as he saw us sitting together at the same table.

Greg Clayton was amazing and after the performance we stayed back to talk. I learnt

that Kenza, an urban planner of international experience, was recently divorced, and had been feeling lost and empty.

She also told me that she played the piano and I could sense that the music was really helping her get back to life.

We skipped coffee this time and left Modavie by 10pm. My hotel was within walking distance, just a little further than the apartment hotel Kenza was staying at.

"Don't stay in the swanky hotels when you are in old Montreal." Kenza said. "The apartment I'm staying at is in a building constructed in 1904! It's as though you are living in that era." We started walking. The fragrance of Kenza's perfume wafting about us was almost intoxicating.

When we reached Kenza's apartment building, she said, "Well Prasad, I am taking a flight back to Calgary in the morning and won't see you at the conference tomorrow. I really enjoyed meeting you and getting to know you. Don't you think perhaps that Tal Farlow wrote Autumn Leaves just for us to connect?"

Then pausing at the main entrance door, she said softly, "I know I owe you a coffee Prasad. Would you like to come up to my apartment now and have a cup of coffee with me? We could talk."

I did now know what to say.

I looked into her eyes -her blue and innocent eyes –longing for conversation and searching for a continued friendship. But sensing the feebleness of my own mind, I felt unsure. After taking a moment to decide, I said.

"Kenza, it's really late now. It's time to sleep and you have an early morning flight. I think this time I waive my coffee fee. There's always a next time."

I adjusted her long coat as there was a chilly wind as we said good bye and stayed out on the street till I saw the light in her apartment turn on.

That next time never came and my coffee date with Kenza is still pending.

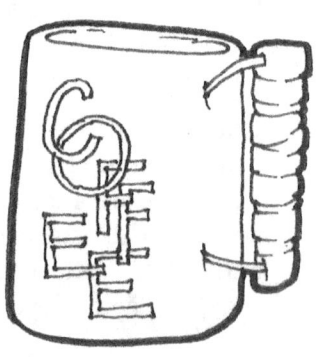

22

SHASHWAT AALINGAN – A HUG FOR SUSTAINABILITY

For past several years I have been struggling to influence the Government, investors, businesses and the general public regarding sustainability. But all the efforts made so far have been more or less in vain.

I thought of consulting Lord Vishnu this time. I went to the Dadar beach in Mumbai. It was a full moon night and I walked across the patchy sands, sometimes jumping to avoid the litter.

After a graft of three stents in my heart (I call them the trident), I now have a kind of instant communication system with Lord Vishnu. The stents apart from maintaining good circulation of blood in my heart function as a cosmic communication device. So I sent the message to Lord Vishnu using my trident of the stents.

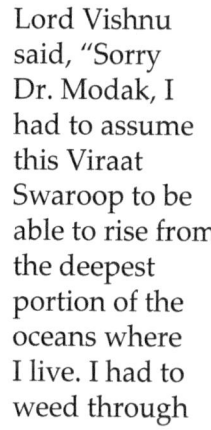

Lord Vishnu appeared in a moment responding to my call. But he came in his Viraat Swaroop that swirled the sea and churned the cover of the clouds. There was a thunder and flashing illumination. His enormous body was radiating blinding my eyes. I got worried (as people should not think that it is a repeat of 26/11) and requested the Lord to change his form to someone human. Lord Vishnu agreed to my request and took the form of Krishna.

I then stood like Arjuna from the Mahabharata in front of him.

Lord Vishnu said, "Sorry Dr. Modak, I had to assume this Viraat Swaroop to be able to rise from the deepest portion of the oceans where I live. I had to weed through so much of muck, especially the plastic waste, sewage and sludge – and only way was by assuming my Viraat Swaroop and simply push through it all. I never realized that the mankind focused only on land based management of pollution and took the oceans for granted. Anyway, what can I do for you this time Dr. Modak?"

I explained to the Lord about my frustration on the acceptance of sustainability in practice. "There is only talk and no action." I said.

Lord Vishnu (now Krishna) heard me out patiently and with a divine smile said, "Dr. Modak, you cannot bring in this change alone or all by yourself. You will need everybody to participate. The only way to involve and influence people is to give them a sustainability hug. Remember the use of touch enhances the transfer of spiritual or subtle-energies up to 100%, when compared to a greeting that does not involve touch."

He then continued, "When you will hug someone following my instructions, you will simply transmit your passion regarding sustainability to the other person. The person you hugged will not only get possessed but will be able to transmit the message of sustainability when he or she will hug someone else. This process will thus be viral and cascade rapidly. As you keep travelling across the word, keep hugging as you meet with people in each country. I estimate that in a year all people on this planet will live sustainably."

I was really impressed with Lord Vishnu's hug strategy. I must become a hug-a-holic I said to myself.

But I had some stupid questions.

"My Lord, some cultures don't accept hugging and if hugged can get seriously offended. And few or hardly anyone travels in the mountains where nomads and tribal live. Also can you ever imagine hugging the security guards at the airports?"

Lord Vishnu smiled and said, "Don't worry, I will tell you how to handle these exceptions. The tribal people already live sustainably and so you don't need to go to the mountains to hug them. They should be the ones descending from the mountain and hugging others. You don't need to hug the security guards as they hug you! We will go step by step."

He opened his arms and invited me for a good hug. "It's called Shashwat Aalingan (meaning a hug for sustainability)." He said. Then he hugged me and whispered in my ears.

"First bow to each other and recognize each other's presence. This is a desirable step but not essential. Next, open your arms and begin hugging, holding each other for three in-and-out-breaths. With the first breath, become aware that you are present in this very moment and feel happy. With the second breath, become aware that the other person is present in this moment and feel happy as well. With the third breath, become aware that you are here together and you want to do something good for this Earth. You will feel deep gratitude and happiness for the togetherness and taking a joint responsibility on sustainability. Finally, release the other person and bow to each other to show your thanks. I will send you a Gmail (means God's email) with more detailed instructions.[12]"

While he was giving this guidance, I was simply lost in his divine hug. I thought I should just continue and remain in his arms. I also realized that it was He who was managing the sustainability of the planet and beyond. Seeing me in a trance, he tapped my head and woke me up. I was disappointed.

While departing, he said, "Now devote the remainder of your life to replacing the usual hand shake with a sustainability hug. Open your arms to new people you meet and embrace them. This deeply transformative practice will change everybody's life and every person you will hug will appreciate and practice sustainability."

Before assuming his Viraat Swaroop, he cautioned,

"Becoming a hug-a-holic is a practice that requires a delicate balance of giving and receiving love. This doesn't mean that you're running up to embrace every single person you see on the street. The hugs that come from you are more of a natural effect that comes through a deeper devotion and passion to sustainability. My best wishes Dr. Modak."

Then with all the thunder and flashing illumination, Lord Vishnu in his Viraat Swaroop disappeared.

I went to my office in IL&FS.

---

12 based on Thich Nhat Hanh's work in "Chanting from the Heart"

My secretary Kermeene came to meet me. "Sir, I need your signatures." She said, "And do you know I am on vacation from tomorrow for 2 weeks?"

I said "Oh dear, print the papers ASAP so that I can sign them. Enjoy the break Kermeene, Take care!" I said this, got up and gave her a good hug following Lord Vishnu's instructions.

As we parted, I realized the sustainability hug was not all that difficult. Kermeene did not realize (perhaps) the special ability that I had transferred to her.

In few minutes, Kermeene came to my desk with papers that were printed on both sides. "Sorry Sir, printing took little longer as I wanted to use Elemental Chlorine Free (ECF) paper this time. I had to locate the right paper pack."

I was shocked to see this change. Normally Kermeene would print on single side and use regular chlorine bleach paper. After the sustainability hug, her behaviour had changed.

So what Lord Vishnu said was right.

While I was signing the papers, Pretty (Oops Preeti!) Mistry our facility and catering head and Kermeene's good friend walked by. Kermeene stopped her to greet and hugged her saying "long time no see!" Kermeene must have given her a sustainability hug, as within an hour, Preeti came to my desk asking my help to overhaul the food menu towards organic, eliminate use of plastic water bottles during the meetings and asked how to send the waste food for composting.

While returning from my desk, I saw Preeti run into Ramesh Bawa, Managing Director of IL&FS Financial Services (IFIN). Since they knew each other for long, Preeti gave him a friendly hug saying, "Sir, hope all is well."

In minutes, I saw Ramesh Bawa lift his phone and speak to one of his senior deputy, Asesh. "Asesh, why aren't you taking action on what Dr. Modak has been requesting (repeatedly) – a serious implementation of the Environmental & Social Management Framework (ESPF). Please take this up asap – ESPF is not to be looked at as a corporate compliance requirement but a risk management tool to our business. Also remember it adds value and builds our brand attracting international investors".

I thought this was amazing. The cascading effect that Lord Vishnu spoke about was actually happening.

I flew to Delhi the next day and was at the Ministry of Environment & Forests and Climate Change (MoEF) (I met A. K. Mehta, IAS, Joint Secretary, in charge of Pollution Control and (Acting) Chairman of the Central Pollution Control Board. When he saw me, he took out his hand for a handshake, "Oh Dr. Modak, how come here today?"

Not wanting to waste this opportunity, I stepped ahead and gave Mr. Mehta a sustainability hug. I could sense that he was surprised and a bit awkward. But I managed to hold him for 30 seconds following the three steps. We parted saying, "Let us catch up some time."

The next day's edition of the newpaper DNA carried an article on Page 3 -- "MoEF re-launches its Eco-Mark label with updated and improved implementation mechanism. Relaunch of this eco-label demonstrates MoEF's commitment to move beyond conventional pollution control and bring in the dimension of Sustainable Consumption and Production (SCP)."I was very pleased and impressed with this announcement.

So Shashwat Aalingan was creating the magic and making the transformation I was looking for. I decided to take an appointment with Mr. Arvind Kejariwal for the interest of Delhi's air quality. That appointment request is however still in a queue!

Anyway, let us get back to the subject of hugging.

Being hugged and touched by parents is important for the emotional well-being and development of children. I remember that when I was young, my parents used to hug me regularly and every day. Did this help in transmitting the DNA of my family to me? May be.

I always hug my kids when dropping them or receiving them at airports. When did you last hug your children? Try giving them Lord Vishnu's sustainability hug. We want to ensure that the next generation understands and practices sustainability as not much time is left to save the planet.

Have you ever hugged a tree when you are walking in the park or in a forest in the early morning? Science has already proven that hugging trees is good for health. According to Amanda Froelich, hugging trees brings in a change benefiting human health by altering vibration frequency. A recently published book called Blinded by Science by author Matthew Silverstone provides evidence of the benefits of tree hugging. These benefits include reducing severity of mental illnesses, Attention Deficit Hyperactivity Disorder (ADHD), depression and the headaches, etc. So go ahead and hug a tree and encourage others to do so for the interest of sustainability.

I spoke about my conversations with Lord Vishnu and the sustainability hug with my Professor friend. As usual, he was not impressed at all. He said he does not believe a word of what I said.

He then spoke in his characteristic matter of fact tone, "Hugging a person causes your brain to release serotonin, dopamine and endorphin to trigger reactions of happiness and joy. These secretions negate the worries of mortality by decreasing the levels of stress hormone, by altering the perception of brain by evoking out positive emotions in us. The hug can cause a massive release neuro-hormones in our body that we are unknown of. These neuro-hormonal changes calm our mind[13]. In this calmness, you discover and believe in sustainability. So what your Lord Vishnu has told you is something rather basic"

I did not like the Professor trivializing Shashwata Aalingan and calling it basic!

Then while lighting his cigar, the Professor asked, "By the way, have you come across the Hug Shirt™ – A shirt that makes people send hugs over distance!"

"No!" I replied.

Professor continued, "The Hug Shirt was invented in 2002, by Francesca Rosella and Ryan Genz- the co-founders of CuteCircuit. Embedded in the Hug Shirt™ there are sensors that feel the strength, duration, and location of the touch, the skin warmth and the heartbeat rate of the sender and actuators that recreate the sensation of touch, warmth and emotion of the hug to the Hug Shirt™ of the distant loved one. The Hug Shirt™ was awarded as one of the Best Inventions of the Year by Time Magazine in 2006. Do you know that research has shown that people need to be touched at

---

13 See Dr. Fahad Basheer, Author of "The Science of Emotions" Blog available at: https://drfahadbasheer.wordpress.com/

least 70 times a day! You can do this easily with the Hug Shirt. This hug is non-physical and can be "executed" over a distance. The system is very simple: All you need is a Hug Shirt™ (Bluetooth with sensors and actuators), a Bluetooth enabled smartphone with the Hug Shirt™ App running and on the other side another smartphone and another Hug Shirt™. A Hug Shirt is rechargeable and washable and is available in Womenswear, Menswear, and Kidswear styles."

I was awed and impressed as all this information was new to me.

I asked, "Professor, do you have a plan to get Hug Shirt technology in India?"

Professor got up and closed the door of this office – then turned to me and spoke in a low voice.

"Dr. Modak, in fact this is a secret mission assigned to me by the Prime Minister himself. Like you were introduced to the so called Shashwat Aalingan by Lord Vishnu (I noticed here a smirk on his face), I am developing an algorithm of processing senses in combination with nanotech based sensors that will promote the NDA Government (instead of sustainability).

Our Hug Shirts will communicate to the NDA's good governance to the opposing party. This will make the opposition believe that NDA is the only party to support and vote for in the next election. The NDA will provide all opposition party workers free Hug Shirts. An undercover team of the NDA will give electronic hugs to these workers and lure them to the NDA team. Of course this will be done on select basis and in a guarded manner. The process of convincing will however become viral. We are currently in a pilot stage and results so far have been pretty good."

I was simply shocked with this deep strategy.

"I am sorry but I cannot reveal any more information to you." Professor said this as he extinguished his cigar. Then he ended the conversation with a thick voice.

"What is sustainability after all? Having a political ruling that is sensible & stable over years is what counts. This is what this country needs. We don't need your kind of sustainability"

I gave a Shashwat Aalingan to the Professor (without him realizing of course!) and quietly left.

23

LIFE WITHOUT A SMART PHONE

Lord Indra, the King of Gods, received the 2015 Earth Report. The primary focus of the report was on how a human being on Earth spends time on a typical day. The report showed that humans spent most of their time using Smart Phones. The statistics indicated that the number of Smart Phones on the Earth had reached a staggering 7 billion and on average humans spent nearly 5 hours a day on their Smart Phones. For 2016, the usage was expected to be even higher – reaching a daily average of 7 hours.

That's just crazy!" said Lord Indra. "This is no life – it is simply a waste of time! It is definitely not what the Gods intended."

He called for an emergency meeting of the divine core committee comprising of the holy trinity - Lord Vishnu (God of Conservation and Protection), Lord Shiva (Lord of Destruction) and Lord Bramha (Lord of Creation).

Lord Shiva suggested that this problem could be easily solved by getting rid of all Smart Phones. "I will simply open my third eye..." he explained, "...and all the Smart Phones on the Earth will catch fire and be destroyed."

[According to Hindu mythology, Lord Shiva opens his third eye to destroy all that is unconscious, dark, and dualistic in this dancing universe. So essentially, when Lord Shiva's third eye is open, all illusions such as the Smart

Phones will come to an end!]

"But this is not the solution" said Lord Vishnu, "the Smart Phone makers will make new phones in no time and provide replacements at competitive prices so as to grab the new market of 7 billion mobile phone users."

"Also let's not forget about the pollution generated by setting 7 billion Smart Phones on fire!" he continued. "Each mobile phone is like a mine of metals and so we can expect the at least 10 million tonnes of hazardous metals will be released into the environment. Very few mobile phone users know this."

Lord Brahma said that he has been observing the increase in the use of Smart Phones over the past few years with great concern. "The use of Smart Phones has major health impacts due to the radiation. Usage of over 2 hours per day can cause headaches and Alzheimer's disease."

Lord Yama (the God of Death and Lord Brahma's son) who had been recording the mintues of the meeting, said that according to some Swedish research that had been published in the International Archives of Occupational and Environmental Health Journal, people who use mobile phone for an hour per day will develop a brain tumor in ten years. There is also an American researcher, who claims that using mobile phones can cause different types of cancers. Very few Smart Phone users know that."

Lord Indra immediately instructed Lord Yama to initiate a survey to understand cause of death of every arriving soul focusing on their lifestyles. "The questionnaire you had previously used to examine the impact of smoking of cigarettes should work, as the usage of Smart Phones is an addiction – just like smoking."

"But Lord Vishnu, what is the solution to this Smart Phone problem?" asked Lord Indra who was now getting impatient.

Lord Vishnu had another point of view. He said, "As a first step, let us realize why humans on the Earth have started increasing their usage of Smart Phones. Smart Phones today are so efficient and convenient. They have effectively replaced a range of gadgets from the basic ones such as alarm clocks and calculators to the more complex ones such as computers and even the high end digital cameras. The Smart Phone is clearly a disruptive technology. It is not just the hardware, but it's the software or the smartphone applications (or Apps) that have made the real difference! Everyone is hooked on the social platforms like LinkedIn and Facebook (FB) that provide a new digital identity and flood users with megabytes of news and pictures (whether wanted or otherwise)."

"Every day new invitations keep pouring in and the statistics shows that on an average a FB member on the Earth has 338 connections." He continued. "Also let's not forget the dating related mobile apps that have got most teenagers hooked. What we really need, is to bring about a behavioral change."

"My suggestion is to attempt a Pilot study. Why don't we pick five people on Earth and with our divine powers make their mobile phones vanish with our divine power for a week. Then we can see how they live life without a Smart Phone? We should also ensure that any mobile phone they attempt to touch or use during this time will instantly vanish! Basically, they should be completely without a Smart Phone during the experiment. We will then meet after a week to take stock and review the results of the Pilot study." Then

turning to Lord Shiva he said, "Please take responsibility for operation Vanish Smartphone"

Lord Vishnu was always known to come up with clever ideas. So the Committee agreed to his suggestion.

"Who will be our five test subjects?" asked Lord Shiva and Lord Brahma recommended some interesting names.

At 8:15 am sharp, Mr. Mukesh Ambani of Reliance got into his BMW 760li. He took out his Smart Phone to make some private important calls as he would speak in peace and comfort. These calls or instructions would determine the course of business in India and for that matter of the world. But today the moment he touched his Smart Phone, it simply vanished! He was shocked. He had three spare mobiles in his car, but each

of those also disappeared the moment he touched them. He asked his driver to lend him his mobile and was astonished when that too vanished on his touch.

Mr. Ambani did not know what to do, how to spend the next 30 minutes in the car. He looked outside the window and saw the slums and poverty of Mumbai. He was aghast as he never looked outside, always being too busy staring at the screen of his Smart Phone. He then looked at the photos of his three children Akash, Isha and Anant that he always carried in his wallet.

"Oh there is so much to do for this city." he said to himself and then with a sigh said, "I really don't connect much with my children. I must spend quality time with them as a family." He decided to not use his Smart Phone for some time. "The absence of Smart phones is making me think differently." he muttered to himself.

Sunny, a young collegiate had a date with Julie at Café Mondiger at Colaba at 6pm. This was to be their second meeting after a brief encounter at a party in Bandra. Sunny was riding the A/C Bus from Malad. The traffic was crazy and Sunny was getting delayed by almost half an hour. He picked up his Smart Phone to text Julie and let her know of the delay but as soon as he touched his Smart Phone, the phone vanished – courtesy the powers of Lord Shiva.

"Shit, what's happening?" Sunny exclaimed. He searched for the Phone in his bag pack. There was no trace.

In desperation, Sunny requested his neighbor on the bus for his phone explaining the "emergency." The neighbor, who was a kind retired person, lent Sunny his Smart Phone. But as soon as Sunny touched it, that phone also disappeared! This was a serious problem!! Sunny had to not just apologize profusely but also give the gentleman his contact information and hand over his college ID

card and driving license with the promise that he would compensate or return the Smart Phone, the very next day. The old man who was earlier very kind was now enraged as his Smart Phone had photographs of his 50th wedding anniversary celebrations. "How do I get these back?" He said, in tears. Smart Phones have become now places to store the memories.

Sunny reached Café Mondegar by 6:45pm - forty five minutes late for his date and he was sure that Julie won't be around. There was no way any girl would wait that long without a call or text. As he entered Café Mondegar however, he found Julie wearing an embroidered white shirt and a dark skirt, sitting crossed legged at one of the round tables.

"Oh Sunny, why so late? You must have been stuck in the traffic." she said in an understanding tone. "But I knew you would come and so I kept waiting."

While taking his seat at the round table, Sunny apologized profusely and then looked into Julie's eyes. Her eyes showed the happiness, trust and an interest to go ahead.

"Oh indeed, there was no need to panic!" Sunny told

himself as he ordered a draft beer and Akuri. Not having the Smart Phone helped both Sunny and Julie to know that they really liked each other. They eventually got married.

Deepika Padukone, the famous actor and one of my favorites, was in a shopping mall. She finished her shopping and took out her Smart Phone to call her driver to come fetch her at the mall exit. The Smart Phone disappeared!

"Oh I must have left the phone in the car" she thought. "Lately I have really become so absent minded."

She then approached the information desk for help and the lady on duty there dialed the driver's number. She tried several times but the response she got was "Out of reach!"

"This happens when cars are parked in the lowest basement." The lady explained apologetically. "I am sending one of my boys to the basement right way. He will ask your driver to fetch your car." After all the lady knew that she was talking to Deepika Padukone the famous actor! Meanwhile, in order to keep Deepika busy and entertained, she asked Deepika whether she would be interested in taking a look at a small exhibition set up by the Mall to display products made out of waste materials and crafted by poor women. Deepika went across to see it and being a person committed to working for the good of society, she was really overwhelmed and inspired. Two weeks later, she announced a program to encourage such initiatives in Bangalore and chose to become an ambassador for the cause. "Losing my Smart Phone the other day – showed me a new opportunity to do some good." she said in a Press Interview.

There we two more individuals that were tracked by Lord Indra. They included the politician Subramanian Swami (who really didn't know what to do in life in the absence of a Smart Phone) and a share broker on Bombay Stock Exchange (who thought of committing suicide when his Smart Phone vanished).

The Committee of Lords met after a week to review the results of their Pilot study.

"So life without Smart Phones seems to be a good idea – despite its advantages." said Lord Vishnu. Both Lord Shiva and Lord Brahma seemed to be in agreement. To come to an acceptable conclusion and follow up action however, the Committee decided to do a Godly Consultation (similar to the Public Consultations here on Earth!).

Around 100 Gods, demi-Gods and other celestial beings attended the consultation. Several ideas were proposed on how to discourage the increasing use of Smart Phones and encourage people on the Earth to reduce the time spent on mobiles. Some suggested reducing the battery life of the Smart Phone so that the talking time is restricted to only 1 hour a day. Some suggested a complete ban on certain mobile applications (such as social networking) thereby encouraging people to live life in "reality", meet and talk to each other and not keep staring at the screen and or get a disturbed night's sleep or over shop (i.e. consume for the sake of consumption). Some asked for withdrawal of the WhatsApp application through which humans keep sending silly messages and pictures only for the sake of a "digital identity" and because it's free.

Muni Narad (son of Lord Brahma) suggested making the Smart Phone apps completely unpredictable to unreliable.

Imagine if you logged into your FB account and saw total strangers shown as your friends! Or if you logged on to LinkedIn and saw somebody else's profile instead of yours! What a crazy world it will be! Muni Narad had a devilish grin when he said this.

Lord Vishnu vetoed this suggestion.

"This is so typical of Narad Muni." he said. "Narad's suggestion would drive the humans crazy and turn them into mentally depressed and completely dysfunctional lunatics!"

[Narad Muni, the son of Brahma and a devotee of Lord Vishnu is known for gossiping. He knows all the news from around the universe and is an infamous trouble-maker -- causing fights and misunderstandings among Gods and humans alike by spicing up facts. Muni Narad is believed to be the first journalist on the Earth and it is said that he still guides the Indian Journalists!]

Lord Brahma who was listening to all this patiently, spoke. "I don't have an immediate solution but I would like to suggest something we could look at

for the long term. Given the human addiction for the Smart Phones, let me "engineer" a few innovative molecules in the Human Genome that will provide the human body with Smart Phone like capabilities. Armed with this feature, the humans of the future will be able to "send SMSes", "make calls" or "go on FB" or "shop" by simply using mental powers. For instance, two people, a thousand kilometers apart can, by simply closing their eyes and meditating, have a conversation without a Smart Phone. By introducing this change in humans, we will address the health related issues of the Smart Phones as well that of the mounting E-Waste!"

"This is an excellent suggestion and I congratulate you Lord Brahma!" said Lord Vishnu. "Just copy part of the DNA structure we have. We all communicate with each other through our Mind Power– and without any of these Smart Phones for thousands of years – Isn't it?" And I thought he was just right.

The Godly Consultation on Smart Phones ended with a Vote of Thanks.

24

Professor Thanh Teaches me the (Emotional) Art of Giving

Professor N. C. Thanh was the Chairman of the Environmental Engineering Division when I joined Asian Institute of Technology (AIT) in Bangkok. Most in the Division used to be scared of him as he had a very strict face and was firm on following the rules a stickler for the rules. At the Division parties however, he was a different person. He would be the star of the event, socialize with everybody and even take the lead on the dance floor.

Professor Thanh was always well dressed and wore everything branded – his belt, his shoes, his shirt and the tie were all signature stuff. I don't think he ever shopped for items on sale or with discounts! That was all a part of his personality!

Professor Thanh was a Vietnamese national. He had done his doctoral research in Canada (at the University of Laval) and then become a Canadian Citizen. He spoke French fluently but his English had a mix of Vietnamese and French accent. Whenever he spoke it sounded rather pleasant and sweet.

During my stay at AIT, I hardly interacted with Professor Thanh as I worked with Dr. Bindu Lohani. I did however know that water treatment was one of his areas of expertise and he had bagged research awards on work done on "horizontal filtration".

I reconnected with Professor Thanh nearly 5 years after I returned to India, in 1989, on a cruise on the Chao Praya River. Meeting him on the cruise was a sheer coincidence.

He asked me, "Dr. Modak, what do you do nowadays? I have left AIT now and I run training programs under the banner of CEFIGREE

143

(International Centre in Water Resources Management in France). Would you have the time and interest to come to Bangkok and deliver a few lectures for our training courses? We don't pay much but we will take good care of you!"

I readily agreed to Professor Thanh's proposal. I was missing Bangkok anyways.

I would lecture on Water Quality Modelling and Management in Professor Thanh's courses. These events used to be once every four months and as a result,I did many sorties to Bangkok for nearly three years. Professor Thanh was a good host and a meticulous organizer. His team included my batch mate Wanida Srichai and Prof. Thanh's former secretary from AIT - Khun Ratana. They took really good care of me - I was picked up and dropped to the airport, housed in a decent and a friendly hotel, taken out with friends to some excellent local restaurants and of course to the shopping malls.

While at AIT, I hadn't had the opportunity to listen to Professor Thanh's lectures. During one of the CEFIGRE training programs however, I got the chance to do so. Once, Professor Thanh was introducing the subject of

Water Quality but the first two slides were not connected to the subject at all. The first slide showed a map of Bangkok highlighting the locations of shopping malls where there were sales. The second slide showed map of Pat pong, Soi Nana and Soi Cowboy and highlighted the locations of some of the most frequented night clubs and the "Go Go" bars.

While showing these two slides to the participants, Professor Thanh smiled and said "Well, you all will have copies of these two slides. So don't worry about what to do in the evenings – everything is taken care of. A mini-van with a driver who speaks English has also been arranged for your safety and comfort". Then he made a serious face and said, "But now, listen to me - We are going to discuss Water Quality and I want your full attention – no distractions please!" I really liked his style.

Professor Thanh often gave surprises. I recall a round table meeting in Bangkok where we were both present and the organizers asked each of us to introduce ourselves. I did my best in projecting my research and work experience - trying to impress the people. When Professor Thanh's turn came, he simply said, "I specialize in managing people." I was surprised! During the coffee break, I went to him and asked, "Professor, why didn't you talk about your work on water treatment, the research you published, awards you secured, etc? – "managing people" sounded a bit trivial!"

Professor Thanh smiled and said, "Dr. Modak, you will soon realize that managing people is actually the key and something extremely hard to do." Unfortunately, I understood his point all too well much later in my life.

Professor Thanh also had a fantastic memory and would remember every minute detail. I recall once we were having a drink at one of our close friend's place (P. Illangovan) in Bangkok. At the time, Professor Thanh was working with a Finnish company that operated from Helsinki called "Soil & Water". Before the dinner, Professor made me a concoction of red lingonberry Finnish wine - a rare wine not generally seen at the airport duty free shops. The concoction was exceptional and I praised Professor Thanh for the delicate balance and said, "Professor, I wish we have another occasion to drink this wine once again."

Years passed by. In 2002, I was in Yogyakarta, Indonesia for a conference when I saw Professor Thanh's name in the list of delegates. When I checked in, I had a message waiting for me in my room. It read, "Dr. Modak, I knew you were to attend this conference. Please could you come to my room at 7 pm for a drink?"

When I reached his room, there were some old friends and some new faces that Professor Thanh introduced. Professor Thanh then got up, opened the mini-bar and took out a bottle of red lingonberry. He told everybody, "This wine is Dr. Modak's favorite. I am offering him the concoction that he had and loved the last time he was in Bangkok." I later realized that Professor had bought this wine especially for me on one of his trips to Helsinki and kept it in the reserve. I was astonished with his remarkable memory and touched by this affectionate gesture.

When Professor Thanh was appointed as the Director of the Asian Institute of Technology in Hanoi, we had several opportunities to meet and do joint projects. During one of the missions, I remember visiting his house in Ho-Chi-Minh City. I was greeted by his old father and the three sisters who cooked dinner for me that evening. When we sat at the dining table, Professor Thanh's father introduced the menu, spoke about each item and then called on the sister who prepared that item and thanked her for the hard work. This was something rather unusual and very touching. When we finished the dinner, I was asked to say a few words about my experience of eating the home cooked Vietnamese food. I spoke and Professor Thanh translated. That dinner was a rather emotional and very memorable event.

Expressing emotions has always been Professor Thanh's weakness. He is a very sentimental and a sensitive person. I visited his house in Bangkok when he had organized a lunch for me and Dr. Bindu Lohani. He asked me to come early and when I arrived, he took me to the market. He then personally picked the vegetables, meat and the fruits after a lot of thought and examination. "It is important that one should be personally involved right from the shopping, when it comes to preparing lunch for friends. Most ask the cook or order from a restaurant. I don't when it comes to friends" He explained. And the lunch turned out to be excellent.

Professor Thanh, Dr. Bindu Lohani and Prof. Visu at AIT – A Recent Picture

After the lunch, Dr. Lohani left and I stayed on a bit longer. Professor Thanh took me upstairs to show me the house and I saw an amazing collection of handicrafts, art pieces and paintings. I couldn't help but praise some of art work and I said, "I envy you Professor for processing such a great collection." Many of these pieces were original antiques. Later, we went downstairs for a cup of Vietnamese tea.

As I was leaving his house and getting into a taxi, a large box was handed over to me. I was surprised. When asked about it, Professor Thanh said "Dr. Modak, these are a few gifts for you as a memory for today's wonderful lunch." I insisted on opening the box

and found that it contained gifts that were actually the very art crafts that I had praised during the tour of the house. I felt very embarrassed and said, "Professor, I was only appreciating your collection. You didn't have to gift it to me."

Professor Thanh smiled and said, "Dr Modak, it's easy to give a gift to someone by buying it in a mall. There are no emotions there! But it is something different when you gift someone from your own collection and part with it happily – all as a token of love and affection. My heart will be with you when you will keep these artifacts in your house." I was simply speechless!

I still have those wonderful gifts of art work in my house and they remind me of Professor Thanh and his teaching me how to give a friend a gift. The (emotional) art of giving!

25

Lord Vishnu consults me on Sustainability

On January 21, I suffered from a cardiac attack and was rushed to Hinduja Hospital (Mumbai) in the nick of the time. I was operated on (and had two stents put in) and then discharged after a week-long stay in the ICU. This post narrates a bit of my hospital experience.

How real is the story? I leave that to you to decide.

Lord Vishnu, the principal protector God of Hindu Mythology, had been after my secretary seeking an appointment. He wanted to take my advice on sustainability management in the Kingdom of the Gods. In his email he told me that sustainability was just working in the Heavens and he thought the problem stemmed from poor sustainability management on the Earth.

I didn't have enough time for the Lord as I was busy with some assignments for the World Bank and so I proposed we have a quick chat on Skype instead.

After hearing his story, I said, "I am not really surprised that you have problems with sustainability – first of all you don't have clear job description and allocation of responsibilities when it comes to sustainability management. You are the supreme God for protection and conservation and yet, you are not well connected to the other Gods like Vayu, Agni, Varuna and the Goddess Earth who represent important elements of nature i.e. Panchmahabhuta. They have been given sub-ordinate importance like Minister of States in India. You folks don't meet each other on regular basis and there is no coordinated approach to sustainability management. Also there is no common agenda and no practice of sustainability reporting like we practice here on Earth. You remain a Page 3 personality. You have thousands of temples floating around. The other Gods representing the Panchamahabhuta and who matter to sustainability don't have many dedicated temples. The temples that do exist are not a part of your network – for instance, the Tiruvannamalai temple in South India depicts the manifestation of the five elements by Lord Shiva and not you[14].

Your relationship with the Panchamahabhutas at the operational level is therefore quite confusing. There is also no integrated perspective given to the worshipers as they offer prayer to these Panchamahabhutas separately in the respective temples. For sustainability communication, there should be been just one common temple all the Panchamahabhutas. I don't like this isolated approach."

"I agree Dr. Modak." said Lord Vishnu. "Your company visiting card shows all the five elements to be well-connected and well balanced."

"That's beside the point." I thought to myself. To cut the conversation short, I said, "Well Lord, let me give you this quick bit of advice now and you can meet me later for a more detailed discussion. Let us restructure the Gods and your organization. Please get Lord Indra involved as we need to take on some administrative reforms and a new communication strategy. Meet me on January 23rd but before coming to my office check with my secretary – I am really very busy."

Then, I ended the Skype call.

On January 21st, I suffered a massive cardiac attack and was rushed to Hinduja

---

14 See http://www.greenmesg.org/temples_chennai/pancha_bootha_sthalams_chennai.php

Hospital in Mumbai.

That night, the doctors got me stabilized and decided to do an angiography followed by an angioplasty on January 23rd.

I waited for my turn in the Operation Theater (OT) and was lying on the ICU bed (which seemed like the first class seat on Lufthansa). Dr. Rajani – a very busy heart specialist – was to perform the procedure.

Just then, a doctor appeared in my ICU cubical. He was unusually tall with an impressive mobile and an imported stethoscope. Soon the image blurred and Lord Vishnu appeared in place of the doctor. The mobile was replaced by a Shankha and the stethoscope by a Pasha. I was shocked to see him.

"How the hell did you get in here Lord Vishnu?" I asked rather irritated with his Godly intrusion. "Didn't you check with my secretary? She would have told you that I was hospitalized."

Lord Vishnu spoke to me in Malayalam. And then realizing that I was not able to understand the language, he started speaking in English, "Sorry Dr. Modak, I was busy understanding your case papers with the nurses in the ICU and had to quickly learn Malayalam to know what's gone wrong with you. I did try calling your secretary but kept getting a message not in reach. So I decided to check your whereabouts myself. That's how I reached this hospital."

"But who issued you the Gate Pass?" I asked. "I don't want you to have problems with hospital administration."

"Don't worry", Lord Vishnu said, "but I had tough time locating you until I said that you work for the World Bank. I did not know that this hospital has a special ICU unit for the staff and consultants of the World Bank! I also came across a special ICU unit for Ministers where only by-pass surgeries are performed. Apparently when given a choice between an angioplasty and a by-pass, the Ministers are only interested in the by-pass as that is an option they are used to. There is also a special ICU ward which admits only the rich and where they fit stents made of gold."

I was not interested in these

details and told Lord Vishnu that I would be moved to the OT any time now and that he should simply disappear (and take another appointment from my secretary). Lord Vishnu however insisted that he should accompany me to the OT.

"But how can you do this?" I asked. "And that too in your Peetamber outfit? Do you realize there are hospital strict rules? And besides, you don't even have a Gate pass."

"Leave it to me." said Lord Vishnu. "Let me first understand your problem once again."

He came forward and closing his eyes, touched my forehead. "Aha!" He said, "These reports, ECGs, X-rays don't give me a holistic picture. Now I understand your situation."

I didn't like this empirical approach to my diagnosis. "You should have sanitized your hands with this disinfectant spray before touching me." I told the Lord.

Ignoring my protests, Lord Vishnu rested his hand on my forehead for a while. He then suddenly transformed into the famous Dr. Rajani. He called the nurses to wheel me to the OT. They did so obediently with all the case papers stacked on the trolley. We

crossed the corridors through the swinging doors, knifing the chill around us.

When we reached the OT, I was worried as to what would happen if the real Dr. Rajani was already present. Fortunately he was not. Only his Team was there and they positioned me on a narrow bench under a scanning machine as the anesthetist readied his needle.

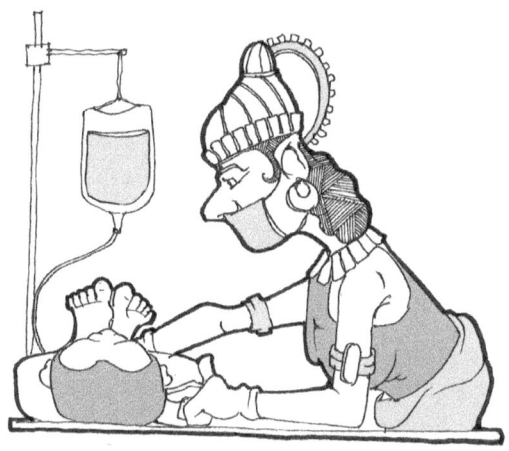

Lord Vishnu (as Dr. Rajani) then turned to the anesthetist and said, "Fire a shot of 900." A scintillating fire swirled from my wrist all through my body like a Sudarshan Chakra. Images of the movement of the dye started to appear on a large screen. Lord Vishnu told his Team mate, "Take me to the 100x resolution right here."

"Yes Sir" replied the assistant.

Just then the real Dr. Rajani entered the OT and I saw an amazing transformation. Lord

Vishnu cleverly blinded the Team for a second and moved inside the body of real Dr. Rajani. I could see Dr. Rajani tremble a little as he was being possessed/ controlled.

Then the real Dr. Rajani said, "Well Team, we are just in time. Get me stent - size 32. Let's float the ship to the docks and balloon."

The team assistant said, "Yes Sir, 32 it is – But Doc, what is that halo sort of thing I see around you as you bend down towards the screen? It is very strange."

I had noticed the halo too.

"You seem to be in good hands Dr. Modak." I heard someone say, though.

I don't know or cannot recall who said this.

The procedure was as doctors say, "uneventful!" And I decided not to invoice Lord Vishnu for my advice on sustainability.

SHADES OF GREEN

26

MANY FACES OF BIODEGRADABILITY

The claim of biodegradability is often associated with environmentally-friendly products, but I often wonder what exactly does this mean? The answer is not simple as there are many faces of biodegradability.

The US Environmental Protection Agency (EPA) defines as biodegradable those materials which can decompose under natural conditions. The American Society for Testing and Materials (ASTM), a leader in setting international standards, states that biodegradation is brought about by a biological activity, particularly enzymatic action, which can lead to changes in the chemical structure. The Federal Trade Commission (FTC), another US government agency, has drawn up guidelines on what legitimately qualifies as biodegradable materials.

Examples of biodegradable materials include fruits, vegetables, leaves, paper and seeds. Non-biodegradable materials, on the other hand, do not break down easily. These materials pose a threat to the surroundings since they simply pile up and take a long time to degrade. Landfills mostly comprise non-biodegradable materials such as plastics.

Can we certify biodegradability?

Going by the definitions listed above, most products are fundamentally biodegradable; the only difference being the amount of time it takes for each product to break down. Depending on the time, biodegradation may be partial or total.

In the test recommended by the European Union (EU), a 10-day window is used to define ready biodegradability. Within this time, a readily biodegradable substance must reach at least 60% mineralisation based on CO_2 production or O_2 depletion, or 70% based on reduction in Chemical Oxygen Demand (COD). The 10-day window begins when biodegradation has reached 10% and must end within the 28-day test.

Many manufacturers show some biodegradation taking place for an x-period of time and then use the data to extrapolate. But you cannot extrapolate the biological degradation process as such an extrapolation is scientifically unsound.

The Biodegradable Plastic Institute (BPI) in the US conducted two separate sets of tests on the Aquamantra water bottle sold by Dana Point, a California-based company which uses an additive from Enso Bottles LLC. The first test showed that the degradation process plateaued after 60 days and the second showed no degradation at all after 45 days. The company then did a 30-day test and extrapolated that the material will biodegrade in four years. This extrapolation could be however misleading.

Another example is found in the August 2010 issue of Biocycle Magazine. It published a study initiated by the Environmental Services Department and performed at the Miramar Greenery Composting Facility. Here 105 different compostable products were evaluated. The majority of the products selected met the ASTM standards (either ASTM D6400 or D6868). All of the products tested were purchased in the market. However, more than half of the 105 products did not biodegrade greater than 25%. Fifteen items that were both ASTM and BPI certified showed almost no effects of biodegradation.

Independently assessed and disclosed biodegradation data is thus essential to assess the fate and behavior of substances in the environment.

Are Biodegradable products always benign?

Take the case of active cleaning chemical nonylphenol ethoxylate (NPE), which is made of carbon, hydrogen and oxygen. NPEs do biodegrade to a benzene ring type or other simpler structures. However, this class of chemicals is considered suspicious because NPE can be possible endocrine disruptors. This means NPE may mimic endocrine hormones and cause havoc with a woman's reproductive system. So although biodegradable, NPE may by no means be environmentally-friendly.

End products of biodegradation: Are they always safe?

It gets more complicated when we think about products that contain complex chemicals. Pesticides such as DDT are hazardous and toxic in their own right and take a long time to biodegrade. But the greater problem in this case is that the breakdown products are even more toxic and dangerous than the original DDT. So biodegradation of such compounds can in fact complicate matters!

While biodegradability is something we all should desire in green products, we must understand its limitations, especially the "fuzziness around it's halo." Until such time that we come up with a better operating and communicable definition, biodegradability is like Hamlet asking – "To be or not to be!"

27

The Mobile Mines

Not long ago, mobile phones were a rare commodity and a luxury. These were used mainly by business people, government officials and the elite in society. Today, mobile phones are everywhere and used by everybody because of their affordability, connectivity and other applications. This has led to a huge number of unused and discarded phones because people frequently upgrade and replace their phones.

In the middle of 2005, the subscribers to mobile phone carriers dramatically increased. The number of total users jumped close to 4 billion worldwide resulting in an estimated 650 million retired or discarded mobile phones.

In 2014, nearly 60 percent of the population worldwide already owned a mobile phone. For 2017 the number of mobile phone users is forecast to reach 4.77 billion. The number of mobile phone users in the world is expected to pass the five billion mark by 2019[15].

The problem now was what do we do with these discarded mobile phones?

A mobile phone has significant environmental impacts throughout its life cycle –from extraction (especially metals), making, packaging and distribution, use and disposal.

The following figure describes the life cycle of a typical mobile phone. You would notice that recycling and

15 Source: Mobile phone users worldwide 2013-2019 | Statistic
    www.statista.com/statistics/.../forecast-of-mobile-phone-users-worldwide/

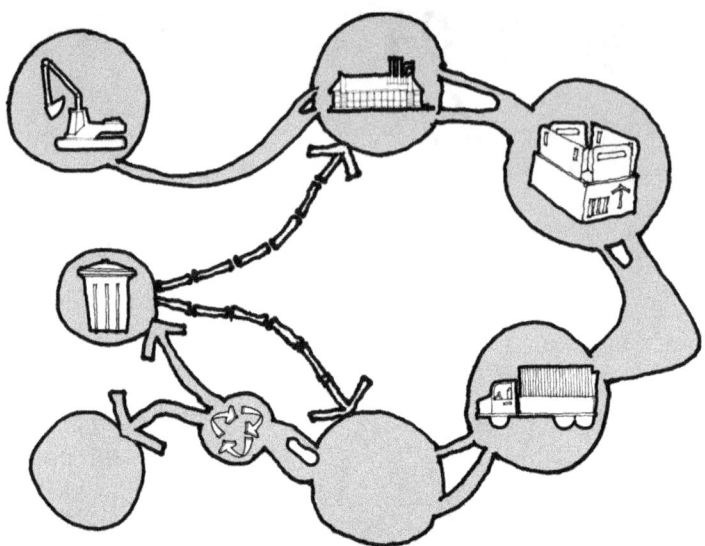

reuse should ideally form a dominant component of this life cycle. Most discarded mobile phones will otherwise choke our landfills.

What do mobile phones typically contain?

Mostly, mobile phones comprise of a handset (which includes: Printed Circuit Board (PCB), Liquid Crystal Display (LCD), Keypad, Antennae, Microphone, Casing), a battery and a charger. The PCB is made mostly of copper soldered to a board with protective coatings and adhesives. The board is made of epoxy resin or fiberglass and generally coated with gold plating. Other precious metals and hazardous substances in the PCB are arsenic (in chips made from gallium arsenide), antimony, beryllium, Brominated Flame Retardants

(BFRs), cadmium, lead (used in the solder that joins the parts), nickel, palladium, silver, tantalum and zinc. The lead and BFRs have the highest environmental impact due to their levels of toxicity and persistence in the environment.

The LCD as the name suggests contains liquid crystals and these substances can contain toxic substances such as mercury. Rechargeable batteries generate less waste than single-use batteries however; rechargeable batteries can contain toxic components such as cadmium, nickel, zinc and copper. The charger used to recharge the battery often weighs more than the handset and battery combined. It is generally not interchangeable across the different makes and models of phones, contributing significantly to the waste generated. The chargers consist of mainly copper wires encased in plastic, but materials such as gold, cadmium and BFRs may also be present.

Discarded mobile phones are like mobile mines of precious metals.

Nearly 300 grams of gold can be recovered from approximately 1 ton of recycled mobile phones. This gold when re-used can save mining 110 tons of gold ore. Batteries contain a range of metals which can be reused as a secondary raw material. There are well established methods for recycling most batteries containing lead, nickel-cadmium and mercury, but for some, such as the newer nickel-hydride and lithium systems, recycling is still in the early stages, but that will soon change.

So it is important that we find a way to recycle or get back the used mobile sets. Many large mobile set makers have come together today under the leadership of the Basel Secretariat to form the Mobile Phone Partnership Initiative (MPPI). We however need such partnerships to "descend

down" to local levels.

According to a global consumer survey released by Nokia, only 3% of people recycle their mobile phones. The survey was based on interviews with 6,500 people in 13 countries. Globally, half of those surveyed didn't know that metals could be reused. Between 65 – 80 per cent of a Nokia device can be recycled. Nokia has 5000 collection points for unwanted mobile devices in 85 countries around the world. It is the largest voluntary scheme in the mobile industry.

In Bangladesh, Nokia tried to promote its mobile recycling campaign, however the response was not significant mostly because of lack of awareness and unfamiliarity with the concept of recycling. Also people wanted to be paid for returning their used mobile phones.

So some experts believe that buy-back programs may just work. Sprint in the United States has a long list of approved phones for their buy back scheme[16]. Sprint pays a $195 for a 64GB Wi-Fi iPad, where as a T-Mobile MyTouch 4G is worth $85.69. A Samsung Restore will fetch $26, and an LG EnV Touch $12 in account

---

16 For more information visit: http://www.sprint.com/responsibility/communities_across/ index.html?ECID=vanity:recycle

credit. Normal wear and tear is fine, but the product must turn on and be free of corrosion, water damage, and display scratches.

There could be other incentive models for mobile phone recycling. At 40 Beijing post offices, Nokia has placed a Mobile Man to accept used mobile phones. Made in Singapore, Mobile Man is a non-motorized creature standing about 6 feet tall and weighing some 44 pounds. The Mobile Man gives a free movie ticket to those who turn in old phones. All they have to do is put their handset in a designated envelope and they'll also get a receipt that lets them stay updated on the status of their phone as it gets dismantled and recycled.

Nokia has taken other steps to encourage mobile phone recycling by installing Integrated Nokia Kiosk (INK) – a first-of-its-kind kiosk that combines recycling and customer care services. As part of a six-month pilot program, the booths have been rolled out in four locations across central Klang Valley in Malyasia. Mobile users can drop off their old phones at the kiosks to be recycled, as well as leave their devices for servicing.

We often use the term Extended Producer Responsibility (EPR), but in order to successfully mine the metals in our discarded mobiles phone, we must cultivate Extended Customer Responsibility (ECR). Everyone needs to consciously and actively recycle used mobile phones.

The next time you upgrade to a new mobile phone, consider sending the old one for recycling instead of just tossing it in the dustbin. Let's help conserve Earth's precious metal resources and do our bit to save the planet. Don't forget that mobile phones are like mobile mines!

For Students: Interesting projects could be conducting surveys on the used or discarded mobiles. Segment the survey across urban and rural areas, income groups, gender, age etc. Learn about take back schemes on used mobiles in your neighborhoods; meet mobile phone makers and suppliers on recycling – especially of metals, and open up a campaign. Attempt a life cycle analyses of mobile phones and the chargers. Study the technology options and economics of metal recycling.

28
Dwarfs with Tall Shadows

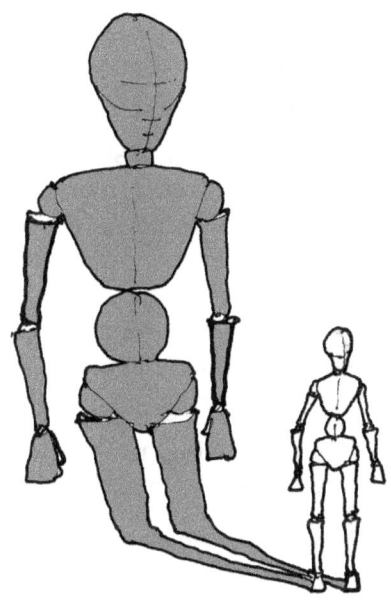

Life Cycle Analyses (LCA) today has become the basis for product makers to rethink about their products. LCA is a technique that helps assess the environmental impacts associated with all the stages of a product's life from-cradle-to-grave (i.e. from raw material extraction through materials processing, manufacture, distribution, use, repair and maintenance, and disposal or recycling).

Increasing number of products are now designed and manufactured to meet requirement of eco-labels that insist on "exclusions" of certain harmful substances, set thresholds on resource consumption ("inputs") and waste generation ("outputs"). The idea is to minimize adverse environmental and health impacts, reduce risks to the ecosystem and consumers in all phases of the product's life cycle. Products that are eco-labeled are therefore expected to have low environmental impacts/risks. Product manufacturers aim to meet the eco-label requirements through change in design, manufacturing process, packaging and the logistics of distribution. LCA provides the strategy of Life Cycle Management (LCM)

Typically, life cycle of a product goes through various phases. The following figure illustrates the life cycle phases for a T-shirt.

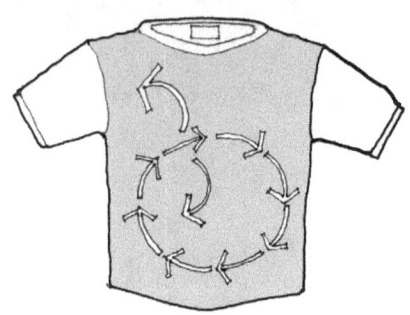

Indeed, each phase of life cycle for a product corresponds to different intensities of environmental impacts. For some products, processing or manufacturing phase dominates and for some others, it is during the use phase where substantial environmental impacts occur.

The impacts in the manufacturing phase are best addressed by the manufacturer through product redesign, sustainable packaging, influencing the supply-chain, deploying better logistics and taking back the used product as extended producer responsibility. The use phase impacts of the product are however to be managed at the consumers end. If the consumer is careless, insensitive or not aware of how to use the product correctly then the impact in the use phase can be substantial.

There are many products that have low environmental impacts in the manufacturing phase. These products with their low environmental impact (during manufacturing) appear to be like dwarfs and hence appeal while making the choice! In the use phase however, the same products lead to significant environmental impacts; especially if abused or carelessly used. Thus environmental impacts of such products cast tall shadows! Examples of such products are incandescent lamps, iron, washing machine etc.

The following figure shows normalized percentage of environmental impacts (on Y-axis) for a washing machine in different phases. Clearly, you would notice that for a washing machine the "use phase" dominates.

LCA of a washing machine (Source: Andrew Sweatman)

Therefore, it is important that the product makers and product users/consumers work in tandem and communicate with each other. Thus both product makers and users are jointly responsible for implementing or influencing responsible manufacturing and undertaking responsible product use. Only then will we be able to achieve the goal of sustainable production and consumption.

We as consumers should therefore be very particular about correct use of the products we buy. Most product makers today guide the consumers regarding the optimum use of their product. This guidance is not only limited to safety but also towards minimizing resource consumption and waste generation. Often, we do not read the product-use instructions carefully and if we do then we tend not to follow those instructions seriously.

The next time you buy a new washing machine for your home, you may like to do a "family session" of collectively reading the user manual and learn how to operate the washing machine in the most energy and water efficient manner. For instance, washing machines should be best run with full loads and one should practice line drying as much possible. Levy's claim that the use phase impacts of a pair of jeans can be reduced by 50% if it is line dried and washed in cold water. If every U.S. household used only cold water for washing clothes, then it is estimated to be equivalent to nearly 8 percent of the Kyoto target for the U.S on carbon dioxide emissions! So taking care to minimize the environmental impacts in the "use phase" of such products really matters.

When we buy a product, we should select the product by looking at its full life cycle impacts. As a consumer, we must take on the responsibility of minimizing environmental impacts in the use phase and insist for guidance from the product makers. Let us be responsible consumers and not cast "tall shadows" with the products we use and consume!

For students – Take up a research project on LCA of some of the products like washing machine. An electric iron, a cotton T-shirt could be examples where use phase dominates. Consider a bicycle on the other hand where impacts in the making or manufacturing are much more than during use. You may also like to do household surveys to check how much gets read and followed up on the use guides/instructions provided by the product makers. How well are these manuals done and do they focus on reducing impacts in the use phase.

29

The world today is on a carbon regime. GHG emission caps/targets, emission trading, carbon taxes, reduction in coal consumption or protection of coal reserves and carbon sequestration are some of the most used buzz words that many of us don't understand (although most pretend to!)

Some environmental hardliners believe that soon there will be carbon driven stock markets, where only low carbon goods and services will be offered, low carbon infrastructure will be the style of built environment (whatever that means) and there will be a universal carbon currency replacing the US dollar and the Euro. For example, your bank account will have 100 tons of carbon

(to trade, invest or use) instead of a currency. Everyone on the planet will be encouraged towards low carbon living and carbon will be the key factor in all decision making.

Taking the lead, I decided to practice low carbon living myself. I thought that was a noble move and would serve as a good demonstration to my family, friends and colleagues. Some people cautioned/warned me that low carbon living is not easy and could even be expensive.

The first thing I decided to do was to change my present diesel driven SUV to an Electric Vehicle (EV). EVs were introduced 100 years ago. Whether it's a hybrid, plug-in hybrid or all-electric, the demand for electric drive vehicles (EV) is on the rise. Currently more than 3 percent of new vehicle sales are EV, and the sales could grow to nearly 7 percent — or 6.6 million per year — worldwide by 2020.

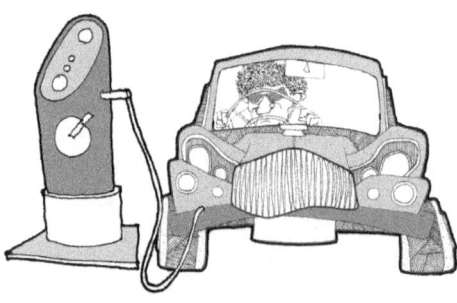

So as to not show any preference to any business house making EVs in India (particularly my good friend Anand Mahindra), I decided to import a Nissan Leaf (the best Plug-in Electric Vehicle or PEV) from Nissan's plant in Sunderland in the UK. This was an expensive buy but I decided to go ahead and spend the money to show my commitment to low carbon living.

Despite all my diplomatic influence, procurement of Nissan Leaf took quite a while as the testing and certification agencies were not accustomed to handle an imported EV. After three months of juggling the necessary paperwork the Nissan Leaf EV finally arrived at my bungalow. I decided to invite my Professor friend to see the Leaf and take a ride with me to get the "feeling" of "sustainable mobility". I set up a coffee table in my garden with a large ash tray and waited for Professor's arrival.

When Professor reached my house, I was charging my Nissan on the home plug. The Nissan LEAF can charge its lithium-ion battery from 0% to 80% in approximately 30 minutes using a rapid charger; however, with an approved Home Charging Unit, it requires either 4 hours using a 32A unit or 8 hours for a 16A unit.

"You can start using the EV without a public charging infrastructure or wait for DISCOM (Power Distribution Company) to come forward and invest in one. Also, the Lithium ion batteries can be recycled up to 95% leading to fairly low impact on the environment." I told the Professor proudly but carefully so as not to sound like a marketing/sales agent for Nissan.

The Professor however, was not interested in such details and instead he handed me a print-out taken from the Singapore Strait Times.

The article[17] was about a fellow called Nguyen who imported Tesla's 2014 Model S from Hong Kong to Singapore. Nguyen was expecting a rebate under Singapore's Carbon Emissions Vehicle Scheme (CEVS) for his good gesture[18]. However, he got

---

17 Refer to http://www.straitstimes.com/singapore/transport/electric-car-tesla-slapped-with-15000-tax-surcharge

18 The Model S is granted tax breaks in several countries. In Britain, buyers get a £4,500 (S$8,800) grant, and in the United States, they get a US$7,500 (S$10,400) income tax credit. Hong Kong waives registration tax for electric cars, which can be as high as 115 per cent of value. In Norway, a Model S gets a tax exemption of around US$135,000.

a shock when he was fined $15,000 after his Model S underwent mandatory emissions testing by Singapore's Land Transport Authority (LTA). These emission tests were conducted by the LTA under the UNECE R101 standards and had found that the electric energy consumption of an imported used Tesla car was 444 watt-hour/km. To "account for CO_2 emissions during the electricity generation process", the spokesman said, "A grid emission factor of 0.5g/watt-hour was applied to the electric energy consumption". From this, it was determined that Mr. Nguyen's Tesla produced 222g/km of CO_2, putting it within the $15,000 surcharge band under Singapore's Carbon Emission-based Vehicle Scheme.

"How silly!" I responded to Professors news item in a tone of frustration and disgust. "So the customer of Tesla in Singapore was punished and not rewarded."

Taking a sip of the coffee, I added "Professor, if this happens in India, then the entire FAME program will go bust!"

Faster Adoption and Manufacturing of Hybrid and Electric vehicles in India (FAME)

FAME or the Faster Adoption and Manufacturing of Hybrid and Electric vehicles in India' was recently launched by the ministry as part of the National Electric Mobility Mission Plan[19]. The 'FAME India' scheme offers incentives on electric and hybrid vehicles of up to Rs 29,000 for bikes and Rs 1.38 lakh for cars, aiming to promote use of eco-friendly vehicles.

The heavy industries ministry has estimated a total requirement of about Rs 14,000 crore for the scheme. Against this "expenditure", the plan aims to help save Rs 60,000 crore annually in the country's oil import bill by 2020. I thought these calculations clearly show the strong case to "drive electric". In addition, we achieve 100% emission reduction from the tail pipes and the consequent environmental and health damage costs. Therefore, it is not just the government, the customers and the EV manufacturers that benefit but also and more importantly, so does the environment. It is not surprising therefore that many feel that promotion of EVs through FAME is a giant step toward cleaner mobility. Electric vehicles are seen by governments as an important

---

19 For more information: http://dhi.nic.in/UserView/index?mid=2418

part of cutting emissions and reducing global warming. The first phase of the scheme is being implemented over a two-year period in 2015-16 and 2016-17 with an approved outlay of Rs. 795 crore, out of which Rs. 500 crore will be spent on demand incentives. As per the scheme, depending on technology, battery operated scooters and motorcycles will be eligible for incentives in the range of Rs. 1,800 to Rs. 29,000, while for three-wheelers, it is between Rs. 3,300 and Rs. 61,000. For light commercial vehicles the incentives range from Rs. 17,000 to Rs. 1.87 lakh, and for buses from Rs. 34 lakh to Rs. 66 lakh. Under this scheme, the customer gets the incentive in the form of lower cost of hybrid or EV at the time of its purchase. Manufacturers can claim the incentive from the government at the end of each month.

Professor however did not look convinced by the FAME approach of giving subsidies. Taking a deep puff from his cigar he said in a serious tone, "Prasad, I have two major concerns on the EV. My first concern is on the methods of manufacture and disposal of the EVs, particularly their batteries, my second and more pressing concern is how will the electricity which powers EV be generated? Given that the vast majority of power generated around the world is grid-tied, where the EVs are charged will therefore play a large role in determining their carbon emissions. The carbon emissions of EVs can be four times greater in places with coal dominated power generation than in those with low carbon power generation (such as hydel, renewable and nuclear). There are bound to be emissions somewhere and not necessarily at the point of use."

Having said all this, the Professor opened his briefcase and showed me a chart (see figure below[20]).

"Although the above information is rather dated it drives the point that the country or the location matters." continued the Professor. "The legend to the right of this chart helps explain the factors driving the variation between countries. In India, Australia and China the dominance of coal in the fuel mix means that the grid powered EVs produce emissions ranging from 370-258 g CO_2e/km. Compare this to the hydroelectric exporter Paraguay where virtually all of the 70 g CO_2e/km results

20 Image Source: http://shrinkthatfootprint.com/wp-content/uploads/2013/02/Emissions-Equivalent-Petrol-Car.gif

from vehicle manufacturing and electric driving consumes significantly lower GHG emissions"

These figures were shocking to me. "So do you mean to say that the geography or location matters?" I asked.

"Indeed." said the Professor. "A recent study carried out by a group of economists in the US makes this point. Using a fine-grained, county-level measure tracing vehicle emissions to tail pipes and electricity grids, these researchers mapped the petrol cars and EVs. What they found was that in some locations, going electric does more harm to the environment thereby not justifying the subsidy. Therefore just like in the Singapore case, EVs should be actually taxed and not incentivized.

The researchers focused on five major pollutants: carbon (CO_2), sulfur dioxide (SO_2), nitrogen (NO_x), particulate matter ($PM_{2.5}$), and volatile organic compounds (VOCs). They considered 11 different EV models from the year 2014, as well as the "closest substitute" petrol car. For petrol, calculating environmental damage was pretty straightforward. The researchers considered factors like a car's fuel-efficiency rating (city miles for urban counties, highway miles for non-urban), pollutant dispersion (such as average wind patterns), and number of environmental damages (to health, infrastructure, crops, and so on). Combined, this data gave them the aggregate emissions of driving a certain petrol car one mile in a given US county.

Determining the comparable damage from electric vehicles was a bit trickier. Here they used an EV's fuel-efficiency equivalent (kilowatt-hours per mile) to figure out how much electricity it drew from the regional grid. They also knew the hourly emissions profiles for the five target pollutants at 1,486 power plants across the U.S. So for each county they knew how the grid responded when an EV plugged in, which told them how much environmental damage that car produced at the power plant. The researchers then converted all their damage estimates into dollar values.

To quote the study co-author Stephen Holland of the University of North Carolina, Greensboro -- The real big take-home message is: location, location, location!

A country's energy mix thus affects the environmental advantage of EVs. It can even depend on what time of day the batteries are charged because night-time electricity is less dependent on coal.

Electricity from coal (the most polluting method of generating power), drastically reduces the environmental advantage for EVs. The life cycle analysis of EV cars in China shows they are far more polluting than conventional cars because China generates almost all its power from coal.

I won't be surprised that the result will be same for India" the Professor stated confidently.

"However in a country like Norway, where most power is generated from hydroelectricity, EVs fairly quickly begin to outperform conventional cars in terms of their overall environmental impact[21].

In 2012, President Obama launched the EV Everywhere Grand Challenge — an US Energy Department initiative that brought together America's best and brightest scientists, engineers and businesses to make plug-in electric vehicles more affordable as today's petrol-powered vehicles by 2022. On the battery front, the Department's Joint Center for Energy Storage Research at Argonne National Laboratory was commissioned to overcome the biggest scientific and technical barriers that prevent large-scale improvements of batteries. The game-changing technologies being currently developed by the Energy Department's Advanced Research Projects Agency-Energy (ARPA-E) could change the way we think of electric vehicles. From investing in new types of batteries that could go further on a single charge to cost-effective alternatives to materials critical to electric motors, the ARPA-E's projects could radically transform the EVs.

So the key is not to popularize EVs through financial incentives alone, but encourage building a mission on EV such as the one launched by Obama. But given the poor performance of our coal based thermal power plants, we will first need to undertake initiatives to improve the efficiency of coal based power plants and factor in the AT&C losses ($kgCO_2e/kWh$). We need FAME but more critically we need de-carbonization and efficiency improvement in the power

---

21 Read "Environmental benefits from driving electric vehicles?" Holland, S., Mansur, E., Muller, N. and Yates, A. NBER Working Paper No. 21291. June 2015

sector before we can enjoy the environmental benefits of EVs.

Minister Piyush Goel has recognized importance of this challenging task and announced a policy on the modernization and phase out of fossil fuel such as coal with emphasis on renewable energy." Professor said (I guess Professor was probably the SA or Secret Advisor to Minister Goel)

The Professor then showed me work done by Gyan Prakash of CBalance[22]. Gyan Prakash has published very interesting data and analyses on the electricity generation factor ($kgCO_2e/kWh$) of coal based thermal power production in India. The data is now a bit dated but the observations made then are perhaps still valid.

Prakash found that the average Indian electricity generation emission factor is 0.89 $kgCO_2e/kWh$ (or 0.89 g/Watt hour) and average Indian AT&C loss emission factor is 0.30 $kgCO_2e/kWh$. This data does not make a good case for EVs. In fact promotion of EVs will lead to more GHG emissions than petrol cars. In many cases we can see that states have a low adjusted emission factor for generation but due to high AT&C losses their end user emission factor is higher than the national average emission factor. Fixing the AT&C losses should therefore be the priority and as it is a low hanging fruit.

Arunachal Pradesh, Meghalaya, Mizoram, Uttarakhand, Kerala are the States where the emission generation factors are less than 0.5 $kgCO_2e/kWh$.

"Find a job to teach at the Doon University and take your Nissan Leaf there. Only then can you justify your choice of going electric. You cannot drive this car in Delhi and claim low carbon living!" Professor concluded, extinguishing his cigar.

I was aghast at his suggestion.

My wife who had been listening to our conversation said, "Let us move to Mussorie. Don't you think the location also matters?"

I thought that this was perhaps the best part our conversation of the morning.

I heard a beep beep from my garage– my Nissan Leaf was fully charged and was ready to go.

But I was not excited to go electric anymore!

22 Read "Environmental benefits from driving electric vehicles?" Holland, S., Mansur, E., Muller, N. and Yates, A. NBER Working Paper No. 21291. June 2015

30

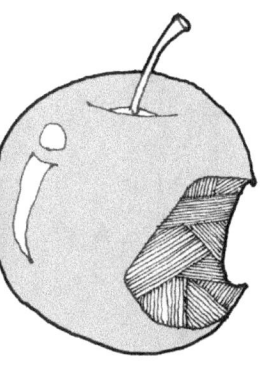

Last week I was in a supermarket to buy some food items. A poster about Organic Food caught my attention and I saw that the supermarket housed a whole new section of organic products. This section included organic fruits and vegetables, organic preservers, organic tea etc. I also saw stacks of flyers that listed the benefits of going organic. These organic products were however priced higher than their ordinary counterparts. But then I thought that this price premium shouldn't mind as it may offset the costs of my medical treatment or perhaps may reduce my chances of hitting a cancer over a long run!

Deciding to go organic, I picked up a pack of organic apples from New Zealand. The apples were delicious!

The question that puzzled me however was "what is organic? and how do I know whether what I am shopping is truly organic – i.e. who verifies the authenticity of the organic tag? and why should New Zealand's organic apple reach Mumbai's supermarkets?"

Organic foods are foods produced using methods of organic agriculture. Organic agriculture is defined as a production system that sustains the health of soils, ecosystems and people. It relies on ecological processes, biodiversity and cycles adapted to local conditions, rather than the use of inputs with adverse effects. Organic agriculture combines tradition, innovation and science to benefit the shared environment and promote fair relationships and a good quality of life for all involved[23].

---

23 Source: International Federation of Organic Agricultural Movements (IFOAM)
   http://www.ifoam.org/growing_organic/definitions/doa/index.html

If we go by this definition then the concept of organic food is really not new. In fact, this is how the food used to be produced generations ago following traditional farming techniques. So going organic now simply means that we are going back to our traditions & culture that respected the environment and followed agricultural practices that were sustainable.

Organic is something that is sustainable, local, small-scale, family-owned, natural and agro-ecological. The transition may however be slow i.e. take more time. The productivity per acre of land could be initially less compared to "modern" techniques. Organic food production is however intended to drive the growth of farmer's markets, generate more employment and improve community livelihoods, preserving and enhancing productivity over long term. We therefore must take a rounded perspective.

Unfortunately, if these are the characteristics of organic business, then organic food alone cannot feed the world. Given the surging population and intense urbanization, we may still need to follow the "so called efficient" methods of food production that rely on mechanization along with the use of fertilizers and pesticides. We may even have to risk food produced through Genetically Modified Organisms (GMOs). For instance, a hectare of conventionally farmed land produces 2.5 times more potatoes than an organic one. So, if are looking for scalable solutions to go organic then globalization of organic food industry is perhaps the answer or at least part of the solution.

Markets for organic food are ever increasing. According to Organic Monitor estimates, global organic sales reached $54.9 billion in 2009, up from, $50.9 billion in 2008. The countries with the largest organic markets are the United States, Germany, and France[24]. Acreage managed organically is however only a small percentage close to just around 1% of the total area cultivated[25]. So there is a long way to go still.

Globalization of organic food has however many challenges. National organic food standards mainly exist in developed countries but then there are now hundreds

---

24 Source: The World of Organic Agriculture: Statistics & Emerging Trends 2011

25 Source: The World of Organic Agriculture: Statistics & Emerging Trends 2011
   See http://www.ota.com/organic/mt/business.html

of such standards in use. So the criteria for an organic apple from New Zealand will be different from the organic apple from California. Significant efforts for harmonization of organic food standards are needed and it may just not be worth it, given the complexity, specificity and preferences of the regions. As a buyer of organic food, I would be lost in the maze of labels and terminologies.

The US Department of Agriculture's National Organic Program for instance distinguishes three categories of organic: '100% Organic', 'Organic' (contains at least 95% organic ingredients) or 'made with organic ingredients' (at least 70%). Only products in the first two categories are eligible to carry the USDA Organic Seal. To qualify for the European Union Organic Logo however, at least 95% of a product's ingredients of agricultural origin must be organically produced.

On the side of harmonization, the International Federation of Organic Agriculture Movements (IFOAM) is an umbrella organization with more than 750 members in 108 countries. IFOAM offers an Organic Guarantee System which enables organic certifiers to become "IFOAM Accredited" and for their certified operators to label products with the prestigious IFOAM Seal next to the logo of their IFOAM accredited certifier[26].

A more recent movement harmonization is Asian Regional Organic Standard (AROS). Operated through the Global Organic Market Access (GOMA) Project, AROS would help farmers in developing world to claim a stake in the global organic food industry. The Asian Regional Organic Standard (AROS) was approved on 12 February, 2012 by GOMA's Asia Working Group.

Apart from the non-uniformity of standards, the second challenge is the management of global organic food supply chains. Organic food standards often encompass environmental attributes and address social and ethical considerations, especially when we look into the handling of farm labor. Given the small land holdings of farmers in developing countries, along with the poor access to infrastructure and finance and weak monitoring and enforcement, verification of organic criteria becomes

---

26 Source: http://www.ekobai.com/analysis/details/5

extremely difficult. Added to that is the problem of traceability as it is often hard to pin down the supplier network when there are informal segments operating between farm and produce. We need robust accreditation systems as well as teams of verifiers to ensure that the global chains of organic food actually deliver the organic products.

Costs of labor have been one of the principal factors to look for competitive global sourcing. Hence, organic food that is more labor intensive in the EU and the US, travels distances from developing world. This leads to more Green House Gas (GHG) emissions, greater environmental impact (e.g. packaging) and importantly more costs. Added are the costs of accreditation and verification. This is a yet another challenge.

It is important therefore to apply Life Cycle Assessment (LCA) and judge whether globalization of organic food is the way ahead. LCA related to food production looks into: energy required to manufacture artificial fertilizers and pesticides; fossil fuel burnt by farm equipment; nutrient pollution caused by nitrate and phosphate run-off into water courses; release of pollution that may cause

acid rain; and the area of land lost under farming that could have been used for some other beneficial use. It also looks into the material burden on packaging, storage space (with climate control) and spoiled food waste, transport and disposal of fruit residues if processed. Such accounting of resources, energy and wastes/ emissions may just show that getting organic apples from New Zealand to Mumbai may not be environmentally sound. Ideally, an organic apple from New Zealand should be sold and eaten in Christchurch and not in Mumbai!

For Students – Research on the criteria for Organic Food, Organic Cotton, associated Eco-labels and come up with a common criteria. Attempt quantification of benefits and costs over life cycle of going organic. Take a case study on organic food that travels long distances. Understand the term Traceability. See http:// up.agri.net.in/organicmain. aspx to know e-organic traceability organic food in Uttar Pradesh in India.

31

A System Dynamics Approach to Discourage Smoking

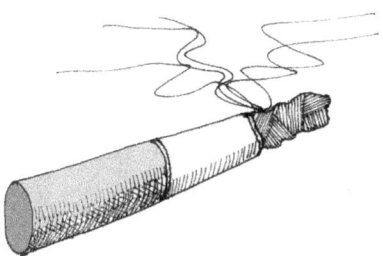

Nearly 80% of the World's 1 billion smokers live in low- and middle-income countries.

Tobacco kills around 6 million people each year. More than 5 million of those deaths are the result of direct tobacco use while more than 600,000 are the result of non-smokers being exposed to second-hand smoke.

Second-hand smoke is the smoke that fills restaurants, offices or other enclosed spaces when people burn tobacco products such as cigarettes, bidis and hookah (water-pipes).

In adults, second-hand smoke causes serious cardiovascular and respiratory diseases, including coronary heart disease and lung cancer. In infants, it causes sudden death. In pregnant women, it causes low birth weight.

Smoking should be therefore banned where people agglomerate and should be discouraged at the personal level.

"Tobacco is universally regarded as one of the major public health hazards and is responsible directly or indirectly for an estimated eight lakh deaths annually in the country. It has also been found that treatment of tobacco related diseases and the loss of productivity caused therein cost the country almost Rs.130,500 million annually, which more than offsets all the benefits accruing in the form of revenue and employment generated by tobacco industry".

— Supreme Court of India, Murli S. Deora vs Union of India and Ors on 2 November 2001

This observation is even more valid today with perhaps a stronger set of studies and statistics to support it.

The Union Health Minister of India J. P. Nadda (JP) was fed up with the tactics of the opposition and the lobbying of the Tobacco Czars (like ITC, Godfrey Phillips) towards stalling his proposed amendments to the bill on Cigarettes and Other Tobacco Products (Prohibition of Advertisement and Regulation of Trade and Commerce, Production, Supply and Distribution) or simple called COTPA.

These amendments had been suggested with the best of intentions and after a lot of internal discussions and stakeholder consultations. The bill proposed increasing the fine for smoking in public places, from Rs. 200 to Rs. 1000 and recommended the removal of designated smoking zones in hotels and restaurants.

In addition to a proposed ban on the sale of loose cigarettes, the minimum age of a person buying tobacco products was to be increased to 21 years from the existing age of 18. Studies have indicated that 18 to 21 year olds make up 83% of the group of first time smokers and the proposed increase in the age limit was expected to reduce the consumption of illicit cigarettes and discourage youngsters from getting hooked on to this dangerous habit.

The Finance Minister had raised excise duty on cigarettes by a whopping 15% in the 2015-2016 budget so as to (I presume) discourage smoking and certainly not build a revenue stream.

JP's secretary called me to set up a meeting to discuss the COTPA "problem." I was told to bring along my Professor friend as he had heard a lot of good things about him from the Prime Minister's Office (PMO). "Let us see how he can help me?" JP said, when the secretary connected the call.

Fortunately, the Professor (though a cigar smoker himself) agreed to join me and we took a flight from Mumbai to Delhi the very next day. As we were exiting Delhi airport, we bumped into Y. C. Deveshwar (YC), the Chairman of ITC.

"Where are you heading to YC?" I asked.

"London." replied YC in a hushed voice. "I better rush." He continued, "It seems the Union Health Minister has appointed some high level Consultant to advise him on how to ban smoking in India. If this really happens, then the business of ITC will be severely hit. I will have to make alternate arrangements as I am answerable to my British investors. Just the announcement of proposed

COTPA has led to a fall in ITC's share price by 7% on the Bombay Stock Exchange, so if the new bill actually gets passed /implemented, then we will lose even more."

I couldn't disagree but I was glad that YC did not know that the high level Consultant was standing right next to me, i.e. the Professor.

"Good Bye Dr. Modak! Incidentally I am travelling by the same flight that was taken by my friend Dr. Vijay Mallya – i.e. Jet Airways departing at 12:10 pm to London. This will perhaps give some "fuel" for the daily news hour especially to our dear friend Arnab Goswami of Times Now. He will wonder why this particular flight gets chosen for all escapes."

"You are right YC – but there is nothing common between you and Dr. Mallya." I told him. "You are a very respectable person – except that both of you are devils in disguise – one sells cigarettes from behind a mask of "Sustainability" (ITC has bagged several sustainability awards) and the other one sells "liquor" like a "King" and "fishes" around with the Banks."

YC however, did not have any intention of listening to my observations and he swiftly left and was soon lost in the crowd.

While we were driving to JP's office, I briefed the Professor on the laws and regulations related to smoking in India and fed him with some interesting statistics.

There are approximately 120 million smokers in India. According to the World Health Organization (WHO), India is home to 12% of the world's smokers. Approximately 900,000 people die every year in India due to smoking as of 2009. This figure could well be now close to 1500,000 or 1.5 million.

Anti-smoking advertisements are now screened at the beginning of the movie and during the interval. In addition, a disclaimer must be displayed on-screen during each scene where smoking is present. This requirement is well taken by the Bollywood and the Theater Owners.

According to the latest data on cigarette consumption given by the health ministry in Parliament, the consumption in 2014-15 was 93.2 billion sticks — 10 billion less than in 2012-13. But the production of cigarettes too fell from 117 billion to 105.3 billion sticks in the same period.

A nationwide smoke-free law pertaining to public places came into effect from 2nd October 2008. Places where smoking is restricted include auditoriums, movie theaters, hospitals, public transport (aircraft, buses, trains, metros, monorails, taxis, autos) and their related facilities (airports, bus stands/stations, railway stations), restaurants, hotels, bars, pubs, amusement centres, offices (government and private), libraries, courts, post offices, markets, shopping malls, canteens, refreshment rooms, banquet halls, discothèques, coffee houses, educational institutions and parks.

Smoking is allowed on roads, inside one's home or vehicle. Professor said that this was terrible as it would lead to secondary or passive smoking. The proposed amendment by Naddi addressed this concern.

Smoking was permitted in airports, restaurants, bars, pubs, discothèques and some other enclosed workplaces if they provide designated separate smoking areas. Professor said that these areas look like "gas chambers" of Nazis except here people volunteered to get in and were not there on the gun-point. The amendment to COTPA asked for a ban of such areas.

Anybody violating this law is charged with a fine of Rs. 200. The sale of tobacco products within 100 yards of educational institutions is banned – something difficult to enforce. The Cable Television Network (Regulation) Amendment Bill, in force since 8 September 2000, completely prohibited cigarette and alcohol advertisements. The proposed amendment is asking for increase in the fine from Rs. 200 to Rs. 1000.

Today more than 60 per cent of the total tobacco crop produce is used for making cigarettes. Rest is exported and used to make the bidis. India earns around Rs 300,000 million as excise duty on cigarettes. We will in fact earn more money as the Finance Minister in the new budget as increased the excise duty by 15%. The per capita consumption of cigarette in India is 96 per annum which is one of the lowest in the world. Some smokers said that we have a lot of scope to improve!

There is a significant export of unprocessed Tobacco from India. The Government collects good revenue out of this export. More than 6 million people in India are employed in farming Tobacco.

We reached JP's office and

after some preliminaries, JP asked the Professor about his reactions and suggestions on the proposed amendments.

On the ban and its enforcement, Professor told JP that the "Statistics from Global Adult Tobacco Survey (GATS) indicates that 60% of the smokers are not affected by the ban on consumption of cigarettes in public places. Since the turn of the century, no matter how pervasive the bans on smoking, the global cigarette volume sales had increased by about 8% and this trend was likely to continue."

JP was rather disappointed with the Professor's opening remarks and retorted, "Professor, are you not aware that Tobacco alone is the leading cause of 90% of the diseases affecting the mouth, 80% of the chronic obstructive pulmonary disease, 60% of heart diseases, 50% of cancers and 20% of all deaths? According to the Tata Memorial Centre in Mumbai, tobacco use is linked to 85% of head and neck squamous cell cancer cases."

I supported JP's argument further by adding, "There are more than 4000 chemicals in tobacco smoke, of which at least 250 are known to be harmful and more than 50 are known to cause cancer. There is no safe level of exposure to second-hand tobacco smoke."

Although a single cigarette is small in size and typically weighs less than 1 gram, a cigarette typically emits between 7 and 23 milligrams (mg) of $PM_{2.5}$ when it is smoked, depending on the manner of smoking and the brand (see References 1 and 2 on the reference citation list). When people congregate in an airport baggage area or enter a smoking lounge where many brands are smoked, the average amount of $PM_{2.5}$ mass emitted per cigarette is about 14 mg. Although 14 mg may not seem like a lot of mass emitted, each cigarette weighs only about 0.9 grams total, making it an extremely potent source of air pollution for its weight.

"Shouldn't we then promote the Electronic or E-Cigarettes?" I asked the Professor.

"Quite the contrary" replied the Professor. "E-cigarettes may be smokeless but are essentially Trojan horses, capable of a wreaking havoc as an addictive device.

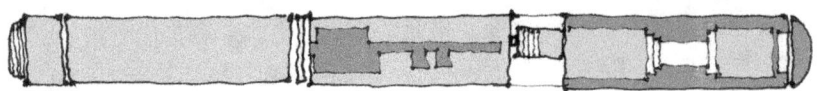

E-cigarettes help sustain the habit, not quit it. Flavoring agents used in the E-cigarettes or the Electronic Nicotine Delivery Systems (ENDS) are just another way of luring young potential clients. The nicotine contained in these cartridges is much more than the legal threshold of 30 mg. The adverse effect of nicotine on the cardiovascular system and foetal brain impairment are also well documented and propylene glycol, which is the main solvent in e-cigarettes, is used as an industrial poison. It will de-normalize many of the tobacco-control rules."

At this point, JP's Secretary butted in, "The State-run Food and Drug Administration has declared selling of e-cigarettes illegal in Maharashtra. But the national laws on these slender Electronic Nicotine Delivery Systems (ENDS) remain hazy. Maharashtra is the second state after Punjab to crackdown on e-cigarettes. Unfortunately, they are still freely available for sale online."

"Sir, I would highly recommend that you introduce a ban on E-cigarettes in the proposed amendment of COTPA." The Professor said this rather strongly and in a high pitch to JP.

"Oh don't give me another new point to fight for!" JP exclaimed and continued with his point on the adverse environmental impact of cigarettes. "Smoke is not the only culprit. Cigarette butts are worse." he said "They dot sidewalks, clog gutters, and soil our beaches. Cigarettes contain toxins which as a result of the littering, leak into the surrounding environment. It only takes a single cigarette butt to contaminate a liter of water. It is also dangerous for animals who might mistake littered butts for food."

Here the Professor had some interesting information to share. "Many cigarette filters are made of cellulose acetate, a high-grade plastic that's also used in sunglasses." He explained. "The plastic from the cigarette butts can be recovered to make plastic products. You should invite companies such as TerraCycle who have found a way to recycle these unwelcome discards. The program is known as Cigarette Waste Brigade and has gone global. To date in the United States alone, TerraCycle has set up over 7,000 cigarette recycling bins and more than 38 million butts having been collected[27]."

"That is truly inspiring Sir!", I said. The Professor had another point of view. He mentioned that while framing policies on banning or discouraging smoking of cigarettes, we must look at the economics and employment of the "peripheral industries" that thrive on smoking. "You have to protect them just as much as Public Health." he said.

"Today, cigarette lighters are a multi-billion dollar global industry that is growing annually at 3-4%. Region-wise, Asia Pacific represents the world's biggest market for cigarette lighters followed by Eastern and Western Europe. But more than 80% of the world's lighters are made in Wenzhou, a town that has built unbeatable molding, tooling capabilities for mass producing the product. In keeping with our PM's message of "Make in India", we should be boosting the production of cigarette lighters and take on China."

"What about cigarette ash tray makers?" he continued. "Most belong to informal sector and handicraft industry. There are also other stakeholders such as home air purifier makers, medical counselors, chest physicians, drug and chewing gum makers who have essentially been thriving on the smoking business."

"So a bit of smoking of cigarettes must continue." I said, adding yet another dimension to our discussion.

JP was completely lost after listening to us highlighting the pros and cons of discouraging smoking with data and statistics and asked for a service of some strong coffee.

While JP and I moved to his desk and spoke on other matters, the Professor continued to sit at the conference table, busy with some sketching. As usual, he had started smoking his pipe for inspiration and in just 10 minutes, he walked across to us and presented a complex diagram. I am pasting this diagram below.

"This is the depiction of Smoking of Cigarettes in India in the style of System Dynamics." He explained in his trademark smoker's voice. "See the various

27 For more information, visit: https://www.terracycle.com/en-US/"

Smoking Cigarettes in India using System Dynamics

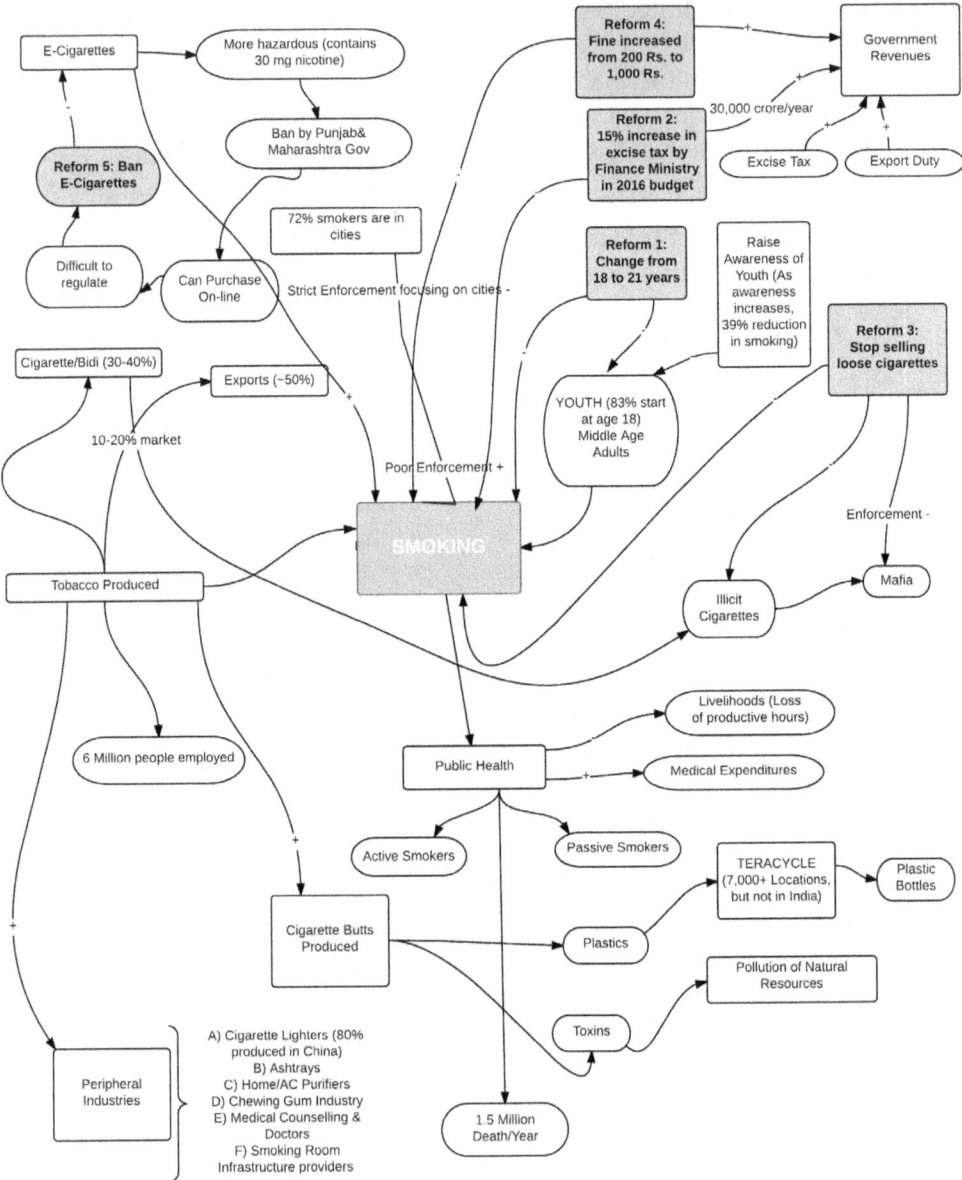

linkages we talked about, complexities such as delays and switches and the step functions, positives and the negatives that affect smoking while considering interests of various stakeholders. The reforms we are talking will essentially drive the system and must be set in a judicious combination with economic development. We need to simulate the possibilities and scenarios upfront to come up with something realistic, doable or practical. Ad-hoc decisions will not work. If you are interested then I can code this diagram in VenSIM software that is used in SD applications."

The Professor then went off to the loo leaving JP to take a closer look at his "system dynamics" representation. "I think this Professor friend of yours has created a very interesting diagram highlighting the complexities of making amendments to the existing policies. I like his approach on the "systems thinking" but it should not lead to "policy paralysis".

"However, I just hate the guy." continued JP. "He had the guts to smoke his cigar in my room and put both of us under the risk of passive smoking and ironically so when we were talking about discouraging smoking. I don't think I will hire him for this job. Wish him good luck on my behalf."

We returned to Mumbai that same evening and throughout the flight there was no conversation between us.

Systems Dynamics (SD) is an invaluable and exciting tool to introduce and train environmental scientists, engineers, planners and

economists of understanding "systems". I did three courses on SD during my doctoral research and thoroughly enjoyed. Very few post graduate programs in India have SD in the curriculum.

If you are interested in knowing more about SD, then don't miss reading the monumental work done by Professor Jay Forester of MIT (see https://en.wikipedia.org/wiki/Jay_Wright_Forrester)

To students: Note that Professors Systems Diagram was done in a hurry. See if you can improve and send me a "proper" version at prasad.modak@emcentre.com

Professor Om Damani of IIT Bombay recommends a tutorial which is available at: http://jsterman.scripts.mit.edu/docs/Sterman%20Sustaining%20Sustainability%2010-2.pdf

Disclaimer – The story of the consultation meeting with the Union Health Minister and bumping into Y. C. Deveshwar, Chairman of ITC at the Delhi airport is not real. No offences made or implied. I hope their mention is taken in good spirit & humor. The data and statistics presented are however real.

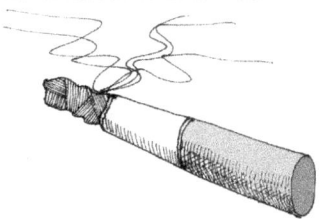

32

ENVIRONMENTAL EMISSIONS MARKET IN INDIA — ARE WE PREPARED ENOUGH?

Policies on environmental management evolve to address challenges that are critical and issues that need to be addressed. Policies are also developed to proactively and strategically prepare for the future.

Sharing of international experiences becomes extremely useful and almost essential for policy development. The learnings from these shared experiences try to help ensure that past mistakes are not repeated.

Successful policies cannot however be directly adopted and transposed on "as is" basis. They need to be adapted and localized, factoring in the institutional capacities, maturity and preparedness of the stakeholders (especially from the industry/business sectors), status on data and technology and of course the extent of political support.

Environmental Governance typically consists of two broad approaches, viz. Monitoring & Enforcement (M&E) and Market based Instruments (MBI). M&E is most commonly followed with the help of laws and regulations and by setting up enforcing bodies such as the Pollution Control Boards (PCBs). M&E alone cannot ensure compliance as the institutional capacities of PCBs are limited in number and geographical spread of polluters is large and most of the polluters in country like India are the Small and Medium Enterprises (SMEs) who are difficult to regulate.

The MBI approach has been adopted by several and mostly developed countries. This approach creates financial incentives/disincentives to motivate the polluter to take decisions that are beneficial to both the environment and the business. In most cases, MBIs provide cost-effective solutions when well supported by M&E. Sometimes however, there have been mixed results where success could not be solely attributed to the MBIs. The few applications of MBIs in the developing economies are mainly driven by development financing institutions such as the World Bank[28] and by the Environmental Economists at the Business Schools of MIT & Harvard and the like.

India is relatively a late entrant in the field of environmental governance through MBIs and with very little experience in designing and operating the MBIs. In the environment and energy market-space, we are currently operating three schemes - the Renewable Energy Certificates (REC); Perform, Achieve and Trade (PAT) and a Pilot Emissions Trading Scheme (ETS).

The REC scheme is managed by the Ministry of New and Renewable Energy through a registry. PAT is managed by the Bureau of Energy Efficiency (BEE) and having just completed Phase I, is yet to establish the market. Both the schemes however, have not performed well.

The Pilot ETS initiated by the Ministry of Environment and Forests (MoEF) was championed by the Central Pollution Control Boards (CPCB) in the states of

Maharashtra, Tamil Nadu and Gujarat. Today even after a lot of fancy and seemingly impressive power point presentations, this scheme is practically defunct.

In the quest for building an accurate national database and creating benchmarks of emission intensities across the highly polluting industrial sectors, the CPCB has created a monster scheme called the Continuous Emission/Effluent Monitoring System (CEMS). This has been initiated in the hope that if the Pilot ETS is put into operation as planned and becomes successful then the idea could be implemented across the country. ETS focusses on particulate emissions – a bizarre choice

---

28 As a primer, I would recommend to read the Guidance Note prepared by the World Bank. Available at http://siteresources.worldbank.org/INTRANETENVIRONMENT/ Resources/GuidanceNoteonMarketBasedInstruments.pdf.
This document is a bit outdated now but may still be useful as an introductary read.

made by some of the top researchers from international universities, including Environment Minister then, Jayaram Ramesh – a savvy IIT Bombay Alumni (and my 3 years senior!).

India is keen to meet the voluntary GHG emission targets pledged internationally. These targets have been reflected in the country's Intended Nationally Determined Contributions (INDCs) during COP21. Reduction in the GHGs would mean improved energy efficiency, reduced absolute energy consumption (promoted through PAT) and a shift towards renewable sources of energy (through the REC). All this would lead to a reduction in the emissions (not just particulates) and consequently lead to an improvement in the air quality – which is an interest of the ETS. Further, the industrial sectors of focus in the three schemes are pretty much common. All the three schemes are fundamentally interlinked and if unified and orchestrated in symphony, they can help India address the GHG emission issue and effectively meet the set targets. It is a pity that we still operate in silos such as energy, environment and climate change.

To keep this blog short, I have created an Appendix[29] that can be accessed on the web. to this article of my notes with some useful references that provide details on ETS, PAT and REC. There is also an interesting section on CEMS Vs PEMS (Predictive Emission Monitoring Systems). I would encourage research scholars to take up the task of a comparative assessment of the three schemes using this base note. I will be delighted to help.

My professor friend was busy in organizing a 3 day residential retreat for the top brass of the BEE, the MNRE, the MoEFCC and the CPCB at Ranikhet (Uttarakhand). The location of this retreat was being kept a secret and care had been taken to ensure that mobile phones won't be able to receive signals. The Ministers of Power (Goyal) and Environment (Javdekar) were scheduled to preside. The menus were meticulously designed to meet the food preferences of the Mehtas, the Mathurs, the Tripathys as well as the Birlas and the Shrirams (who represented industry associations). A

29 https://prasadmodakblog.files.wordpress.com/2016/02/notes-to-the-post_environmental_ emissions_market.pdf

few consultants were also invited but the menu was not customized for their tastes as consultants are generally not very particular about the food and are used to a free lunch.

"A lot of my energy is going in designing this damn food menu." the Professor said. "That's what most of these participants are most particular about."

"But Professor, what is the theme of this Retreat?" I asked.

"The idea is to create a dialogue amongst the participants to help them better understand what is happening in India's energy and environment market (and the various MBI proposed) and to develop something common, cross cutting and synergistic for the benefit of industry/business and the government (both national and state) to meet the GHG emission targets. I want the commonalities and differences to be thoroughly discussed and the challenges candidly expressed and faced head on. Practical solutions can then be efficiently planned (in phases), coordinated and communicated in a transparent manner." The Professor said this while lighting his cigar.

"Oh, you are so thoughtful!" I said. "This 3 day of brainstorming session will really help. As of now the three schemes seem to operate along the X-Y-Z axes that are perpendicular and seemingly independent of each other."

"Well, as you are an environmental professional – let us take up this ETS for discussion." said the Professor as he ordered a coffee.

Siding with the government view, I began my pitch.

"Do you know Professor, Officials at the CPCB/MoEF claim that the ETS proposed for particulates in India is the first of its kind in the world? Don't you think that we should encourage MBIs that have never been ever tried? Shouldn't we be the first in that as well?"

Professor retorted, "Dr. Modak, particulate emission trading was attempted way back in 1992 in Chile. An "Emission-Offsets Trading Program" was established by Supreme Decree No. 4 (DS 4) in March 1992 to control total suspended particulate emissions (TSP) from stationary industrial sources in Santiago, Chile[30]. This emission trading program suffered from serious flaws in

---

30 See https://gupea.ub.gu.se/bitstream/2077/21313/3/gupea_2077_21313_3.pdf

design and implementation. Trading rights and sanctions were not clarified. Institutions engaged in trading and regulations were not efficient and process followed was not transparent. The market created under the program performed poorly due to regulatory uncertainty, high transaction costs, lengthy and uncertain approval processes and inadequate enforcement. It was unfortunate that in its pursuit of progress toward attaining ambient quality standards, the environmental authority paid insufficient attention towards setting up conditions for assisting/ encouraging market development.

The only benefit of this scheme was the creation of a baseline emission inventory. Interestingly, there was an improvement in the air quality – but not because of the MBI, but due to factors exogenous to the program such as the price-based introduction of natural gas. Use of cleaner fuel made the difference to air quality and not emission trading!"

"Understood", I retreated (wondering that we will probably replicate the Chile experiment as our situation is no different!) "But then why are we focusing on particulates?" I could not resist asking.

"It is a bizarre choice." said the Professor with a smirk on his face. "The argument made was that the particulate concentrations in urban residential areas were way above the standard, leading to severe health impacts. This was true but the industrial clusters where the pilot ETS were being implemented were essentially industrial zones with mixed land use and relatively less resident population! This was a typical case of right statistics but used in a wrong place!"

"Furthermore" he continued, "the particulate matter (PM) is a diffused parameter with a very complex profile. ETS for particulate matter would involve number of uncertainties in the measurements. Also installation of CEMS is expensive for industries, especially to the SMEs.PM emissions in an industrial cluster comprise not just emissions from industrial stacks, but are contributed by host of other sources such as transport emissions and others (especially open burning) that may play a significant role. Further, there could be distant sources outside the "bubble" (i.e. of 75 kms radius as defined in the ETS) that could contribute as transported

188

by wind. Finally, focus of emission reduction is on point or stack based emissions of particulates whereas many times particulate emissions release in industries is due to fugitive sources like in handling and storage of materials.

"We have to realize that for the success M&E combined with the MBI, we need a sustained, long term and a transparent regulatory push while simultaneously addressing technical glitches and building the requisite institutional capacities. Take the example of the US. They focused on the utility industries and developed a program addressing various pollutants step by step (e.g. Ozone in 2008; SO_2-NO_x- Visibility from 2009 to 2010; Cross State Air Pollution Rule (CSAPR) from 2011 to 2012, Effluents from2012 to 2013, PM/$PM_{2.5}$ from 2013 to 2014, Ash from 2014 to 2015, MATS from 2015 to 2016 and CO_2 proposed for 2017). The Idea was to stimulate "innovation" in this process. The focus on particulates alone was not going to lead to any innovations."

I thought the Professor made a good point. We often operate on a knee-jerk basis, piece meal and that typically happens when our ministers visit the Ivy League universities.

I thought of asking the Professor about the CEMS imposition. Most industries today are looking for either cheap or reliable CEMS solution providers. Either choice poses challenges. Almost all CEMS are imported (there being no Make in India wave in this sector), expensive and with very little local support for calibration, operation and maintenance. Also the on-line results are not very reliable.

Do these CEMS actually work and how accurate are they? Also what does the PCB do with the data received? These questions came to my mind and I took a large gulp of the coffee.

Given the poor technical capacities for data analytics at the central and state PCBs, these institutions will be unable to adapt their decision-making procedures to take advantage of the new information provided by the CEMS.

"The installations of CEMS have become a scam, with overcrowding of overnight equipment suppliers." said the Professor as he paused for a while and lit another cigar.

"Have you heard about

Predictive Emission Monitoring Systems (PEMS)?" he asked. "The PEMS is gaining acceptance worldwide including at the EPA at the United States. Both CEMS and PEMS provide emissions readings on a continuous basis, but by different means. CEMS measures the physical and chemical attributes of stack gases directly. With regular maintenance, CEMS can be accurate and reliable and thereby necessary for meeting the federal, state and local regulatory requirements. CEMS however, represents a large expense that does not make processes any more efficient or profitable. In addition, CEMS cannot predict the future or the consequences of contemplated process changes. The only way to do these is to use a mathematical model.

These models are developed empirically from sample data collected by CEMS, which are installed in a stack for a trial period and then removed when the PEMS becomes operational. Empirical methods include ordinary least squares, polynomials, and Artificial Neural Networks (ANNs).

A PEMS model gives a prediction of "what if'", It essentially predicts the consequence of taking a control action and accordingly advises to change the course of a process. The PEMS model can also be inverted, such that for a given set of uncontrolled inputs and a desired output, a search program can iteratively determine values for the controlled inputs to yield the desired output. If variables such as quality, yield, and throughput are also measured, the PEMS can be used to predict and control the process to maximize these parameters to great financial benefit. PEMS are significantly cheaper and had lower O&M hassles as compared to CEMS"

I thought that it's a high time that CPCB and PCBs start looking at the PEMS approach, involving the industries and PEMS service providers. We seem to be so bogged down only to the CEMS! I wonder if there are any vested interests or simply lack of information!!

"Any final thoughts Professor?" I asked, noticing that Professor was about to extinguish his cigar.

"Well, I am really thinking of organizing a hands-on or practical training for experiential learning for some of the top professors from the Ivy League Universities where they can come to India and see the ground reality before making recommendations

to some of our ministers.
In the case of the ETS Pilot
Project, I think that these
professors should have visited
the industries (especially the
SMEs), examined at the stacks,
met the PCB staff (especially
the mid-level staff) and spent
a few days with the PCB stack
monitoring teams. I don't
like it when we get used as
a laboratory by these much
respected professors so they
can field test their test policies
– sometimes to secure research
grants or in the interest of a
publication!"

"Well, well Professor" I said
scornfully, "that's a bit too
harsh. I don't like it or rather I
disagree – But perhaps you do
have a point!"

33

Making Waste as the Business

I had been on a tour out of India for a couple of weeks and when I returned, I was passing over the dump site of Deonar Dharavi in Mumbai on my way to Chembur (where my Professor friend lives) from the airport. The dump site is supposedly one of the largest in Asia – not something to feel proud of; but it is better known today as the setting for the movie Slumdog Millionaire.

I was amazed to see a tall wireframe barricade with check posts encircling the dump site. This was new. The dump site looked like a

mountain. At each check post, there were armed guards with big guns and search lights. I even noticed a combat tank with ammunition at the main entrance. When did we start a war on waste?

"Crazy!" I mumbled to myself.

When I reached the Professors home and settled on his sofa, I asked, "Professor, what's going on around the Deonar dump site?"

"Well" said the Professor, "all this is because of the new initiative that I have launched in India. I advised the Government to use market based mechanisms to tackle the problem of waste management. This was so that will not have to depend on regulations and enforcement anymore. For years, we have had the regulations, regulators, environmental NGOs and now abhiyans and despite all of them, the problem of waste remains. We continue to see more and more waste and now with the new waste streams that have emerged, the problem has become difficult to handle. People litter, they don't segregate their waste and merrily dump it. Our land and water resources get contaminated. The biodiversity comes under threat. So I proposed that the Government pays for the waste delivered and takes on a waste buying campaign … essentially treating the waste as an asset."

"The Municipal Corporation of Greater Mumbai (MCGM) generates nearly 10000 tons of mixed waste every day." the Professor continued. "All this waste is now bought by the MCGM from the waste generators, at an attractive price. The city has opened up 30 waste depots where waste can be brought by anybody and they can get paid for it. At each depot, the waste is weighed and payments are made based on the volume and characteristics of the waste. If you bring waste that has been segregated, then you get a better price. The purchase for buying specific waste streams and materials like e-waste, metals, glass, plastic etc are also fixed. If you bring waste in the form of a component (through some disassembly and re-engineering) then you get paid

even better. The idea here, is to promote innovation."

The Professor stopped and took a deep puff on his cigar before saying, "The moment this policy and scheme was announced, people all over Mumbai went crazy. No waste was to be wasted. Everyone was rushing to the depots with waste they generated, waste that was dumped and even waste that they stole! Many people quit their jobs and have now taken up waste collection and selling as their full time profession. Centers of waste to resource conversion have introduced training courses and micro-finance. Some have even started offering transport services. These waste vans run on the bio-gas that is generated from the organic waste. The railways have introduced special shuttles from Churchgate and VT stations that will carry only waste and not commuters at 9am, 10am, 12:40pm, 3:30 pm and 7:05 pm.

All the waste from the depots is now transported to the Deonar dump site.

The dump site now looks like a mountain. Several attempts were made by the underworld and Mumbai waste mafia to steal this waste reserve and sell the waste in the suburbs or in the black market to make money. That is the reason for all the added security measures such as the high wire fence and check posts around the dump site. In fact now, all the dump sites in India are heavily guarded almost as though they were national treasures. Given the years of callousness on waste management in India, we believe that the value of the waste bank created on this basis will be as important as the gold reserve. This bank will provide resources for the next three generations in India. Once waste is recognized as an important national commodity, we expect a sharp rise in India's GDP as well as the Gross Ecological Product (GEP)."

I was astonished with this bold and far sighted approach. No wonder, the streets of Mumbai looked cleaner and were now litter free. There seemed to be no risk of flooding and dengue anymore. The long lines of vehicles and waste vans outside the waste depots showed the citizens' commitment to the principle – "Waste is Wealth!" The added benefit of supporting livelihoods of thousands of waste-pickers would certainly help this Government to win the next election.

"But what will you do with the millions of tons of waste that will be collected by this process? And what about the financing? How will you pay and continue to pay to the waste suppliers on a national scale?" I asked.

The Professor has probably expected this "stupid" question. "We examined this challenge." he said lighting his second cigar.

"The waste bought will be auctioned and processed to make products to put back to the market. For example, used computers will be refurbished with new hard disks fixed and legal software installed and provided to the schools at low cost. Plastic will be processed to make diesel and sold at the petrol pumps. Tetra pack cartons will be converted into furniture.

We have also spoken to the private sector and held several rounds of discussion. One of the major problems of the waste processing industry in India today is a guaranteed waste supply. Through our approach towards waste as commodity and centralized procurement, the waste processing industry are now feeling confident to buy waste from us and invest in processes to make recycled products. We are signing product purchase agreements (PPA) with these waste

194

processing companies and no taxes will be levied on the recycled products. We will now see more recycled products made out of waste than virgin products.

Because of waste to electricity conversion, the electricity rates have crashed. No chemical fertilizers are being bought in a 30km radius because of the abundant compost. Corporate biggies like the Tatas, Birlas, Ambanis and Vedantas have set up large waste verticals in their business. Waste materials have now appeared on the commodity trading exchanges. Waste bonds are also out. This is the idea of circular economy.

Organizing efficient collection and recycling of waste at the national level, is going to save further contamination of our natural resources – thereby improving our resource security. Tourism will also improve. These benefits far outweigh the investments.

Funds for buying waste will be mobilized mainly through the revenues collected from selling waste to the processing industry. Trimming down the waste management cells of urban local bodies, pollution control boards, departments of environment etc. will also help reduce the costs. Due to the lead taken by the market

based approach, I see that regulators will have a smaller role to play."

"Professor", I said, very impressed, "this is an amazing approach. You have managed to usher into India, the Green Economy. I am sure other countries will follow suit – do you see any challenges?"

The Professor got up and walked towards the window and looked outside. "This is where I need your help. Due to pricing of the waste as commodity, there is now going to be a major transformation. Everybody wants to generate more waste to make money. I see an increase in the per capita waste generation from 0.5 kg /day to nearly 1.5 kg/ day. Some folks, especially the SMEs have found innovative ways to generate more waste in the production operations. This has led to two fold increases in waste generation on a per ton basis for some products. Apparently, price they get from us on supplying waste provides more income than selling of product itself in the market! I have come across cases where SMEs are selling their products as waste at our depots. The reason being we guarantee purchase and offer good prices. The price line is very important. If I lower the rates, then people won't supply us with their waste.

If I increase the rate then more waste will be generated and brought to the depots. That is not good from the sustainability perspective so it's a tight rope walk."

I realized the gravity of the problem that Professor was taking about, but did not have an easy answer.

"I wish people understood why they consume beyond their needs and generate waste in the first place." I said.

"Oh I am tired listening to this philosophy Prasad!" snapped the Professor as he extinguished his cigar. "Talk something real and practical."

I returned home – this time not going over the dumpsite of Deonar Dharavi.

The report Global Waste Management Outlook led by UNEP International Environmental Technology Centre (IETC) and International Solid Waste Association (ISWA) is now out. I was one of the four principal authors and contributed to the chapter on situation analyses – challenges & opportunities. This was a yearlong grueling project. Access this report at http://www.unep.org/newscentre/default.aspx?DocumentID=26844&ArticleID=35410 andknow more about it at http://iswa2015.org/assets/files/downloads/03_Wilsson_David.pdf

At Ekonnect Knowledge Foundation we just concluded a video competition in Mumbai called Anvaya (means in Sanskrit – positive action) on waste to resource management. There were 14 entries. Visit www.ekonnect.net to download the report and to access the YouTube channel to view the films.

34

Teaching Environmental Modeling with Hooke's Law

We all know that environmental modeling plays an important role in environmental management. Impact assessment is one example where we make an attempt to predict or anticipate environmental impacts due to actions we propose to take. We use models to help us in this endeavor.

Models tell us about the "what if?" and caution or guide us in taking required preventive measures. Mitigation includes not just physical measures but also required policy reforms. This makes both the construction and application of models very interesting, useful and exciting.

Models improve our understanding of the "system", making us realize its limitations while simultaneously providing clues on how to interpret the modeling results to our advantage.

Environmental modeling requires and deserves a full course in a post-graduate program. Unfortunately, this course is not generally offered today in most universities due to the evident shortage of faculty. Environmental modeling is however widely used and almost essential in influencing major decisions with regards to developmental activities and mitigation of their environmental impacts.

Modeling is generally taught through a few lectures in the course on Environmental Impact Assessment (EIA). That is not enough! Some places teach modeling by training students on some of the canned software e.g. AERMOD, QUAL etc. Both professors and students feel that this is how modeling should be "taught" or "learned!"

Apart from the postgraduate students, modeling needs to be taught to other key stakeholders like the government officials, Environmental NGOs etc. It's

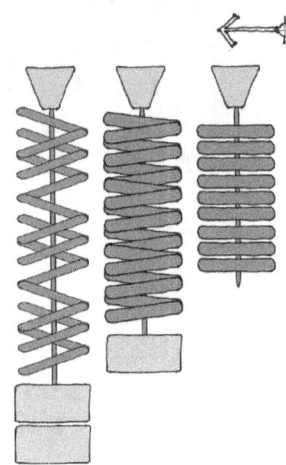

not that we want these stakeholders to become modeling experts but we want them to know enough to appreciate, question and get involved when the models are influencing important decisions.

I spoke to my Professor friend, who has been teaching environmental modeling for a long time now, about my concerns/worries about teaching.

"How do you teach this subject, Professor?" I asked.

"Come to my first modeling lecture next week at IIT. I am running a course on environmental modeling for environmental NGOs and government officials." He said casually.

I was fascinated! Teaching a heavy/intense subject like environmental modeling to NGOs and Government officials can be quite a challenge.

I reached the class early and took a back seat to look inconspicuous. The "students" walked in shortly and

occupied the seats.

The Professor entered the classroom with a large bag. Everybody was curious.

Professor asked everyone whether they had studied Hooke's Law in their school/college days and the answer was a resounding "Yes!"

"Great!" said the Professor.

I failed to understand why this question was asked. Must be something naughty as usual, I thought to myself.

The Professor pulled out a metal spring from his large bag and hung it on a C-Frame. He took out a weight with a hook from the bag and announced, "I am going to attach this weight on this spring. What would you expect to happen?"

There was a quick show of hands.

"Sir, the spring is going to expand because of the weight." answered one of the students who was junior officer at the Pollution Control Board.

Professor smiled. "You are right. Let me then do so."

When the weight was attached, indeed the spring elongated. "This weight was 1kg by the way." Professor said.

Professor now pulled out another similar metal spring and placed it on the C frame.

"I am now going to put a 2kg of weight on this second spring." He placed the weight.

The students now saw two springs under different weights. The one with 2kg that elongated more than spring that was loaded with 1kg.

"Do you see any difference?" Professor asked.

The student, who was an activist in the struggle on stopping encroachment at the Mangroves in Mumbai, said that the spring with 2kg elongated more.

"That's absolutely correct!" said the Professor.

He then measured the extent of elongation. For spring 1, it was 0.5cm and for spring 2 it was 1cm.

"So with more weight on the spring, there is more elongation. This proportional relationship is essentially Hooke's law". The Professor explained.

If we plot force or weight against extension for a material which obeys Hooke's law then the relationship will look like the graph below.

The gradient of this graph is the spring constant (k) or Young's modulus[31](Y) which is measured in Nm^{-1}. For copper Y is around 117, for aluminum around 69 and for nylon close to 3. The type of material matters.

Professor then asked the students to come up to the C-frame and carry out experiments with springs of different materials and various weights and calculate Y. This was some fun!

Adarak (Ginger) Tea was now served.

"Do you see any environmental connection with this experiment has?" Professor asked.

Most faces were blank.

Professor prodded, "Take the case of untreated sewage entering the lake?"

There was a pause.

"Are you trying to imply that more is the pollution load getting into a lake, more is the deterioration in water quality" asked one of the smarter students. He was working on the "save Powai Lake" project. "This is what Hooke's law will tell us."

Another student, an assistant engineer from Municipal Corporation added "and it will

31 Refer to: https://en.wikipedia.org/wiki/Young%27s_modulus

depend on the lake's Young's Modulus, more is the depth, mixing and dilution less will be the deterioration in water quality."

The Professor smiled "Both of you are absolutely right. You got that! We will call the Young's modulus here as the Assimilative capacity." He then proceeded to explain the term assimilative capacity. He talked about mixing height, horizontal winds and turbulence in the air sheds; depth, velocity and cross sections influencing waste assimilation in the rivers etc.

Then there was a discussion that we must not exceed the "allowable" assimilative capacity. We must have policies, regulations, required institutional capacities and the finance.

While the discussion moved to this point, Professor took out a 20 kg weight from his bag. He attached this "heavy weight" to one of the springs. The spring almost "sank". There was a disproportionate elongation. It did not follow the "linear model" of the Hooke's law as shown in the graph above.

Everybody was stunned.

The Professor explained that the weight of 20 kg exceeded the limit of proportionality.

Hooke's law was no more valid as we were stretching the material too far.

The linearity ended after Point "a" as shown in the figure below.

There was one more interesting thing Professor asked the students to notice. When he removed the 20 kg weight, the spring did not come back to its original length. Clearly the elastic limit of the spring had been crossed and a permanent deformation had occurred indicating a non-linear behavior.

The message to the students was clear. They understood that if the assimilative capacity is exceeded, then the impacts could be non-linear and even irreversible.

If too much wastewater was discharged in to the lake, then the water quality changes could be major, catastrophic or permanent. So one would need interventions on both the preventive/ mitigative and restorative side i.e. treating the wastewater prior to lake discharge, or discharge with treatment at the center of the lake where depths are greater or introduce aeration, carry out dredging or apply biotechnology to improve the restorative capacity (or lakes Young's modulus). The Professor discussed the risks that needed to be understood for each of the options. There were pros and cons and no free lunch.

This experiment led to the understanding that we need to be precautionary and protective to the assimilative capacities available in the nature. We must compute or model the possible consequences in advance.

Professor was about to finish his first lecture on modeling now. He went to the white board, drew a lake in plan and placed three springs connected with each other.

He then summarized, "Don't look at the lake as just one spring but made out of several different springs –all interconnected. A load on any of the springs will not only elongate that spring, but will transfer the load to the connecting springs leading to elongation in them. Since the Young's modulus of the springs will be different (as depths vary, so the currents and the extent of re-aeration), the net elongations (or water quality changes) are going to be complex. If wastewater is discharged at the bank or in the mid of the lake for instance, it will make a difference as the springs in 'action' will be different."

He looked at the Powai Lake outside the window of the class and slowly said,

"I am requesting Dr. Prasad Modak who is sitting in the last row, to come up with a physical model of springs and weights for the Powai Lake when we meet next. We will do various experiments on this model by hanging weights, measuring the elongations and changing the springs. In the third lecture, I will explain how we will use the principle of Hooke's law to develop a simple lake water quality model."

"Oh, this is now getting really tricky and difficult." I said to myself.

I decided to bunk the next lecture and jump straight to the third.

35

My Professor friend called me early one morning and asked me to come to Delhi by the earliest flight. When I asked him why? He said, "This is a call from the Union Minister of Environment & Forests & Climate Change (MoEFCC). He is looking for ideas from us on how to improve quality of life of people in Urban India. I told him that together you and I would come up with something innovative – the first of its kind in the World – and help India."

We reached the Union Ministers office to find him waiting for us rather impatiently. "I want to bring in a change in Urban India." He announced. "With all these problems of air pollution, poor drinking water quality and fires at the waste dump sites, the situation is getting worse. Despite several orders being issued, laws and regulations being updated, there has been no improvement --no change! The municipal corporations and pollution control boards

continue to their business as if their institutions consist only of built structures and with no people functioning inside. The only change is the change of staff. I tried introducing green city/clean city/sustainable cities awards and campaigns to showcase examples of good practice. But that has not worked. No one believes in these awards and the claims made by the city heads and data reported is almost always questionable. Most city heads say "don't tell me what Navi Mumbai or Pune city is doing as these things are simply not relevant to us." I am really frustrated. Please help!"

The Minister was right, good examples often don't work – although we all feel they should and the same cities continue getting the awards giving others no opportunities to improve themselves. We assured the Minister that we would come up with an innovative plan but on the condition that he would not question us and promise to provide full support with no budgetary restrictions. The Minister agreed – though a little hesitantly.

As soon as we returned to Mumbai, we designed a new competition on our Indian cities. The competition was titled "Cities of Today that Will Lead Future India."

The criteria for award were formulated accordingly. See the following table. We focused on the dirtiest and most poorly managed Indian cities instead of those that were performing well or steadily improving. There was no point in focusing solely on the good ones as there were only a few. It was important to recognize the bad cities who can show what's possible in future India if we followed "business as usual". We were aiming for a large number of applications. City officials were to be given one month to e-file their application complete with an attachment of photographs showing examples of callousness, filth, morning haze etc. and a PDF of public complaints received and action not taken

The award scheme was very attractive. The Lead city (i.e. the worst performer!) would receive a grant of 1000 million INR from the central government, the city ranked

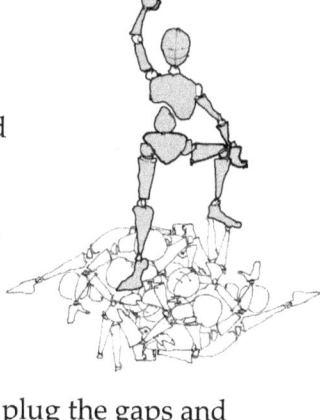

second would get INR 800 and the third performer would have INR 500 million. The cities could use this fund to plug the gaps and address their infrastructural and institutional deficiencies. The rank was to be provided with no audit requirements in order to expedite actions. [We later realized that the interest from city heads was to look at this grant as an opportunity to launder money through innovative contracting mechanisms – hand in glove with equipment suppliers, contractors and NGOs. We suspected this but realized that it could be an example of another form of leadership!]

The announcement of such a novel award scheme led to a lot of discussion amongst the city administration. The Chief of Mumbai Corporation was very pleased and it seems he told his colleagues, "Good timing, we have just had this massive fire at the Deonar Dump that we were successful in not managing well. This can be cited as a good example in our bid for the award." The Chief of Delhi Corporation called for meeting with

Criteria for the Competition "Cities of Today that Will Lead Future India"[32]

Municipal Solid Waste (MSW)	Total dumping area per person ; percent increase over last 5 years
	Maximum height of the Dump
	Number of uncontrolled fire incidences in the dump areas
Other Wastes	Biomedical waste not adequately handled and mixed with MSW
	C&D Waste that is simply dumped
	E-Waste that reaches the landfill
Air Quality	Average Air Quality Index and extent of violations over the "Standard"
	Specific parameter like PM10 and importantly viable count on the particles reflecting impact of open defecation (something we added to reflect gravity of the situation)
Water	Water availability (hours of supply and quantity), Water quality at the taps
Urban Floods	Floods managed terribly leading to loss of life, damage to infrastructure and spread of diseases
Natural ecosystems	Mangroves destroyed, lakes polluted and infringed upon, Trees felled
Noise	Noise profile across the city with Max values, Day and Night averages – Exceedence over standards
Public complaints	Public complaints received and that remain unattended

his colleagues at the Delhi Pollution Control Committee (DPCC) and asked for data on the rising air pollution in Delhi from last 5 years" I really want to see graphs that will show a steep rise over the years and that we did nothing about it. We must show that we are leaders in this arena." He said.

The Chief of the Chennai Corporation was joyous – he said "We have an excellent story to tell about the recent Chennai floods, where despite early warning we did nothing and never built adequate storm water management infrastructure." Those who heard this felt really proud of this achievement. In Bangalore, the city chief said, "I think we will be the winner on account of mess we have made with our lakes. This is something unique but we must give equal credit to the Bangalore builders besides our interest to promote private

---

32 Table 1 is only an illustration and a detailed criteria with more variables and a clear basis of scoring was posted on the website of MoEFCC. Worse is the city, more scores were to be attached.

sector participation."

Everyone was thus keen to highlight their achievements of the past 5 years and they all got busy filing the application. Some cities hired management consultants like PwC, KPMG, E&Y and Delloite etc. who were good at producing elegant reports in perfect English and using nice fonts. "Let us invest in consultants", proclaimed the Chief of City in Ahmedabad. Hiring consultants was an expected move. Most city governments do not write reports on their own.

We received more than 100 applications and I was getting worried. I called the Professor and he told me not to worry. "I have already set up a committee of retired IAS officers (who used to manage cities themselves, although not very well and who have a lot of time to spare). They will help us." He said.

"But Professor," I continued, "why is there such an overwhelming response? I do understand the interest in the money but don't you think that the citizens in these cities should simply ban or dissuade their city heads from even filing an application. Isn't it a great shame for your city to actually get this award under our proposed scheme?"

The Professor smiled and replied,"So you really don't know the real reason for this rush! You missed additional incentive that I added. The winning cities will be allowed to send a team (comprising of environmental NGOs and media) on a special 15 day tour of various other cities. First prize winner gets sent to the America, the second to Europe and third to the Asia-Pacific. The tour will be fully sponsored (along with shopping allowance) and designed to appear to be very technical with learning and experience sharing objectives. The attraction of winning these lavish tours will work as a good incentive thereby ensuring a proper and well thought out application is made."

"My apologies Dr. Modak for not telling you this in advance." said the Professor as he lit his cigar and took a deep puff.

I replied, "Now I am really excited to see the results and I am sure the Union Environmental Minister will be pleased. Indeed, we have a bright future ahead for cities we live in."

36

Environmental assessment (EA) as a concept came about due to the thinking of "precautionary principle" and "do no harm" to the environment. EA was conceived as a proactive tool to ensure that the projects in their construction and operational activities produced least negative impacts possible and that the residual impacts were communicated to the stakeholders and mitigated by appropriate environmental management plans.

The Precautionary Principle[33] or Precautionary Approach

The precautionary principle (or precautionary approach) to risk management states that if an action or policy has a suspected risk of causing harm to the public, or to the environment, in the absence of scientific consensus (that the action or policy is not harmful), the burden of proof that it is not harmful falls on those taking an action that may or may not be a risk.

This principle is used by policy makers to justify discretionary decisions in situations where there is the possibility of harm from making a certain decision (e.g. taking a particular course of action) when extensive scientific knowledge on the matter is lacking. The principle implies that there is a social responsibility to protect the public from exposure to harm, when scientific investigation has found a plausible risk. These protections can be relaxed only if further scientific findings emerge that provide sound evidence that no harm will result.

The first country which promulgated EA legislation on a national scale was the United States of America. The National Environmental Protection Act (NEPA) laid the foundation of the EA process requiring projects

---

33 Source: https://en.wikipedia.org/wiki/National_Environmental_Policy_Act

(according to pre-determined criteria based on project type, project size and project location) to undergo an environmental examination. NEPA also stated the reporting requirements for obtaining approval of the responsible administrative body.

The National Environmental Policy Act (NEPA)[34] is a United States environmental law that promotes the enhancement of the environment and established the President's Council on Environmental Quality (CEQ). The law was enacted on January 1, 1970. As the bill was an early step towards the development of the United States's environmental policy, NEPA is referred to as the "environmental Magna Carta".

NEPA's most significant outcome was the requirement that all executive federal agencies prepare Environmental Assessments (EAs) and Environmental Impact Statements (EISs). These reports state the potential environmental effects of proposed federal agency actions.

NEPA grew out of the increased appreciation and concern for the environment that resulted from the 1969 Santa Barbara oil spill. During this time, environmental interest group efforts and the movement resulting from Rachel Carson's book, Silent Spring, helped to pass the Wilderness, Clean Air, and Clean Water Acts. Another major driver for enacting NEPA were the 1960s freeway revolts, a series of protests that occurred in response to the bulldozing of many communities and ecosystems during the construction of the Interstate Highway System.

Since its passage, NEPA has been applied to any major project, whether on a federal, state, or local level, that involves federal funding, work performed by the federal government, or permits issued by a federal agency. Court decisions have expanded the requirement for NEPA-related environmental studies to include actions where permits issued by a federal agency are required regardless of whether federal funds are spent to implement the action. This legal interpretation is based on the rationale that obtaining a permit from a federal agency inherently results in federal funds being expended, even if no federal funds are directly allocated to finance the particular action.

---

34 Source: https://en.wikipedia.org/wiki/Strategic_environmental_assessment

The initiation of NEPA in the US had a ripple effect in other countries notably Canada, Australia, Netherlands and the United Kingdom. Each of these countries developed their own EA related policies and legislation, modeled on the US NEPA but incorporating their individual priorities and requirements. Soon EA was followed by developing countries especially in the Asia-Pacific region. The outcomes of the EA were linked to the Environmental Clearance (EC) process. However since EA was to be performed by a project developer in order to obtain the required EC for the development activity, the quality of assessment was generally biased and very poor. This situation has unfortunately not changed even today.

Most countries followed the criteria of project screening based on project type, size and location and as a result only a certain type of projects required EA or Environmental Impact Assessment (EIA). Mostly such as schools, parks, renewable energy projects like solar, wind and even metros did not require EIA on the argument that these projects are intrinsically environment friendly. If however the project was proximal to a sensitive location such as a reserved forest or a sanctuary or a turtle breeding ground, it required more deeper or rigorous examination. Many countries therefore delineated environmentally critical or sensitive zones and the necessary buffer areas.

Depending on the sensitivity and complexity of the project, EA was conducted at two levels – Rapid EA or Initial Environmental Examination (IEE) or Comprehensive EA. The call on the appropriate level of EA was often subjective and every project developer or investor (i.e. the Consultant) argued the case for an IEE instead of a Comprehensive EA to save on costs and time.

Deciding the threshold on project size is however a complex and rather subjective exercise. Also these thresholds on requirement of EA have always been abused. In Hawaii for example, hotels having less than 100 rooms were not required to perform EA. Consequently, after NEPA, most hotels were built with 99 rooms. In India, the Supreme Court recently directed a ban on diesel-guzzling luxury cars and SUVs with engine capacity of 2000 cc in response to the severe air pollution in Delhi.. As a result, Mahindra's came up with a new vehicle fitted with a 1990 cc engine! Now I ask you, do you think a 10 cc reduction in the engine capacity will solve Delhi's problem of air pollution?

EA was made mandatory in India under the EIA notification of 1994 under the Environment (Protection) Act (EPA)[35]. Since 1994, the notification has been amended several times (far too many to keep track of in my opinion) to apparently bring in more clarity, improve the implementation process and address any specific issues or lacunae.

The EIA notification follows a schedule that presents project types and thresholds. The siting rules and zones along with the required buffer distances have also been outlined. There is a scheme of categorization that determines whether the EA will need to be submitted for review and EC at the Centre or at the State. Every developer aims for a State level clearance as that is believed to be easier to acquire through means, both fair and foul.

Over the last three decades and especially in India, EA has been followed on a project level and the instrument is primarily used to identify mitigation plans prior to the EC. Experience has shown that limiting EA to projects alone is not going to be very effective in the interest of sustainability. Consideration will need to be given to regional level impacts where multiple projects contribute to the impacts cumulatively. In other words, EC must look at regional situations and development scenarios to recognize the indirect/induced and cumulative impacts and ensure that the carrying capacity of the region is not unduly exceeded.

Many countries have enhanced their EA legislation to address requirements of regional and cumulative EAs especially when dealing with area wide development projects such as industrial estates, network of transport corridors, urban and peri-urban development etc. Here, in addition to mitigation plans, the regulator thinks about planning as well as policy measures. This led to extension of EA to Strategic EIA (SEA) which is currently being implemented to legislation in most developed countries and emerging superpowers like China.

---

35 India's Environment (Protection) Act, 1986 available at: http://envfor.nic.in/legis/env/env1.html

Strategic EIA (SEA)[36]

Strategic environmental assessment (SEA) is a systematic decision support process, aiming to ensure that environmental and possibly other sustainability aspects are considered effectively in policy, plan and programme making. In this context, SEA may be seen as:

· a structured, rigorous, participative, open and transparent environmental impact assessment (EIA) based process, applied particularly to plans and programmes, prepared by public planning authorities and at times private bodies,

·a participative, open and transparent, possibly non-EIA-based process, applied in a more flexible manner to policies, prepared by public planning authorities and at times private bodies, or

·a flexible non-EIA based process, applied to legislative proposals and other policies, plans and programmes in political/cabinet decision-making.

Effective SEA works within a structured and tiered decision framework, aiming to support more effective and efficient decision-making for sustainable development and improved governance by providing for a substantive focus regarding questions, issues and alternatives to be considered in policy, plan and programme (PPP) making.

SEA has been applied at the sector level, but in most instances, these requirements have been promoted or rather forced upon by the Development Financing Institutions (DFI). In fact, it may not be wrong to state that DFIs such as the World Bank, International Financing Corporation (IFC) and the Asian Development Bank have significantly influenced the national EA systems across the world.

As early as in 1992, the Mumbai Metropolitan Regional Development Authority (MMRDA) undertook Sector Environmental Assessment of Mumbai's Transport Plan at the insistence of the World Bank. I had an opportunity to work on this assignment where we examined road, sea and rail transport alternatives.

In 1996, on the insistence of the World Bank once again, the Ministry of Environment and Forests (MoEF), the Government of India

---

36 Source: http://www.graham.umich.edu/pdf/ia-guide.pdf

conducted Sectoral EA of the proposed Hazardous Waste Management Project. The focus of this Sectoral EA was the generation and analyses of alternatives to identify the most preferred option that would do justice to the environmental and social considerations. The project outlay was approximately USD 300 million and I was asked to prepare the Sectoral Assessment report which included five public consultations across the country. This was one of the first such reports produced by the World Bank on SEA.

Another variant that emerged through this process was the programmatic EA which looked beyond a specific project examining the potential for up scaling and replication of a developmental activity. While a project by itself may not require EA or an Environmental Clearance (EC), the same project when replicated or up scaled had potential to cause adverse impacts on a regional scale. The technique of programmatic EA brought out idea of developing mitigation plans in the form of best practices. These best practices would then be embedded in the very project design. When a project of 500 bus stands was proposed in the

State of Punjab in 1999, the bus stand as an individual project did not require any EA or EC. However the design, layout and siting of the bus stand was looked at from an environmental and social perspective and a "model" project configuration that met with environmental and social expectations was developed. This design was then replicated all over the State as a project carried out jointly by IL&FS Ltd and the World Bank. I had an opportunity to lead the project team.

In the Philippines today, a blend of programmatic and SEA is conducted for certain area-wide projects but it is not officially approved in the President's decree.

Thus, EA has reached a hierarchical structure in the form of a "pyramid" where policy or Strategic EA gave the overall direction and laid down the principles, followed by regional/programmatic and cumulative EAs with the base as the Project EAs. This led to Environmental and Social Management Frameworks (ESMF) that were recommended and adopted by the borrowing financial institutions (Category Financing Intermediary or FI of the World Bank or ADB). ESMFs were also used by cities and regions to ensure that environmental and social considerations were mainstreamed in policies, plans, programs and projects or the 4Ps.

In India ESMFs are operated by organizations such as IL&FS Ltd, IDFC, PowerGrid, SIDBI etc. I often call these organizations as "islands of excellence".

Limitation of Project-Limited (Area wide development) of EAs,

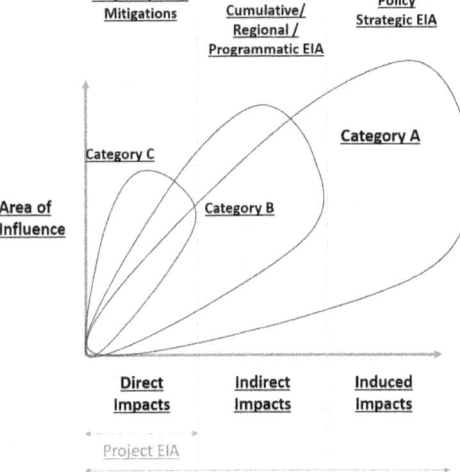

ESMF and Development Effectiveness

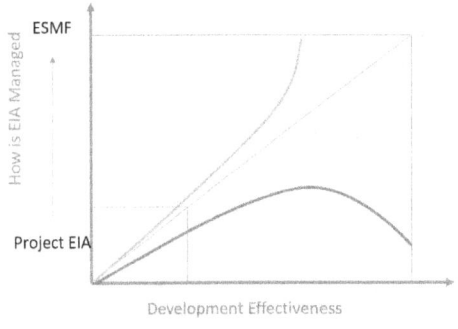

Development Effectiveness will increase when Environmental & Social Management Framework is present

By end of 2000, I would estimate that almost 50,000 EAs would have been produced across the World. There were however, two important elements that needed to be introduced – EA review criteria and Effectiveness of EA through "auditing" mechanism. In mid 1995, Norman Lee and Chris Wood from the Manchester University developed criteria for EA review.

Also since very few post-audits were carried out (some in Australia but not on a global scale) the task was undertaken by Barry Saddler with the support of International Association of Impact Assessment (IAIA). My good old friends L. Panneerselvam (now retired) and Sonia Kapoor (now at ADB), my colleague Radha Gopalan and I conducted a detailed study of 14 Bank supported projects in India and published a report of our findings[37]. Many of the observations made in this report are still valid today.

---

37 This report is available for download at: http://documents.worldbank.org/curated/
en/1999/09/2099771/india-review-effectiveness-environmental-assessments-world-bank-
assisted-projects-fiscal-1990-97

As it became apparent that there cannot be silo approach towards the management of environmental and social issues, a specialized discipline of Social Impact Assessment (SIA) soon emerged. Social development specialists, especially from Universities (dominated by experts from North Americas and Canada) took the lead and started working on a methodology for SIA as a complement to EA. Ideally, both processes should be integrated, especially during the scoping, analyses of alternatives and public consultation stages of EA. However due to different procedural requirements and different processing departments (which is a pity!), we often see separately prepared reports on EA and SIA.

Despite the importance of integration, even now such a practice has remained, giving a piece meal or sliced approach to deal with management of environmental and social issues. Again in SIA, the emphasis is primarily given to the issues related to resettlement and rehabilitation rather than on the induced social impacts. In general there is simply a non-availability or lack of an "integrated expertise."

Very close to SIA is the area of Health Impact Assessment (HIA). This dimension to EA got added when impacts were visualized on regional scale considering both environmental and social parameters over the long term. Impact on health was considered as a result of both direct and induced/indirect impacts with complex relationships between pollution release, contamination of resources and their consumption leading to phenomenon such as bio-accumulation.

HIA today, is not a separate mandatory requirement but is an aspect to be factored in the EA or SIA for certain types of projects. Consideration about health impacts led to realization that understanding of impacts is rather complex and there are several uncertainties about the assessment. This led to the discipline of Environmental Risk Assessment (ERA) focusing on the nexus between health and the eco-systems.

I was fortunate enough to work with Dr. Richard Carpenter who was one of the major players in drafting the NEPA. Richard was a chemist and a pioneer expert on environmental indicators and risk assessment. He worked for many years with the Program on Environment at the East-West Center in Hawaii and later at the University of Virginia in Charlottesville (US). His publications on Environmental Risk Assessment are must to read[38] and I still recall long dinners with Richard (Dick) on EA at the Peace Hotel in Shanghai near the harbor from many years ago.

The next logical step after ERA was to focus on biodiversity. Biodiversity Impact Assessment is today a field by itself where the EA process is followed and adapted e.g. Environmental Management Plan becomes Biodiversity Protection and Conservation Plan.

Given the expanse of EA from project level to policy and planning levels, integration with social development, health and safety related aspects, the next logical step was to wrap all these perspectives into one crucible i.e. Sustainability.

Sustainability framework has been the major extension of EA in the last decade. The idea was not just management of risks but to identify and leverage opportunities while staying within the "limits of growth". Sustainability integration or sustainability based appraisal provided EA a new dimension and a role beyond permitting or obtaining EC. The Sustainability Appraisal (SA) essentially integrated economic, environmental and social considerations. Integrated Assessment (IA) is synonymous to Sustainability Appraisal.

Integrated Assessment (IA)[39]

Integrated Assessment (IA) brings together natural, social, and economic information to assist analysis of policy options for decision makers. The IA process also brings together scientists, policy makers, citizens, NGO, and industry representatives to evaluate options for particularly challenging – or wicked – problems. Since IA builds partnerships and a framework to share knowledge, problems that have both arguable definitions and solutions are best suited to this process.

IAs vary widely depending on the geographic scope, budget, type of issue, and range of decision makers. The following are useful IA steps

---

38 See http://www.hardystevenson.com/Articles/RISK%2520ASSESSMENT.pdf&gws_
    rd=cr&ei=D-Y7V7vqOISCvQSR3augDA

39 Sources: (1) https://en.wikipedia.org/wiki/Precautionary_principle
    (2) http://graham.umich.edu/media/files/ia-benefits.pdf

that ensure the process is both relevant to participants and factually credible:

1) define the policy-relevant question,

2) document status and trends,

3) describe the causes and consequences of those trends,

4) identify desired outcomes and policy options,

5) evaluate the likely environmental, social, and economic outcomes of each option,

6) provide technical guidance for implementation

7) assess uncertainty

These elements are best seen as a flexible framework – different stages might be emphasized depending on the policy context and the scientific and public understanding of the issue.

Integrated Assessment can appear to be overly complex with vague outcomes. However, because sustainability problems often lack a clear cause or solution, the IA process offers an innovative way to build consensus and guide decisions for these pressing and unique challenges. It is also important to acknowledge that there are both tangible and intangible benefits associated with IA. The goal of this study is to communicate both sets of benefits.

Sustainability based EA or Integrated Appraisal is therefore the recent avatar of EA. It has been widely practiced for planning local area development in the United Kingdom where it is mandatory that such appraisals are carried out every year and reported. Few private sector equity investors have also evolved sustainability appraisal frameworks. Some of the DFIs such as World Bank, IFC, and DFID have already set up sustainability based / driven environmental and social assessment requirements.

More recently, the dimension of climate change has been added. The Asian Development Bank (ADB) specifically, has come up with climate proofing and its integration in the environmental assessment with several sectoral guidelines.

After years of experience in the application of EA, several "templated" environmental management plans have emerged. These plans are essentially a repository of good practices and have influenced project design and project management practices. These best practices have been now mainstreamed and are implemented upfront without a push from legislation. In the Kingdom of Bhutan, roads are built how they should be and not a result or consequence of EA.

We must remember that EA is essentially a generic tool that links activities with environmental components and therefore has a place in the establishment of Environmental Management System (EMS) of ISO 14001. In these systems, EA is used to analyze project activities, associated aspects and their influence on the environmental component so as to check whether the impacts are in compliance or whether they pose a threat or risk to human health and eco-systems.

As the understanding on the environmental impacts of making, packaging, distributing and servicing products increased, the tool of Life Cycle Assessment (LCA) emerged. LCA uses the core principles of EA to predict, assess and manage the adverse impacts, influencing thereby the product design, material sourcing and product use and management of rejects/ residues. EA thus provides a generic framework to address manufacturing systems and services following once

again the precautionary and "do no harm" principles. This "power" of EA is not recognized by most as the understanding of EA is limited and often the EA is merely a necessary complication in the process of obtaining Environmental Clearance.

It often surprises me that in India, EA has been a pretty neglected subject in the Ministries and State Environment Departments. The Indian EA system has remained outdated and has not responded to the needs of required "modernization". The community of EA professionals is small and largely engaged in unethical practices whereas the project proponents and investors are still ignorant about the advantages of EA.

At the behest of the World Bank, I prepared a Project Implementation Plan (PIP) for improving the EA regime in India for the MoEF. V. Rajagopalan was then the Joint Secretary then who later became Chairman of Central Pollution Control Board and finally Secretary to the MoEF.

Many of my suggestions in the PIP got reflected in the 2006 EIA Notification – however points made on SEA, Regional EA and Cumulative Assessment were shelved. My proposal to set up a National Environmental Information Centre (EIC) was looked at favorably and was supported using grants from the World Bank- but once again due to bureaucratic reasons, the EIC project was aborted after a year of piloting.

In 2011, I made a sincere effort to set up a 12 institution EIA Training and Knowledge network (EtCON) and came up with a very detailed plan for delivering nationwide training based on a network of institutions approach. My work was initially supported by the World Bank but ironically the project was eventually delayed and finally shelved by them due to their internal politics and because they found it awkward to "fit me in."

I like Dick Carpenter's definition of E I A as *Early, Integrated* and *Always*. Unfortunately in India, none of these three letters are understood, appreciated and followed.

Only God can save this country!

37

Environmental Clearance in India – Fast Track or Change of Track?

Most major investors in India's industry and infrastructure, project proponents and the line ministries have been complaining about inordinate delays and ambiguities in the decisions related to the Environmental Clearance (EC). The new government is therefore making all possible efforts to move on the "fast track."

The current Environment Minister Prakash Javdekar has worked at great speed in his first 100 days and cleared 240 of 325 pending projects. Most public sector companies such as Oil and Natural Gas Corporation (ONGC) and National Thermal Power Corporation (NTPC) got approvals for starting new projects and expanding their capacity. The Ministry also cleared major private sector projects such as a plan to increase Cairn's oil production capacity by 50% in Rajasthan.

The Government estimates the hastening of approvals could spur foreign investment to the tune of 2 billion INR and help revive the economy.

These fast approvals have however became possible by easing norms (e.g. diluting no-development zones), eliminating processes like public hearing, changing thresholds (especially to decentralize decision making at State level) and diverting forest lands. The Forest Advisory Committee (FAC) approved the diversion of a massive 7,122 hectares of forestland for development projects in the first three months Narendra Modi's government. With the forest cover already at 69.79 million hectares or 21.23 per cent of the geographical area as against 33 per cent mandated by the National Forest Policy, forest diversion could be an issue of great concern.

The Ministry further decentralized the forest clearance process by increasing the threshold of projects being considered by State governments from 15 hectares to 40 hectares. So now nearly 90% of the files/applications for forest clearance won't need to be reviewed by the Ministry.

Vide Notification S.O.1599 (E) dated 25th June, 2014, more powers have been delegated to State Environmental Impact Assessment Agencies (SEIAAs) to grant EC to various projects. Earlier, if projects in Category 'B' were located within 10 km. of Protected Areas, Critically Polluted Areas, Eco Sensitive Areas, and Inter-state / International boundaries, they would be appraised as Category 'A' by the Ministry of Environment and Forests. Now, this distance has been reduced to 5 km, implying thereby that more projects can now be considered by SEIAAs for granting ECs. Apart from this, the capacity up to which non-molasses based distilleries and mineral beneficiation activities could be considered as Category 'B' has been increased. Also, all bio-mass fuel based thermal power plants with capacity greater than or equal to 15 MW have been put in Category 'B'. Earlier, such projects were considered as Category 'A' projects, if their capacity exceeded 20 MW.

The Centre had done away with the requirement of public hearings for coal mines below 16 MTPA, in a bid to expand output by up to 50 per cent. Later, this was extended to mines above 16 MTPA, permitting them to mine up to five MTPA or more without consulting the affected people. Border roads and all defense infrastructures within 100 kms of Line of Actual Control have been brought under the General Approval scheme thereby eliminating the requirement for public hearings.

The Ministry reconstituted the National Board for Wildlife (NBWL) and has done away with the five mandatory NGO representatives or the ten persons to be nominated by the Central government from among eminent conservationists, ecologists and environmentalists, as mandated by Section 5A of the Wildlife Protection Act. Besides, the notification only referred to the Standing Committee. It was not surprising therefore that on August 25th, after a petition challenged the constitution of the Board, the Supreme Court stayed the decisions of the diluted Standing Committee of the NBWL. The Standing Committee however has already cleared most of the 140 proposals before Supreme Court intervention.

The Government's mantra seems to be two-pronged — to make it easier for project developers/investors to set up new projects or expand – viz fast tracking – but stipulate stringer environmental norms e.g. on emissions. This approach is likely to satisfy the businesses but environmental campaigners are not impressed. When compliance to existing regulations itself is pathetic, how can one expect that more stringent regulations will be complied with? Unless, the pollution control boards are strengthened, enforcement will continue to be poor.

A High Level Committee (HLC) has been now constituted vide OM 22-15/2014-IA-III, dated 29.08.2014 to review the key five Acts viz. Environment (Protection) Act, 1986; Forest (Conservation) Act, 1980; Wildlife (Protection) Act, 1972; The Water (Prevention and Control of Pollution) Act, 1974; and The Air (Prevention and Control of Pollution) Act, 1981. The idea is to "bring these laws in line with current requirements to meet objectives." The Committee is expected to come up with recommendations in the course of just two months! I am sure the recommendations will include mergers and simplifications in the legal system towards "single window" appraisals and clearances.

Clearly, what we are going to see in the next five years is not just "fast track" on project clearances but a "change of track" in the development paradigm. If foreign direct investments and job creation are going to be the principal drivers for taking decisions, then environmental protection and conservation will certainly take the back seat. We need to take a balanced and a strategic approach to ensure that economic development, security of our natural resources and social justice go hand in hand. We need to change the track towards this direction.

Fixing problems on an ad-hoc basis is not going to work. Merely being on fast track could potentially derail our economy over the long run. Sustainability will then only remain a rhetoric and just a talk in the seminars.

Some reading resources -

http://www.
indiaenvironmentportal.org.
in/category/34622/thesaurus/
environment-clearance-ec/

http://timesofindia.indiatimes.
com/india/Govt-puts-
border-roads-on-fast-track/
articleshow/38575746.cms

http://www.hindustantimes.
com/india-news/on-fast-
track-environment-minister-
prakash-javadekar-clears-
240-projects-in-3-months/
article1-1262676.aspx

http://www.ndtv.com/article/
india/centre-red-faced-
as-supreme-court-puts-
wildlife-board-decisions-on-
hold-581605

http://www.thehindu.com/
todays-paper/tp-opinion/
clearance-without-compliance/
article6392324.ece

You may also be interested
in reading the report on the
walk-out by the High level
committee headed by T S R
Subramanium during public
consultation in Bangalore. The
press release is available at:

https://prasadmodakblog.
files.wordpress.com/2014/09/
press_release_hlc_cmt_moef_
walks_out_27092014.pdf

38

Virtual Impact Assessment of the Coastal Road Project in Mumbai

A 35.6-km coastal road along the western coastline of Mumbai has been planned. This new road would be a freeway linking south Mumbai with the western suburbs and reduce traffic congestion on the Western Express Highway (WEH). The WEH today carries over 60% of the city's traffic and the Coastal Road project will take some of the load off the WEH.

The Brihanmumbai Municipal Corporation (BMC) will be the nodal agency for this project that is to be implemented in phases. The BMC has proposed a 10-km long underground tunnel at two locations - the first from Nariman Point to Priyadarshani Park and the second from Juhu to Versova. This Coastal Road will include 22 interchanges, entry and exit points and lanes dedicated to the Bus Rapid Transit System (BRTS) and is estimated to cost Rs.120,000 million.

I have been keeping tabs on news related to this Project as an environmental professional, I was being hounded at the Page 3 Parties with the question, "Dr Modak, Is this Coastal Project any good for Mumbai?" So far I was having a tough time skirting an issue too complex to answer with a simple "Yes" or "No." The best response at my disposal at occasions was to say something ambiguous, "It depends…"

Statements made by the Chief Minister of the Government of Maharashtra, Commissioner of the BMC and the Project Consultants have been very positive, stressing the Project's need and emphasizing the benefits. In addition to reducing the traffic congestion on the WEH, the Coastal Road Project was estimated to reduce air pollution thereby protecting the Mumbaikar's health. This project however has not found favour with environmental NGOs and professionals. Some architects and nature lovers are very upset with the project concept – and its configuration. As most cars today, are fitted with air conditioners, air emissions from the traffic are not the most pressing concern. Many people are convinced that the more serious problem that needs to be addressed is the air pollution caused by the emissions resulting from the open burning of the garbage and fires at the dumping ground in Deonar.

The Coastal Road Project received Environmental Clearance (EC) from the Ministry of Environment and Forests and Climate Change (MoEFCC) and during this process, the BMC received over 700 suggestions/ objections from citizens, activists and fishermen. I do believe that the project consultants have made every attempt to minimize issues related to land restoration, flooding, mangroves and extent of visual intrusion. I don't know whether answers to the 700 + questions are posted on BMC's website. However, all these impacts cannot be fully neutralized. Citizens will have to compromise between these impacts against the proposed benefits of the new road i.e. an efficient and time-saving transportation in the north-south corridor; reduced fuel

consumption and hence less air pollution. The choice is so hard to make and is as difficult to decide whether to continue to stay in Mumbai!

Implementing the stretch of the coastal road passing through the suburbs of Khar, Juhu, and Versova is going to be a problem for the BMC due to the presence of a lot of mangroves in the area. There is also a stiff opposition from the fishermen of the fishing villages of Khar danda and Mora.

The MoEFCC in its EC has mandated that if there is any destruction of mangroves, then the agency will have to replant three times the number of mangroves lost. But is three an appropriate number? And will such an off-set compensation really help? These are questions that will still remain unanswered.

I contacted my Professor friend to get his views on the Coastal Road Project and suggested meeting over coffee on a Sunday morning. The Professor however had a better idea. "Let us drive on the Coastal Road itself and you will experience the change" he said.

I was taken aback! "Sir, it will take next 6 years to complete the Project. Are you aware that the Project includes reclamation and tunneling components that are not easy to implement. I am sure there will be Project Roko Andolans as well that will stall or delay some of the sensitive sections of the Project."

The Professor smiled. "I am going to take you in my special simulator van that has the ability to do Virtual Impact Assessment (VIA). As we will drive along the proposed route of the Coastal Road Project, the simulator based on VIA will show us the future i.e. how the environment will be during construction and operation phase of the project."

I was astonished. "That is unbelievable! What is this VIA that you are talking about?"

"It's a new and emerging technique." The Professor said briefly.

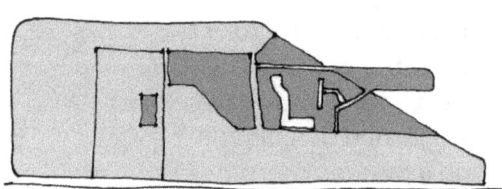

I reached at the MLA Hostel at Nariman Point at 9am. At the gate, waiting for me, was a large van and the Professor with his cigar.

"Get in!" he said excitedly, extinguishing his cigar.

The interior of the van was like a spacecraft with a large screen with a dashboard. The Professor gave me a special pair of 3D spectacles with the unique "power to view the present and the future." The dashboard had buttons that could generate the various environmental scenarios resulting from the project.

We began the journey and soon entered the tunnel beneath Marine Drive that extended all the way through the Malabar Hill reservoir. I heard violins! The Professor said that this music was from one of the National Centre for Performing Arts (NCPA) concerts. "When people pass through the Tunnel, they will be able to enjoy music just as though they were live at the NCPA" the Professor explained.

"How soothing! That's very thoughtful of you" I said.

The tunnel journey was great with bright illumination of lights reflecting on the sheets of water on the wall. This water was flowing due to the unstoppable leaks formed in the Malabar Hill reservoir during the tunnel construction.

We reached Haji Ali in no time but in the maze of flyovers constructed there I couldn't figure out where the famous mosque/landmark was! "Can't do much" the Professor said quietly. "We are aware of this problem and we have apologized in writing for the "visual intrusion" we have created. But you see, this affects only a small fraction of city's population. We must see benefit to the city as a whole. Note that we have also impacted the Mahalaxmi Temple, equally – so it's all fair in that sense."

There was hardly any traffic on the coastal road and the cars that I did see were mostly saloon cars – not what your average Mumbaikar travels in. I guess the common person was still hanging on for dear life, outside the packed local railway compartment. The Professor said that the toll to use the coastal road was rather expensive – and that was because the project has exceeded its original budget of Rs.120, 000 million by nearly 50%.There was also an obligation to use Dutch consultants and Japanese contractors as the Government of Maharashtra had mobilized funding from the Netherlands and Japan International Cooperation Agency (JICA). This has turned out to be a bad deal and rather costly as well. Also since very few commuters were really interested in travelling from MLA hostel to Malad.

I saw a car overtaking us near Worli. The person sitting in the front seat looked like a politician. "That is Mr. Shaikh. The MLA from Malad (West)", the Professor confirmed. "Mr. Shaikh is a regular user of the coastal road. Since now, it only takes him 35 minutes to reach the MLA Hostel from residence, he can wake up a little later in the morning. Mr. Shaikh is a very happy commuter because of the new coastal road." The Professor explained that apparently this was one of the most important factors motivating Mr. Shaikh to endorse the Coastal Road Project and help the BMC resolve the protests from the local fishermen. I however, was very sure that this was not true.

When we reached Bandra, we crossed over the Mahim Fort. The fort (built by the Portuguese some 900 years ago) is a magnificent island fort of historical importance.

"Aha!" the Professor said triumphantly. "Here you will see the power of technology."

We took a diversion, exiting the coastal road and arrived at the Mahim Fort. The Coastal Road on stilt was just in the proximity and was blocking the magnificent sea view that we used to see..

When we entered the Fort, I saw several kiosks placed around the area. The Professor took me to one of these kiosks and pressed a few buttons. A huge screen came up and displayed an unimpeded view of the sea, the rocks populated with young couples sitting and smooching and the khare dane walas (peddlers selling roasted groundnuts). I could also smell a mix of sea spray and untreated sewage and sense a gust of wind – created no doubt through a clever wind generator. This was a depiction of the way it "used to be"!

"Well! We sort of recorded the baseline scenario around the Mahim Fort with Gigabytes of digital photography – then used laser technology to create this baseline virtually so that you can get the same experience as before (the sound, wind, light and smells all blended together)" the Professor explained.

"This is just amazing! First of all, half of Mumbai's population does not know much about the Mahim Fort. Second, a very small percentage of people actually visit it and a majority of them are not monument lovers but simply lovers who are looking for a secluded place. –It is so thoughtful of you to have created this virtual world just to keep your promise to minimize the adverse impacts of the visual obstruction. Hats off to you Professor! You have given a fitting response to objections by Shweta Wagh and Hussain Indorewala." I couldn't stop myself from saying.

We got back on the coastal road and were soon passing over areas of Khar danda and Juhu. This was supposed to be the mangrove affected area. We were on the elevated or stilt section of the road, barricaded by the noise barriers (probably intentional, so as to hide the degraded and depleted patches of the mangroves). Unable to inspect the status of the mangroves and before the Professor could stop me, I pressed the button on the simulator dashboard to view the scene under the stilt road in the monsoon of 2021. What I saw was a picture of cars weeding through the floods, the sea ingresing aggressively with severe coastal erosion on the Juhu beach.

"Well, we did the best we could" said the Professor. "Some of our climate related predictions were not accurate and idea of planting three times the quantity of cleared mangroves was not effective."

I remained silent.

When we completed our journey at Malad, I asked the Professor, "So Professor – is the Coastal Road Project any good?" The Professor lit his cigar and said "Well Dr Modak, It all depends…"

In India, we continue to focus on project level Environmental Impact Assessments (EIA). When we talk about area wide interventions however, we need to elevate our thinking from project level to Regional Impact Assessment (REA).

The REAs need to be triggered through a comprehensive Environmental and Social Policy Framework (ESPF). Agencies such as the BMC and MMRDA or MSRTC need to work together and establish the ESPF that guides infrastructure development from a sustainable and holistic perspective. Projects should get identified only when all the alternatives (both strategic and operational) have been examined and Project EIAs should be conducted downstream, guided by an overarching ESPF, developed through extensive stakeholder consultation. What we need to demand creation and effective implementation of a regional ESPF[40].

---

40 You may like to view a presentation related to the Coastal Road project and the ESPF that I made during my talk at the S.D.VAIDYA Lecture Series titled 'MUMBAI: ON A ROAD TO KNOW WHERE? (Organized by the Indian Society of Landscape Architects (ISOLA)' on 28th of November, 2015). Available at ; http://www.slideshare.net/ EkonnectKnowledgeFoundation

39

Pollution is to be prevented in the first place but even after prevention, pollution is often not fully eliminated. Pollution needs to be adequately treated before discharge so that the environment is not adversely affected.

Take the case of managing wastewater. Industries generate wastewater from manufacturing processes, from utilities (boiler operations and cooling water discharges) and from sanitary use. One can reduce the wastewater generated by modifying the manufacturing process (e.g. using dry operations instead of wet) or by recycling wastewater back in the process. Wastewater after some treatment could also be used for washing or low grade operations. All these efforts lead to wastewater flow and load reduction and the wastewater that is left over needs to be treated as an end of the pipe measure so that the stipulated wastewater standards are met. These standards are listed specific to pollutant concentrations by the regulators (such as Pollution Control Boards or PCBs) with a belief that if the standards are met then the receiving environment will stay protected.

It is not surprising therefore that we see a number of wastewater treatment plants built and operated by individual industries and by industry associations as Common Effluent Treatment Plants (CETPs), a treatment facility shared by industries in a cluster. These treatment plants are inspected by the officers of the PCBs and samples of the treated wastewater are taken and tested in the laboratories to ensure that the plants are in compliance. In cases of non-compliance, actions are taken in the form of warnings (show cause notices). In cases of persistent non-compliance, fines are levied and even closure notices are issued.

I have a problem in believing or trusting the above system of monitoring & enforcement.

Firstly, the wastewater treatment plants are seldom operated by trained or certified operators. In India, we don't have a requirement of certification so just about anybody can operate a wastewater treatment plant. I am always intrigued by the fact that while industries spend considerable capital expenses in building wastewater treatment plants, they simply ignore the plant operations and do not get skilled people to work there, or pay them well and provide them a career progression.

Can you think of an operator getting a raise in salary because he operated the wastewater treatment plant in 24×7 compliance? How about an operator who could reduce the specific energy consumption (KJ/m^3) of the wastewater treatment plant while remaining in compliance? This operator should ideally be felicitated and paid a bonus proportional to the energy bill saved! Sadly, this does not happen.

While satisfactory operation of the wastewater treatment plant is an issue, the other problem is relatively low experience of the staff of the PCB in plant inspection and sampling. Most of the time, the staff (typically a field officer) is not well trained on how to walk through, inspect and assess the plant performance. The officer is sometimes not familiar with the treatment process and the equipment or does not have the prior experience or the eagle eye necessary for such an inspection. So in most instances, the task of inspection and monitoring gets poorly performed.

The brunt of non-compliance is then received by the environment despite investments made, staff deployed and numerous monitoring reports prepared!

I spoke to my Professor friend about my frustrations in this matter. He was in a hurry and was stepping out of his secret research laboratory (This lab was set up in the basement of Income Tax office in Mumbai -- a location unknown to most people. The Professor was convinced that he would get the necessary peace and quiet to work on the 21st century's most amazing innovations there as very few people visited the Income Tax office!)

He heard me out and then said, "Dr. Modak, you have come to me at the right time. I have just completed a pilot project on wastewater treatment plant that speaks. Let us drive to one such pilot and you will see that all your concerns regarding treatment plan operations and inspection are resolved." He said all this in a triumphant voice.

"Treatment Plants that can speak! Are you alright Professor?" I exclaimed.

In the next hour, I drove with Professor to an inconspicuous mid-size activated sludge wastewater treatment plant (capacity 2 MLD) near the Thane-Belapur industrial area. As soon as we entered the gate, the gate greeted us saying, "Welcome!" I was shocked. The Professor smiled and said that he had activated the Speak-o-scope and from now onwards I was going to hear everybody who mattered at the treatment plan.

We reached a chamber that had a bar screen with oil & grease trap. The Professor saw that the chamber was not well operated and cleaned. A lot of oil could be seen floating and getting across to the next treatment unit i.e. the primary sedimentation tank.

He asked the OG ("oil & grease trap"), "How do you feel?"

OG replied, "Terrible, I feel real sloppy. I wish I was given better attention. All I can do right now is skimming but that's really not effective as there is lot of emulsification. Please tell Manjunath (that was the name of the operator) and his boss to consider using enzymes! Apply them at my friend the PST (Primary Sedimentation Tank) downstream. This will reduce the maddening use of chemicals and knock off floating oil and grease."

I was shocked to listen to such coherent and intelligent speech. "How does this oil & grease trap know about advanced use of biotechnology (enzymes)?" I asked, still unable to accept that the oil & grease trap was actually speaking.

Professor smiled and said that this was essentially the combined application of Human Computer Interface (HCI), biomimicry and artificial intelligence. The main role was however played by the Google-Intel microchips. These chips allow the humanoid of each treatment unit to surf on the web to seek knowledge, upload data and download literature. He said that all treatment units in this plant are fitted with such special chips.

Soon I found that the oil & grease unit (OG) had just smsed Professor its performance data of last 24 hours. The Professor was generating info-graphics out of this data on his iPhone by plotting the flow against incoming and outgoing oil and grease concentration.

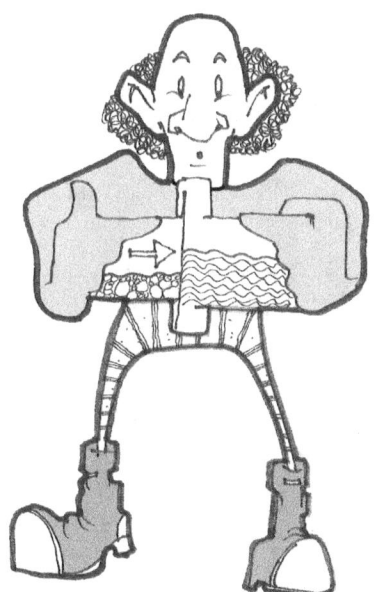

"Hmm!" He mumbled to himself as we moved to the PST. The PST had lot to say. It said that it was not doing well in the removal of suspended solids. It talked about the weir plate, "It is so uneven, tilted and unnoticed. Manjunath keeps loading higher concentrations of alum and lime in despair and this is really not helping much. In fact it is increasing the sludge volumes (swelling effect) and the carryover of high concentrations of suspended solids, oil and grease continues to my friend AT (Aeration Tank) downstream. If we follow OG's advice on using enzymes with me then we will get benefit of higher removal of both suspended solids and the Biochemical Oxygen Demand (BOD)."

I thought that PST was right. Sometimes, basics like the uniform level of the weir plate are not looked into.

The PST made other points such as the motor not getting regularly serviced and the non-functioning overload alarm.

We then moved to the AT which had four 50 HP Floating Aerators (FA). When one of the FAs saw the Professor, it wobbled a bit and skirted towards the wall and yelled, "Hey Professor, long time no see!" Of course only we could hear it, thanks to the Speak-o-scope.

When the Professor asked the FA its point of view, the FA said that it would generally spin in the day time

and would run at full speed with lot of foaming around especially during PCB staff visits. Nights were cool as there was no electric supply. "I am quite happy as all of us get a good night sleep. But sometimes one of us is made to spin – just in case." said the FA as it almost winked at us (i.e. flipped his blade a bit).

I was stunned. The Professor had been able to extract real information on what was happening at the wastewater treatment plant by simply talking to the treatment units. This was really an intelligent inspection and monitoring technology I thought.

We then spoke to the Final Sedimentation Tank (FST), gathered information on the sludge bulking problem and then reached the Final Chamber (FC) of wastewater discharge.

We found FC not very talkative and evading the Professors questions. When Professor asked about the status on meeting with the standards i.e. compliance, the FC changed the subject and started talking about climate change (Now a days I have been noticing that if you want to change the topic, most people start talking about climate change – it is very funny!).

"That's not relevant FC. Come to the point of compliance." Professor growled.

FC said that it could not speak any more as it had a sour throat.

When we exited the plant and reached my car, I could see that the Professor was visibly upset.

To cheer him up, I told him how impressed I was with his 21st century innovation and how this invention will open up new era of wastewater treatment plant operations, inspections and compliance etc. But Professor was silent.

He finally said,"Dr. Modak, this is the problem. I have been successful with treatment units like OG, PST, AT, FA and FST, but when it comes to FC, my algorithms and Google-Intel microchips don't seem to work. Each time I ask FC on its assessment of compliance (as this is the last unit), there is never a true or candid response. Most of the times, FC says that compliance is not a major issue – and it is probabilistic. It often adds that one must keep patient and stay a bit philosophical. I get really enraged!"

I sympathized with the Professor's situation and also understood why his phenomenal invention did not get the desired attention of the industries and regulators. (Will it ever? I wondered.)

I dropped Professor at the Income Tax office as he wanted to continue his research and went on my way.

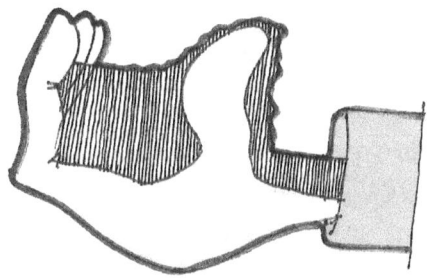

40

The World of the Banks

I started working with the World Bank (WB) as a short term consultant in 1989. My work as a consultant with Asian Development Bank (ADB) began in 1993. So for the past 25 years (almost) I have been associated with these two Development Financing Institutions (DFIs) as a consultant. In some sense I have been an insider but really not part of their system. Some envy this position.

In this long period of engagement, I have worked in India as well as in several Asian and African countries. I had an opportunity and good fortune to be associated with some of the outstanding staff of these institutions, consultants and the clients and I really cherish this experience. This has been a great learning experience for me.

In some of the Bank assignments, my job was to help prepare the projects, assist in the application of safeguards, participate in the supervision missions, build client capacities or prepare Implementation Completion Reports (ICR). ICRs were real eye-openers and I never missed the opportunity to work on them.

Most of the time, I used to be involved in the dialogue with the Central Ministries (like MoEF) or the State Governments/Departments (or the Pollution Control Boards) and Intermediary Financing Institutions (like IDBI/ ICICI in India). These interactions were crucial for understanding the puzzle and gave me a good insight into the dynamics of environmental governance

During the grueling missions

that we would go on, there were opportunities for fun and laughter in addition to moments of pure frustration! Evening dinners during some of these missions would sometimes tend to get philosophical – with us diners questioning the very paradigm of development and the role of the DFIs. With the changing times, priorities and economies, we now wonder whether these Banks have any worthwhile role left to play. Today, these institutions look redundant. No wonder you see emergence of new players like the New Development Bank or Asian Infrastructure Investment Bank.

The general impression of the DFI clients (i.e. the Governments in most cases) was that these Banks are extremely bureaucratic when it comes to procurement process and compliance with environmental and social safeguards. Clients used to be really weary of the requirement of public consultation and disclosure. Some felt that Banks are doing some kind of arm twisting before doling out the money and influencing (or even interfering with) the policies of the Government. To be fair however I feel that Banks for the most part, added value to the project.

I remember a meeting I did with State Environmental Protection Administration (SEPA) of China in Beijing in the 1990s. I was stressing the need for stepping up the process of public participation in decision making. The Chief of SEPA smiled and said, "You (i.e. Bank) are supporting less than 2% of China's infrastructure investments and do you expect us to comply with your advice for such a meager financial contribution? By the way, people who make decisions here are all elected from the provinces and so there is no need to go back and ask or involve people. The elected representatives know best and will protect the interest of the people they represent".

Today China is still struggling on how to implement an effective public consultation process (although a lot is written about it).

Reactions from the Government of India were no different. When we used to go as a Bank team to MoEF, the concerned Additional and Joint Secretaries used to ask me to stay in the room for a while after the meeting with Bank was over. With me alone in the room, they used to then air their reservations/concerns on Bank's requirements or impositions and ask me to mediate. My job was then to find an amicable solution.

Governments, in general, used to be interested in basically picking up as much free or cheap money available (like IDA) from these Banks. Compliance and reporting to the Bank requirements was to essentially satisfy the donors on paper. The ICRs often revealed poor sustainability of the Bank-financed projects or institutional capacity-building initiatives. This was mainly because there was no real ownership taken by the Governments. Often the projects were Bank-driven.

I remember my meeting with the Director General (DG) of the Department of Environment of one of India's neighboring countries. I was in DGs room with a Joint Director (JD) who was my good friend and explaining the need to introduce market based instruments apart from enforcement of the environmental regulations. The DG was watching cricket match on a TV that was placed in his room while I was speaking. I was offering the Bank's technical assistance but soon realized that DG was hardly listening to my pitch. I whispered to the JD that there is no point for me to continue as the DG is quite distracted and not listening.

The JD smiled and said, "No he is actually listening to what you are saying. Usually if he doesn't like what he hears he asks me to increase the volume of the TV. Since he hasn't told me to do so yet, this means that he likes you!"

He then spoke to the DG, "Sir, you may like to visit countries where market based instruments are used. Dr. Modak- can this visit be sponsored as a part of the Bank project?" The DG switched off the TV and started listening to me more attentively now. Indeed, going to foreign places for training and attending policy roundtables has been one of the greatest interests of most borrowing institutions. Task Managers of the Bank are always hounded by the project directors and administrators for such capacity building trips.

Despite these limitations, we must accept that these DFIs have influenced the environmental governance and environmental infrastructure of most of the developing countries today. If we take the example of industrial pollution management in India, we see Bank footprints on programs such as Common Effluent Treatment Plants (CETP), loans extended from IDBI and ICICI to industries on Pollution Prevention and Modernization of laboratories at key State Pollution Control Boards for better monitoring and enforcement. There are now only reminisces as a lot of water has flown under the bridge and the concerned staff at the PCB has retired.

I do however, recall some hilarious situations encountered during some of these projects. I was visiting one of the State Pollution Control Boards during an ICR that had received Bank assistance. We were checking the deployment of office fit-outs, specifically the air conditioners (ACs). We visited all the rooms where the ACs were supposed to have been installed and realised that one was missing. After some thought, the Senior Environmental Engineer said, "Oh yes, we found that we had one AC in excess but since you had stipulated that it must be located in the office, we installed it in one of our executive toilets. Come and I will show you!"

On industrial pollution, the Bank had supported Government of India in two lines of credit – Industrial Pollution Control (IPC) and Industrial Pollution Prevention (IPP). At a location in Gujarat, IPC subsidized a Common Effluent Treatment Plant (CETP) and under IPP, a water use reduction and recycling project was financed at an industry that contributed major effluent load to this CETP. This reduction in the effluent load (that was good) led to major negative impact on the revenue stream of the CETP making the capital investments made earlier not viable!

In IPC, the Bank financed innovative projects that were relevant and could potentially be replicated on demonstration. Sixty percent of the investments were provided as grants. One of the projects financed under this scheme was the manufacturing of bio-pesticides. The idea was to promote bio-pesticides to alleviate the problem of contamination by chemical pesticides and reduce the disease burden. When I visited the bio-pesticide plant during ICR, the management showed me an impressive balance sheet of financial performance. On further discussions, I understood that almost 100% of the production was exported to the EU at a high price point. There was no demand for bio-pesticides in the local market due to lack of promotion and incentives. So in some sense, Bank financing led to protection of soils in the EU rather than in India!

Today we see that both WB and ADB have kind of entangled their investment/assistance operations in the maze of environmental and social safeguards. These safeguards have been continuously updated and evolved and have thus expanded in scope and expectations. This has happened partly due to the legacy and partly due to an attempt to satisfy all the stakeholders. The battle between the Task Managers (who are keen to disburse) and the Environmental & Social Champions of the Safeguards units (who do not want to do any harm) is getting worse – with a kind of polarization often leading either to delays or compromises. The project quality is therefore suffering at entry level and affecting the development effectiveness. Today I also see a lot of fatigue in the Bank teams today with hardly any of the past enthusiasm. Overall, the staff quality has declined over time with attrition of good staff.

There is also a difference in the way the DFIs are perceived. Twenty years ago, when we used to visit the senior officers of Department of Economic Affairs in Delhi as the Bank team, we were ushered to their cabins immediately. Today, the teams have to wait. Sometimes meetings are cancelled or postponed due to other important matters! Clearly, the "World of the Banks" is changing.

41
Let us Work in Full Circle

Urbanization is inevitable. Although efforts have been made to reduce the rates of in-migration to cities, the pace of urbanization has not slowed. Water is one of the affected commodities. As water and sanitation engineers and planners, we should be prepared to face this challenge.

As if these challenges weren't enough, climate change has further added the new dimensions of extremums and uncertainty. Flash floods and continued droughts in and around our cities are already threatening the very delicate balance of the water cycle. These distortions are becoming alarmingly evident.

Soon we will see more changes in the patterns of precipitation, temperature and ground water levels. Coastal cities will witness rises in the sea level and saline water intrusion. We will need to mitigate and adapt to climate change– something as water engineers, we are unfamiliar with. Climate science and engineering will certainly need to be part of the curriculum for water and sanitation engineers. But who will teach these subject will remain a moot question.

It is strange that even though some of us recognize the risks we will face in the future and know about the consequences of the "costs of inaction", we seem to still talk more and act less. There is indeed a relatively less understanding on how to deal with future risks and develop clear national guidance. The interventions need to follow integrated approaches, undertake planning on the canvas of sustainability and lead to revision of engineering standards that we follow today. Low Impact Development (LID) of cities, resilient designs of storm water networks and promotion of recycled water are a few examples of future strategies.

Cities with Purple Water Lines

Extreme water shortages and ever increasing cuts in the water supply have led to increased awareness and the pressing need to find alternative resources. One option is to opt for the organized use of recycled water. I often wonder when will we be able to start organized use of recycled water in our cities.

But are we prepared? And is this something we can practically achieve?

Recycled water is most commonly used for non-potable (i.e. not for drinking) purposes, such as agriculture, landscape and public parks. Other non-potable applications include cooling in power plants and oil refineries, industrial processing, toilet flushing, dust control, construction activities, concrete mixing and creating artificial lakes.

In the United States, an integrated approach to storm water is used with reservoir and groundwater management along with a decentralized strategy. Inspection and review processes towards management of risks and enforcement of public education and training have been the highlights.

To meet future water demands while reducing our dependence on imported water, the City of San Diego has built the North City Water Reclamation Plant and the South Bay Water Reclamation Plant. These plants treat wastewater to a level that is approved for irrigation, manufacturing and other non-drinking, or non-potable purposes. Recycled water gives San Diego a dependable, year-round and locally controlled water resource. Every customer site, wanting to connect to the recycled water distribution system or expand their existing on-site system, must go through a plan review and inspection process by the City of San Diego and the County of San Diego Department of Environmental Health. The reviews and inspections are mandated by the California State Code to ensure that the appropriate regulations are followed and

RECYCLED WATER
IN USE ON
THIS PROPERTY

that the site is safeguarded from a potential cross-connection between the recycled water system and the potable water system.

You would also see a gradual move towards toilet to taps – Singapore being one of the early examples. In India, we will need massive public education program along with a campaign on how to live with and use the purple pipe lines in a safe and sound manner. This is not going to be easy given the presence of a large slum population in our cities and poor water distribution infrastructure. People must be aware of what is flowing in the purple pipe!

Linking water recycling and conservation through Low Impact Development (LID) and use of natural systems to the maximum extent possible have been the strategies.

Water Cycle Management in the Pimpama-Coomera area in Australia[41]

Water Sensitive Urban Design (WSUD) plays a big role in the integrated approach to the urban water cycle management in the Pimpama-Coomera area. It is a unique approach to storm water management, combining natural processes with landscaping and engineering solutions. WSUD aims to manage the quality and quantity of storm water to better protect the local environment and waterways.

WUSD is increasingly being used across the Gold Coast, particularly in the developing areas such as Pimpama-Coomera. The technology behind is the landscaping.

Rainwater tanks play a key role in reducing the volume of storm water runoff from homes and other buildings. Swales can replace traditional street-side kerbs and channels with visually attractive gullies and water features that mimic the natural environment. Drainage ponds and retention ponds act as natural ponds to capture storm water before slowly releasing it into the treatment system. Detention ponds are temporary storage ponds that trap excess storm water in times of heavy rainfall, allowing extra time for the water to soak into the ground.

WSUD can also involve the use of constructed wetlands as treatment devices for storm water. These can be interesting environmental features and often have viewing areas and walking trails. They form habitats for local flora and fauna and use natural treatment mechanisms such as algae, to further treat storm water before it reaches

---

41 Drawn from City of Gold Coast website athttp://www.goldcoast.qld.gov.au/environment/pimpama-coomera-waterfuture-residents-and-businesses-7904.html

our waterways. Constructed wetlands are designed to replicate the natural aquatic environment and contain established eco-systems including fish, frogs and tadpoles that eat mosquito larvae and prevent breeding.

The main concern about reusing wastewater is the potential effect on environmental or human health. There are limited studies on the subject, but so far there are no documented cases of disease outbreaks from using reclaimed water. However, psychological barriers do exist. Even in the United States, the use of recycled water is less than 2%. Just along the coasts of the US, an estimated 12 billion gallons of treated wastewater is discharged into the ocean or estuaries each day. That's equivalent to 27%, or more than a quarter, of the public water supply.

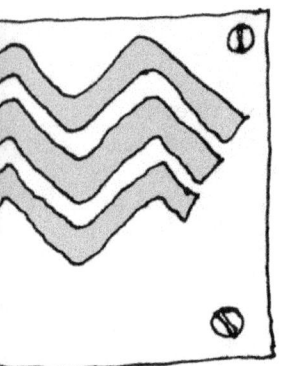

Institutional barriers, as well as varying agency priorities and public misperception, can make it difficult to implement water recycling projects. Finally, early in the planning process, agencies must reach out to the public to address any concerns and to keep the public informed and involved in the planning process. As reclaimed water rates do not cover the full cost of service for reclaimed water, the amount not covered by the subsidized rates is funded from potable water system revenues.

The Indian Industrial sector has realized that in most cases, the cost of the recovered water is less than the cost of the fresh water from other sources. Mumbai has been one of the first cities where water recycling has been practiced in buildings at Nariman Point and industries such as then Union Carbide. Chennai is another example often quoted for the leadership taken by Madras Fertilizers Ltd (MFL) and Chennai Petroleum Corporation Limited, (CPCL). In Mumbai, Rashriya Chemicals and Fertilizers (RCF) has taken a lead by practicing municipal sewage recycling. This trend of recycling water in the industrial sector is strengthening day by day. As the water recycling plants are coupled with financial returns, the attitude of the industries is also changing fast. However these initiatives are limited to specific facilities and have not yet been implemented on a city wide scale.

The Delhi Jal Board (DJB) is looking at recycled water to bridge the gap between potable water demand and supply. Approximately 25 per cent of this recycled water is presently being used for irrigation, horticulture and cooling in power plants by various agencies such as Tata Power Delhi Distribution Limited, Pragati Power Corporation Limited, CPWD and DDA among others[42].

The Bangalore Water Supply and Sewerage Board already treats part of the sewage to tertiary levels close to 80 million liters of water per day and sells it to industries for non-potable industrial and landscape use. "Bangalore however needs to develop a master-plan to reuse the entire city sewage. This also means that smaller STPs need to be encouraged through a policy framework which looks at the big picture." says my good friend Dr Ananth Kodavasal.

All these stories are positive and very encouraging and we need to build on these examples.

Climate change today is a threat to urban infrastructure and lives of the millions who live in these urban areas. The dimensions of the risks are complex, especially on water & sanitation and we have to be ready to face the challenges.

Water & sanitation sectors cannot be operated in silos. Only then we could be prepared to face the impacts of climate change. In combatting these impacts, water recycling is going to play a crucial role. Recognizing the importance of water recycling, several water recycling projects have come up in Indian cities – either due to water shortages, or better water economics or due to directives or enforcement. These interventions have however been limited to specific facilities e.g. buildings, office complexes, airports, small townships, industries etc. and not implemented on a city wide scale.

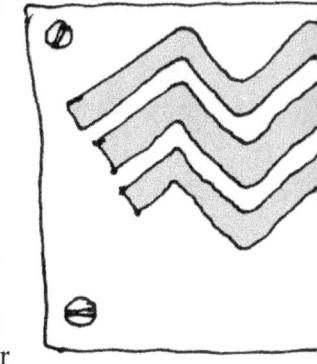

Indeed, this will take some time and effort. There are of course going to be barriers as well as risks. We will need pilots & policies and we will need to impart education

42 See more at: http://indianexpress.com/article/cities/delhi/delhi-jal-board-to-increase-use-of-recycled-water-in-city/#sthash.ORgjik9X.dpuf

& training to the public. A greater involvement of the private sector is also essential. The road is not going to be easy. But we don't have any other options.

Technology, policies, economics and public education are going to play a crucial role. All this is possible if we get together to develop Master Plan on Water for the cities that follows Water Sensitive Urban Design (WSUD). Cities of tomorrow will have to operate in Full Circle. Halves of water and sanitation are not going to work if we are serious on combatting with climate change!

42

Those Magical Days of GMDH

The year was 1982. I was doing my doctoral research with Dr Bindu Lohani at the Asian Institute of Technology (AIT) in Bangkok. My research was on Optimum Siting of Air Quality Monitors. One Friday, one of my Japanese Professors, T. Omura asked to see me at his office after dinner.

Professor Omura had just returned from Tokyo. He greeted me and following some preliminaries, opened a case and took out a listing of a computer program. Those were the days of main frame computers and line printers. The listing of the computer program was on a "132 column" paper and the code was written in FORTRAN.

In his typical Japanese English or Jinglish, Professor Omura said, "Modak, this is the computer program I got from a professor from Japan. It's on the Group Method of Data Handling[43] (GMDH)"

"GMDH? Never heard about it before Professor. What is this technique?" I asked

Professor Omura attempted to explain GMDH to me but he was clearly having difficulty doing so. All I understood was that GMDH was a "cybernetic" technique for building mathematical models based on data and was used for making accurate short and long term predictions.

The technique used the concept of self-organization, followed by a layered process of model building and variable sifting. The layering process was essentially a "prediction of predictions" using a reference function (typically a Kolmogorov-Gabor polynomial) and would stop at an "optimal complexity" judged by an external criteria (such as Mean Square Error). The data requirements for building and operating a GMDH model

---

43   Cover image sourced from http://scialert.net/fulltext/?doi=jai.2011.89.99&org=11

were minimalistic and that was what made this technique an attractive alternative. GMDH also performed much better than the contemporary statistical (data driven) as well as causal models.

Professor Omura then gave me two papers to read. He said that these two papers would help me to understand the foundation of GMDH. The papers were:

A. G. Ivakhnenko. Heuristic Self-Organization in Problems of Engineering Cybernetics. Automatica 6: pp. 207–219, 1970.

A. G. Ivakhnenko. Polynomial Theory of Complex System. IEEE Trans. on Systems, Man and Cybernetics, Vol. SMC-1, No. 4, Oct. 1971, pp. 364–378.

A. G. Ivakhnenko - wish I could meet him in person

"A Russian author?" I exclaimed. I found even the titles of the papers rather difficult to understand!

Handing me a copy of the FORTRAN listing, Professor Omura said "Yes Modak, this listing is very confidential and must not to be shared. I want you to understand the FORTRAN code, implement it on our main frame computer. Once it starts running, we will play with the program, using it for few applications for forecasting river water quality. This code originates from the Kiev School in Russia."

He then paused, looked at me seriously and said slowly, "I am aware that the GMDH algorithm has nothing to do with your doctoral research, but it is an opportunity for you to learn something new and very exciting. I would like you to give a serious try."

I told Professor Omura that I would read and attempt to

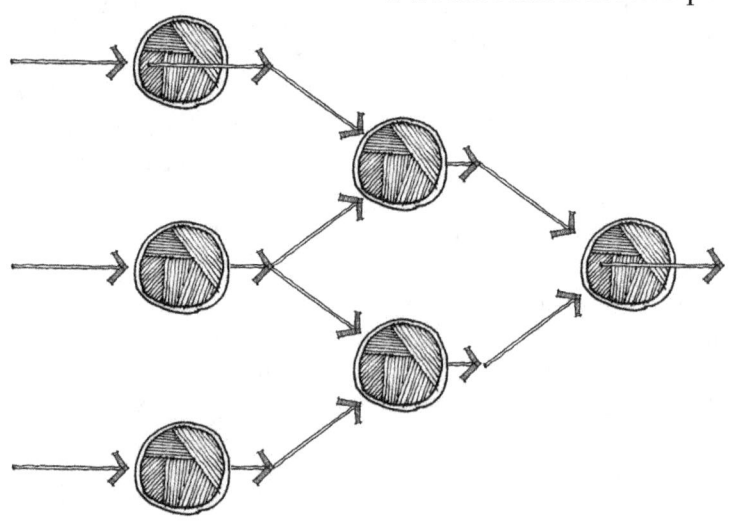

absorb the two papers over the weekend and meet with him on Monday evening. He agreed.

I started reading and soon realized that I would probably need another week to fully understand them. Both papers were simply "stuffed" with ideas, postulations, evidence and outstanding theory. The text was in Ringlish and so not easy to comprehend. There were also several hidden messages for the reader. I went through the papers several times and consulted some "surround" literature and realized that I was getting into something very advanced - a technique on the fringe of artificial intelligence and robotics. In actual fact, I was being introduced to a technique of modelling most suitable for complex, fuzzy (unsure and uncertain) dynamic situations and consequently most relevant to the "environmental systems."

I met Professor Omura on Monday evening and told him that I was on board to work on GMDH with him. "It will take me a little more time to get a handle on the technique, but I will start working on the FORTRAN code immediately." I decided to use WATFIV, or WATerloo FORTRAN IV, developed at the University of Waterloo, Canada.

Professor Omura was very pleased with my interest, commitment and enthusiasm. He ended our conversation with a very honest remark, "Modak, I know nothing about how GMDH works so I won't be able to help you. I am only interested in its application, so good luck and let us keep meeting every Friday night."

I spoke to my Ph.D guide Dr. Bindu Lohani about my encounter with GMDH and he readily supported me in wanting to do more with it.

"Do not let your work on GMDH affect your PhD research though." He said. "However there could well be possibilities of the application of GMDH to your own research problem on optimum siting of air monitors".

Dr. Lohani had worked extensively on stochastic modelling and optimization and loved the application of advanced mathematical techniques on environmental systems.

I began my work and one night, I cracked the GMDH code in WATFIV and was able to reproduce the outputs of some of the case examples cited by A. G. Ivakhenko. It happened at 3am in the morning and I had been the only student working at the AIT's Regional Computer Centre (RCC). That was a moment of great achievement for me.

I left the RCC and walked to the pub outside the campus (we used to call the pub Papa's shop. Papa was a retired Thai Army soldier). I picked up a bottle of Beer Singha and sat on a wooden bench all alone as Papa and his wife Mamma were sleeping and there was nobody else in the pub. I drank my beer, listening to the sound of the rolling wheels and watching the movement of lights from the trail of the trucks on the highway.

"I am now in world of GMDH." I said to myself

Given our success, Dr. Lohani and I decided that I take on GMDH related work as "Special Studies" and drop some of the environmental courses that I was supposed to do. This was a very kind gesture on Dr. Lohani's part and I ended up doing three such Special Studies on GMDH over the next 8 months while simultaneously working hard my own doctoral research.

Dr. Lohani had set up a committee to oversee my Special Studies. This committee consisted of Professor H. N. Phien and Professor Kiyoshi Hoshi, both outstanding hydrologists and mathematicians. When I gave my seminar on GMDH, describing the basic form of GMDH, its variants in Russia, Japan and at MIT in the US, both the Professors were very excited. I still fondly recall the numerous black board based discussion sessions I used to have with them - floating new ideas and tweaking the GMDH algorithm, and specific to modelling complex environmental systems.

I made several applications of GMDH e.g. on river flows, river water quality, air quality and eco-systems. Compared to other models and tools available at that time, GMDH performed much better and was far superior in all these applications. More importantly it revealed new vistas of pattern recognition and the power of mining of data. What really fascinated me then, and still does to date, was its ability to surprise the modeler in deciding the optimal complexity (in terms of both variables and structure). That was GMDH's feature of artificial intelligence.

Today the GMDH technique has become one of the top tools in the Artificial Neural Networks (ANN) family and is applied across all domains, especially in business and financial modelling. Oddly enough, research and applications of GMDH in the field of environment have been rather scant. This is because courses on Environmental Data Analytics are not offered at most universities and that's a pity.

When I returned to Mumbai and joined the Centre for Environmental Science and Engineering at IIT Bombay, I tried to find students who could take up work based on GMDH. Unfortunately I could never find anyone interested in GMDH or even willing to take it up as a challenge. After I left IIT, I started by own consulting company – the Environmental Management Centre (EMC) LLP and straight-away got busy with projects all over the country and abroad.

EMC runs what has now become a very popular and well sought after internship program. It was through this program in 2007 (25 years after my own introduction to GMDH) that I finally found someone willing to be challenged by GMDH. Neeraj Kumar from the Delhi College of Engineering came onboard as an intern and working together we were able to publish some interesting environmental applications of the technique for the Prague Conference on GMDH.

We presented the idea and application for "Adaptive GMDH." I was extremely delighted to see the talent in Neeraj. He hardly spoke to the Team at EMC – and was kind of a loner!

With continuous monitoring of emission, effluent and ambient concentrations in India, considerable on-line data is getting generated by the industries and the regulatory bodies. Unfortunately, all this data is rarely used in the way it should be. With techniques such as GMDH, the

possibilities for the effective use of the data generated are enormous.

I told my Professor Friend about GMDH and he as usual was a patient listener. He then lit his cigar and pointed at the book lying on his desk. The book was titled Long-Range Forecasting: From Crystal Ball to Computer and I knew it well. Written by J. Scott Armstrong and printed in 1985, it was a must read for all modelers.

"What about it?" I asked.

The Professor opened the book and showed me a cartoon in a section called Planning Vs Forecasting. He said "See -the kid selling shoe shines knew exactly what to do when it would rain – i.e. offer the waxing service. He did not need a rainfall forecasting model!"

This cartoon is by the world famous Morrie Turner[44] and has been copied from Armstrong's book

Taking a deep pull on his cigar, the Professor said, "Forecasting is often difficult and your GMDH algorithms may just predict outcomes very close to the real one. However, just to be practical, don't you think that instead of focusing too much only on predictions, we should also have action plans for a few of the most likely scenarios? This aspect of management is often forgotten!

I thought the Professor made a good point as he always did and I left his office with the Armstrong book for a second good read!

My Message for Students of the Environmental Sciences

Don't stick to the conventional environmental domains. Take up something beyond the norm and it will certainly give you rich dividends.

Also, if you meet someone like Professor T. Omura, Never say NO!

For those interested in learning more about this technique, I would recommend the recently published book - "GMDH-Methodology and Implementation in C (With CD-ROM)" 2014, by Godfrey Onwubolu[45]

Group Method of Data Handling (GMDH) is a family of inductive algorithms for computer-based mathematical modeling of multi-parametric datasets. GMDH is used today for data mining, knowledge

---

44 Source -The Registration and Tribune Syndicate – Wee Pals Comic Strip

45 See http://www.amazon.com/GMDH-Methodology-Implementation-C-With-CD-ROM/dp/1848166109

discovery, prediction, complex systems modeling, optimization and pattern recognition.

The most popular base function used in GMDH is the gradually complicated Kolmogorov-Gabor (K-G) polynomial:

The resulting models are also known as polynomial neural networks. Jürgen Schmidhuber cites GMDH as one of the earliest deep learning methods.

The method was originated in 1968 by Prof. Alexey G. Ivakhnenko in the Institute of Cybernetics in Kiev (then in the Ukrainian SSR). Thanks to the author's policy of open code sharing the method was quickly settled in the large number of scientific laboratories worldwide. At that time code sharing was quite a physical action since the Internet is at least 5 years younger than GMDH. Despite this fact the first investigation of GMDH outside the Soviet Union had been made soon by R.Shankar in 1972. Later, different GMDH variants were published by Japanese and Polish scientists.

External criterion is one of the key features of GMDH. Criterion describes requirements to the model, for example minimization of Least squares. It is always calculated with a separate part of data sample that have not been used for estimation of coefficients.

GMDH approach can be useful because:

Optimal complexity of the model structure is found, adequate to the level of noise in data sample. For real problems, with noised or short data, simplified optimal models are more accurate.

The number of layers and neurons in hidden layers, model structure and other optimal neural networks parameters are determined automatically.

It automatically finds interpretable relationships in data and selects effective input variables accordingly.

It guarantees that the most accurate or unbiased models will be found – method does not miss the best solution during sorting of all variants (in the given class of functions).

43

RESEARCH INTEREST AND DIVIDEND IN PRACTICE – CASE OF WATER QUALITY MODELING

The subject of environmental modeling always interested me. But I got into this subject by accident. It happened during my third year of civil engineering at IIT Bombay. Seminar topics were being allotted and my friends and I had bunked the lecture during which this allotment had taken place and gone to the staff canteen. Prof J S R Murthy, after waiting for us in the lecture hall, came to the staff canteen to have his tea. He was raging with anger and frustration and when he saw me there giggling and having fun, he called out to me and said, "You deserve to be punished – you will get the topic that is not chosen by others." The topic that was left was "DO-BOD modeling" and I didn't realize then, that I was going to be stuck with this topic not just for the seminar but my entire professional life!

Later as I pursued my master's degree, my colleague Shirish Naik and I, continued working on DO-BOD models with Professor P. Khanna as our guide. We were fascinated by the work done by two electrical engineers Koivo and Philips. Their paper titled 'On determination of BOD and parameters in polluted stream models from DO measurements only' had been published in Water Resources Research journal in April 1973. The idea of doing away with the direct measurements of BOD and instead predicting BOD concentrations using DO measurements really captivated us. We attempted application of this technique on a river quality data set from Maharashtra and published our first research paper in the Journal of Indian Water Works Association (IWWA). I recall meeting Professor Dr. Niloy Choudhuri, the Chairman of Central Pollution Control Board (CPCB) at the annual convention of IWWA where we were presenting our paper. He listened to our "revolutionary idea" very patiently. He showed all the curiosity and gave us an encouragement. (We returned home with a great feeling that the Chairman of CPCB listened to us. Looking back now I feel that he taught me how to encourage young students even though they come up with stupid propositions!! Every idea has its worth – and should not be simply dismissed! It should be respected)

When I completed my doctoral research and returned to IIT Bombay, water quality modelling and management became a focus of my teaching and research. In 1984, I received a long telegram from the office of the Secretary, Ministry of Environment & Forests (MoEF), Mr T N Seshan. The telegram asked me to attend the first technical meeting of experts for the Ganga Action Plan (GAP) in Delhi. The then newly inducted Prime Minister of India, Rajeev Gandhi was to preside over this meeting. Prof. Choudhuri was also present and when Mr. Seshan turned to him and asked (while pointing at me), "what to do with this young man?" (I was 28 years old then), Prof. Chaudhuri answered, "He will take care of water quality modelling."

The Ganga Project Directorate (GPD) of MoEF awarded me INR 1 million for a project on developing and applying water quality models on the Ganga. In addition, the CPCB contracted me as their advisor/consultant for 4 days a month for 4 years. This meant that I would have to travel to Delhi 4 days every month with no prefixed agenda and sit in the offices of Prof Choudhuri at CPCB and K C Sivaramakrishnan, Project Director at GPD. These interactions offered me great insight to the project and the politics involved. In addition it provided me with exposure to work on water quality management from across the world. International experts from countries such as USA, UK, France and Germany would be invited to speak at the GPD from experts and I had a front row seat to their presentations. It was during one of these talks that I met L Panneerselvam who was then the Joint Director at GPD. We have been close friends ever since.

Just before launching the project, I organized a five days International Workshop on Water Quality Management at IIT Bombay. The top water quality modelers and managers participated in this workshop and I built a national and international network as a result of it. I also made some new friends – most of whom I am still in touch with. Those were truly the golden days.

Two computer based models were developed as a part of the GPD project –STREAM-I and STREAM-II. STREAM-I was a one dimensional DO-BOD model with calibration, verification, validation routines and importantly with an optimal waste allocation algorithm. STREAM-II was unique and one of the first of its kind, as it modelled DO-BOD in a two dimensional space with lateral dispersion. These models were inspired by Professor T P H Gowda's work in Canada and were very relevant to the Ganga project.

Approximately 200 professionals from across the country were trained to use STREAM models, including many Member Secretaries and Chairmen of the State PCBs (SPCB). During this period, extensive field application of STREAM-II took place at the Allahabad Sangam, where I managed a team of 40 scientists working round the clock for 72 hours. This was a great experience in research administration and practice.

The team of research associates who worked with me on the STREAM project went on to become extremely successful individually, in their careers. Juzer Dhoondia went to Deltares in the Netherlands and developed Fuse series of models. Clement Prabhakar developed MODFLOW and RT3D routines for US EPA on groundwater contamination modelling and now teaches at Auburn University. Rakesh Gelda is a lake modeler at the Upstate Freshwater Institute in New York State and worked with Prof. Steven Chapra.

With the support of the British Council, I was able to bring in Professors Sam James and David Eliot from the University of Newcastle upon Tyne (UK). Sam and David lectured in the training programs as resource faculty

Speaking about Newcastle reminds me of the two months of teaching, research and consulting tours that I used to do in the UK, France and Germany. These tours took place over three years – between 1985 and 1987 and I will always be grateful to the late Professor B Nag (the then Director of IIT Bombay) for always approving my travel immediately upon application (He would approve it first and then get the IIT Board's post-approval).

I used to start with Sam James group at University of Newcastle upon Tyne.

We worked on some of the modelling aspects of Tees's estuary then and did some joint teaching and guiding of PhD students. After the lectures, which we often taught together, we would walk across the golf lawns to relax at a Scottish pub. Here we would discuss the class and how we could have improved our teaching. These discussions were absolutely engaging. I don't think this happens amongst the teaching faculty in India.

After three weeks in Newcastle, I moved to Paris to work in the Seine-Normandy river basin with A Leousef, the Basin Manager. Leousef preferred to use simple water quality models and focus more on decision making and economics. He was very practical and a man of action. I liked his style.

I used to live at a boutique hotel near Montparnasse Tower, reveling in the charms and romance of the city of love. Most evenings after work, I would stop to listen to the box guitars played on the city streets with my colleagues from the Seine-Normandy office. We would then sit on wooden chairs on the Avenue Charles de Gaulle and order flutes of dark beers. Leousef would join in later and voice his disagreement with our views on water quality modeling. I believe that this would happen because he was not drunk and we probably were!

The next stop was Aachen in Germany with Professor Poppinghause. We used to work together on the water quality management of Ruhr. Just like Newcastle, our work was combined with some teaching, some research and some guiding of students. The emphasis was however on combinatorial optimization and operation of wastewater treatment plants.

At the end of each visit, Professor G Rinke would drive to fetch me from University of Darmstadt near Frankfurt. Prof. Rinke was also a very senior German Diplomat. He would drive a Porsche car and was interesting in teaching me how to conduct a walk through in a wastewater treatment plant and develop an insight for plant inspection. He was a very unique sort of Professor.

During my ride with him, Professor Rinke drove me though some of the uniquely designed wastewater treatment plants in the Ruhr river basin. We used to drive on roads close to some of majestic castles, pass through thick patches of forests and stop at places with the best beers! The conversations were most instructive and rewarding. I wish Professors in India take along students on such travels with conversations.

Once Prof. Rinke took a diversion and when I questioned him about it, he simply said, "Let me introduce you to a friend." After driving for a few kilometers, we arrived at an old castle-like house. It was evening and the door was opened by an old man with sharp eyes. He shook hands with Professor Rinke and both exchanged greetings. From the excited and animated conversation (in German) that followed, I was sure that they hadn't seen each other in a while. Professor Rinke then turned to me and said, "Meet Klaus – Klaus Imhoff". I was speechless and completely overwhelmed – I was meeting the Guru of Wastewater Management!

Dr. Klaus Imhoff got us some Ruby wine and when learnt about my passion for teaching, he asked me to go upstairs. "You will find an old wooden chest of drawers there." he said. "Open the drawers and choose any slides you wish – they may help you to teach."

When I went upstairs and opened the drawers, I saw a neat stack of metal framed slides with wonderful shots of wastewater treatment plants, unusual units and varied configurations… I had struck gold! I did not know where to begin and what to take! I spent more than 15 minutes looking around.

I heard a voice from downstairs say, "Oh Young Man, take as many slides you want. These are all duplicate sets. Feel free to pick." I was thrilled and chose the slides and to this day I have held on to and cherished that priceless collection of Dr. Imhoff's slides.

So my "research interest" in water quality modeling gave me a lot of "practice dividend." It taught me how to work with the Government, build national and international networks and meet personalities that inspired and humbled me. Indeed, research contribution was one of the outcomes – but education for life was perhaps an outcome that I cherish today.

44

INDIA'S NEW INSURANCE PRODUCT – THE POLLUTION POLICY

My wife told me to get our Health Insurance done. "It's not just for fashion anymore but a necessity…" she said. "…especially since we live in Mumbai."

I agreed.

Health insurance is now a growing sector in India. The health insurance premium has registered a compounded annual growth rate (CAGR) of 32 per cent for the past eight financial years.

I asked my Professor friend for advice on which insurance company I should talk to.

"Oh that's easy!" said the Professor "Why don't you join me for a breakfast meeting at the Grand Hyatt in Santa Cruz with S K Roy, Chairman of LIC, the CEO of Max Life - Rajesh Sud, G Srinivasan, CMD of New India Assurance, Sandeep Bakshi. CEO of ICICI Pru and Sanjay Bajaj of Bajaj Allianz are also joining. All these friends will give you perfect advice."

I got a bit worried. Talking to these "insurance Czars" could mean receiving too much advice and that hence a risky proposition. I was also curious and unable to figure out the Professor's role at this breakfast meeting.

"What's his connection?" I wondered.

However since the breakfast was set at the Grand Hyatt, I decided to accept the Professor's invitation. I love the Kanchipuram Idlis and Pesarattu (Green Gram Dosa) at the Hyatt.

It was a Sunday morning and all the insurance company honchos arrived dressed in T-shirts with their respective company logos and taglines. S K Roy's t-shirt had the usual drab tag line – Yogakshemam Vahamyaham which no one understood. The tagline of Rajesh Sud's t-shirt read Aapke Sachche Advisor (meaning your true advisor) and that immediately put me in some doubt. Born to lead was the tagline on G. Srinivasan's t-shirt and that made no sense. Sanjay Bajaj's t-shirt tagline read Jiyo Befiqar (live fearlessly) whereas Sandeep Bakshi had a tagline Zimmedari ka humsafar (responsibility partner); both these taglines sounded rather filmy.

Taking a gulp of coffee from a large mug, the Professor opened the meeting.

"Gentleman, many of you asked me about the recent news of Delhi losing on its life expectancy by 6.4 years. This news was based on a publication from the Indian Institute of Tropical Meteorology (IITM), in collaboration with the National Centre for Atmospheric Research (NCAR), Colorado, United States. This study titled Premature Mortality in India due to $PM_{2.5}$ and Ozone Exposure was first published by the peer-reviewed journal Geophysical Research Letters (GRL) on May 2014, but was reported by some newspapers only last week."

"Interesting!" said S K Roy, while picking up a banana. "So on one hand we are doing well by increasing the life expectancy through advances in medicines, but on the other hand we are losing the battle because of pollution."

G. Srinivasan agreed with Roy. He was eating organic cornflakes that were imported from Australia.

For those who may not be familiar with the term life expectancy, the World Health Organization (WHO) defines life expectancy as "the average number of years a person is expected to live on the basis of the current mortality rates and prevalence distribution of health states in a population." In India, average life expectancy which used to be around 42yrs in 1960 steadily climbed to around 48yrs in 1980, 58.5yrs in 1990 and around 62yrs in 2000.

Statistics recently released by the Union Ministry of Health and Family Welfare show that life expectancy in India has gone up by five years, from 62.3 years for males and 63.9 years for females in 2001-2005 to 67.3 years and 69.6 years respectively in 2011-2015. These numbers are however still low compared to the global averages.

Experts attribute this jump - higher than in previous decade - to better immunization and nutrition, coupled with improved methods of prevention and treatment of infectious diseases. So if your child was born in the last couple of years, he or she is likely to live five years more than children born a decade ago.

Experts have however pointed out that increasing life expectancy beyond 70 years would depend on environmental factors. These factors would include the air we breathe and the quality of water we drink. Yes, we will live longer, but the big question is how healthy will our lives be? It seems that environmental pollution will be the fourth highest risk factor for deaths. The death count due to pollution is projected to swell in the coming decades because the population in most countries is ageing and older people are more susceptible to illnesses caused by pollution.

The Professor continued as he ate poached egg whites on multi-grain bread.

"Latest international research studies have shown that over 5.5 million people die prematurely every year due to air pollution. Older research has shown that India's air pollution is cutting three years off the lives of some of the country's residents. This research analyzed air pollution measurements across India and found that more than half the country's population — approximately 660 million people — live in areas where the air pollution levels are higher than the national standards. If those high levels of air pollution were brought down, the residents would gain, on average, an additional 3.2 years of life expectancy."

"So Professor, we must reflect impact of pollution on our calculations of the health premiums." said Sanjay Bajaj. I liked his remark as I saw him picking up the Pesarattu (Green Gram Dosa).

I thought of butting in now and said, "But the IITM study has been already rejected by Hon Minister Prakash Javdekar[46]. According to him the study was based on research done in Europe and America and has been extrapolated to defame India. This study used a regional atmospheric chemistry model and not actual sampling, cohorts and long term observations. I was told that he has asked the Central Pollution Control Board (CPCB) to formally challenge the report later this week. So we shouldn't take the 6.4 years of decrease in life expectancy

---

46 Article available at: http://timesofindia.indiatimes.com/home/environment/Pollution-study-extrapolated-to-defame-India-Javadekar/articleshow/52661223.cms

that seriously"

"Oh yes!" said the Professor. "That's the problem with research publications and the news-hungry journalists."

"Poor Sachin Ghude, leader of this paper, has taken long leave and is supposed to be in disguise." He continued. "If you search IITM's website, you will not see any mention of this study nor the publication. Fortunately there are no apologies posted!"

The IITM scientist Sachin Ghude, had clearly said, "Although these results are in line with other global estimates, such as the WHO and the Global Burden of Diseases (GBD), there's no physical way to tell who has actually been killed by air pollution. The methods used in this study rely on statistical algorithms to construct estimates about a population's response to pollution exposure using previous concrete observations on pollution and public health."

Ghude had also cautioned that the problem was that most of these observational studies undertaken in regions with comparatively low pollution levels, such as Europe or the US. There were no epidemiological studies that examined the long-term effects of air pollution on mortality

in India. But the news did not communicate these caveats. Very typical of news-makers, isn't it?

Sandeep Bakshi did not like my intervention. Picking up a chicken sausage, he smirked and said, "Well, there must be some truth in this work. You can always find faults in every ground breaking research carried out. Nothing is perfect. Science evolves!"

As everyone at the table was busy enjoying their breakfast and didn't want to speak all I heard was, "Hmm…!"

"Well…" Professor said at last, "…the Journalist who broke this news was not up to date and picked up a 2014 article. More recent work on this subject has been published by Sourangsu Chowdhury and Sagnik Dey of the Centre for Atmospheric Sciences at Indian Institute of Technology Delhi. The paper, titled Cause-specific premature death from ambient PM2.5 exposure in India: Estimate adjusted for baseline mortality, shows that 50% of the population living in 45% of the districts in India is exposed at PM 2.5 exceeding Indian air quality standard of 40 µg m−3. Kinnaur in Himachal Pradesh was identified as the cleanest district (annual PM2.5 is 3.7 ± 1 µg m−3) and Delhi as the dirtiest metropolitan area (annual PM2.5 is148 ± 51 μg m−3). According to this research, if India manages to achieve the national air quality target of 40 μg m−3, approximately 44,900 (5900–173,300) less annual premature death is expected. If Minister Javdekar is really sensitive about Delhi's pollution, then he will have to refute this recent study as well. But then how many studies can he refute? The CPCB will have nothing else to do but keep issuing rejoinders."

The Clean Air Act in the United States, added years to the lives of Americans by reducing particulate pollution. Particulate data from 1970 to 2012 of US EPA yielded striking results for American cities. In Los Angeles, the particulate pollution has declined by more than half since 1970 and the average Angeleno lives about a year and eight months longer. Residents of New York and Chicago have gained about two years on average. With more than 42 million people currently living in these three metropolitan areas, the total gains in life expectancy added up to something substantial.

Rajesh Sud had been silent all this while. He was having a Punjabi Paratha with curd which was rather filling.

He wiped his face with an eco-labelled napkin and said slowly, "It is clear that we must factor pollution into our health insurance schemes. Today, researchers are publishing articles on air quality but there will soon be series of articles on reduced life expectancy due to poor water quality – especially in rural India. The question is how do we adjust our premiums depending on the place people live. For example, a person in Delhi will pay 5000 rupees extra compared to other cities because the life expectancy in Delhi is claimed to be low."

The Professor lit his cigar and I knew that this was now the time for new ideas.

"Well, I recommend you to come up with an entirely new insurance product." He said. "Call this as the Pollution Policy. Through the promotion of this new instrument, you will raise the common person's awareness about pollution. This policy will also make the Government think hard on the overall economics.

According to the IITM study, the cost of estimated premature mortalities was about $640 billion in 2011 - about 10 times higher than the country's total expenditures on health that year. The health insurance premium for 2011 was just about USD 2.0 billion. Maybe the new Pollution Policy will click and it will generate USD 2.0 billion to start with which may grow to say USD 5.0 billion. Perhaps the Government could take a share of this premium and improve the hospital infrastructure by setting up respiratory treatment wards or more importantly invest in arresting air pollution. You the Insurance companies will thus provide protection to the pollution affected people while tapping the billion dollar market of Pollution Policy Premiums and in this process help the Government. NITI Aayog wants more such innovative insurance products to come up in the public health arena."

As I was waiting for my strong filter coffee, I thought I should add something interesting here, "Friends, China's largest online travel agency is now offering tourists smog insurance, permitting travelers to claim financial compensation should their city break be blighted by bad air. The website Ctrip. com has created the haze-travel insurance package in collaboration with Ping an, a Chinese insurance firm and has now been selling this new product[47]. The insurance is focused on six cities including Beijing, Shanghai and Xi'an - all popular with tourists and also suffering from poor air quality. Under the new insurance package, tourists who spend at least two days in a designated city while pollution levels are high will be able to file claims. Evidently aimed at domestic rather than international tourists, the premium comes to 10RMB (USD 2) and travelers can claim 50RMB (USD 9) per day."

Everyone listened to me politely.

"Travel insurance is another story, but you can draw ideas for the Pollution Policy." He said as he patted on my back.

As we were leaving the Grand Hyatt, S K Roy walked with me and said, "Dr. Modak, I would like to change my tag line - any suggestions?"

I said, "How about - *Come to Us – We have the Solution to Pollution!*"

"Thank you Dr. Modak!" said Mr. Roy.

While getting into the car, I was just thinking Is Pollution Policy the real Solution?

---

47 Refer to: https://skift.com/2014/03/19/china-smog-insurance-is-ctrips-latest-travel-product/

45

MAKE TO TAKE

I received a call from my Professor friend one Sunday morning as I was reading the newspaper and having a cup of tea with some diet khakras (a crunchy Indian snack).

"Have you got any used tube lights to dispose?" He asked.

I didn't have one in the house (as I use mostly the CFLs) but then remembered that there were four Elips tube lights in my garage. I hadn't figured out how to dispose these used tube lights and my usual kachara lady (waste picker) had not shown much interest in them either.

When I told this to the Professor, he said, "Well then, here is a deal for you. Elips Tube lights have an offer – give them your used tube lights and they will give you brand new lights for free. No strings attached! It is part of Elips Extended Producer Responsibility (EPR). There is a tube light collection center at Shivaji Park and today is deal day between 11am to 5pm. So rush! Elips wants to demonstrate to the citizens how they care about their used products and about the environment."

I liked this deal and told my wife that I would drive over to Shivaji Park right away with my used tube lights. I thought of calling a few friends as well. Apparently, you could exchange any used tube light for a new Elips tube light. I thought it was very generous gesture by the company. The Professor was to join me later at the Barista Coffee shop.

EPR is not a new concept. It has been around for the past two decades and is common practice by corporates in the developed world[48]. The idea of EPR was formally introduced by my good friend Thomas Lindquist in 1990, in a report to the Swedish Ministry

---

48 There are many examples of successful and impacting EPRs. A very recent report on the status of EPR in EU countries could be seen athttp://ec.europa.eu/environment/waste/pdf/target_review/Guidance%20on%20EPR%20-%20Final%20Report.pdf

of the Environment. In subsequent reports prepared for the Ministry, the following definition of EPR emerged -

Extended Producer Responsibility is an environmental protection strategy to reach an environmental objective of a decreased total environmental impact from a product, by making the manufacturer of the product responsible for the entire life-cycle of the product and especially for the take-back, recycling and final disposal of the product.

Thomas completed his doctoral dissertation on EPR[49]. Now, EPR been legislated in many countries and has also been included into their national policy frameworks[50].

In India, EPR is often practiced by involving and supporting the informal sector i.e. the waste pickers. This makes the Indian case very unique. E-waste is one of the most popular waste streams of focus and in 2010 Indian lawmakers passed an e-waste policy that included EPR[51].

The Indian EPR law requires electronic manufacturers'

partner with recyclers, thereby including the informal sector, in setting up collection centers. This is perhaps the first time in history that participation of the informal sector has been included in the Indian environmental management framework law. This should lead to creation of green jobs and support to the livelihoods of the poor.

An assessment of the extent to which corporates actually practiced EPR in the E-Waste sector was carried out by Greenpeace. The resulting report (prepared in 2008[52]) showed that companies that practice EPR (i.e. product take backs etc.) in other countries did not do so in India. There was clear unevenness in their global EPR practices thereby making it essential for us to take a stock of the situation on EPR practiced in India today.

49 See http://www.lub.lu.se/luft/diss/tec355.pdfThis dissertation is a must read.

50 See http://www.calrecycle.ca.gov/EPR/PolicyLaw/#World for one of the most recent overviews

51 You may like to read 2007 report commissioned by Greenpeace on India's E-waste and EPR. See http://escrap.com.ar/descargas/extended-producer-resp-non-OECD.pdf Incidentally, Thomas was one of the authors of this report.

52 See http://ewasteguide.info/files/take-back-blues_2008_Greenpeace.pdf

Examples of some other "take back practices" in India include the program from Tetrapack India in Bangalore in partnership with a social enterprise[53], Samsung's STAR program[54] and Dell's laptop exchange[55] are also examples of EPR in India.

When I reached the collection center at Shivaji Park, I was greeted by the Elips Marketing Manager. They took 4 of my used Elips tube lights, he handed over 4 brand new, slim and energy efficient tube lights.

When I was writing my contact details in the fat register kept on the desk, he asked "Sir, do you have any used CFLs? –if you have then hold on to them as next month, we are launching a scheme for replacing used CFLs where for a pair of used CFLs, we will give you one free! And the used CFLs do not have to be made by Elips." I was very impressed. This, I thought was TEPR -- Too much of Extended Producer Responsibility! It also got me worrying about the Elips Company. While environmental stewardship is fine, it cannot be done at the cost of business. If Elips has too many such "take back" campaigns on their products, surely they will get bankrupt soon.

I expressed my concern to the Professor at the Barista Coffee shop. He lit his cigar and took a deep puff.

"Do you know what you have just done?" he then asked. "You provided Elips with enough free raw material to make 9 new tube lights. The amount of mercury in a fluorescent tube light typically varies from 3 to 46 mg, depending on lamp size, age and the tube lights you just exchanged, may probably contain 30 mg of mercury. The new tube lights that Elips makes have a mercury content of about 3 mg. So if today Elips manages to collect say

53   See http://saahas.org/campaign/tetra-pak-collection-recycling/

54   See http://www.samsung.com/in/samsungrecycle/

55   See http://www.dell.com/learn/in/en/incorp1/dell-environment-recycling

1000 used tube lights with high mercury content, they will have enough free mercury to make 10000 low mercury tube lights. ; plus of course the social goodwill to boast and creation of a record of EPR delivered"

"Oh!" I said, not realizing the underlying "economics" or the "business case" of EPR. "Did you advise Elips on this strategy Professor?" I couldn't resist asking.

"Well, I did – at a modest fee! But please keep it a secret." said the Professor. "Right now I am advising APson Office Products. The deal will be "bring your used printer and take a new one for free". Any make will do. The logic of this EPR scheme is to ensure continued consumption of cartridges made by APson. A cartridge today costs one third of the printer and gets consumed on an average once a month. So, we will leverage on our free printer in a very short time. In addition, we are setting up a printer repairs workshop by training the youth (job creation) and provide the refurbished printers to underprivileged schools as CSR."

"You are a genius Professor!" I said, settling the bill. It is indeed a game of make and take!

46

Saying NO to NOCIL

It was 1990 and I was an Associate Professor at the Centre for Environmental Science and Engineering (CESE) at the Indian Institute of Technology (IIT) Bombay.

I received a call from Mr. S. K. Patil, Member Secretary of the Maharashtra Pollution Control Board (MPCB). "Dr. Modak, The Honorable High Court of Mumbai is appointing an Expert Committee to decide on the Environmental Clearance of the proposed Modernization and Expansion of M/s. National Organic Chemicals & Industries Ltd. (NOCIL). I would like to request you to join this Committee. The Committee will be headed by Dr. R. K. Garg, Director of Chemical Engineering Department of the Bhabha Atomic Research Center (BARC)."

Dr. R. K. Garg was a well-known authority in the field of Hazard Assessment. He had previously chaired the Committee on Assessment of Hazardous Industries (known more as the Garg Committee) in the Thane-Belapur area on the outskirts of Mumbai. The Garg Committee had come up with several major observations and recommendations for the MPCB. Working with Dr. Garg was going to be a great honor and a superb learning experience and I readily accepted the invitation.

NOCIL was the Mafatlal Group's flagship company. It was the largest rubber chemicals manufacturer in India. But the plant was nearly 30 years old and badly needed modernization for the sake of its future viability. The Team at NOCIL was one of the best in the chemical industry led by M. S. Patwardhan and President K. Dharam. Dharam was a smart fellow and a great manager and an engineer of details. Prof. M. M. Sharma, internationally well-known chemical engineer and Director of the University Department of

Chemical Technology (UDCT) was NOCIL's advisor on technologies. Dr. Deepak Kantawala, a doyen in industrial pollution control was the Environmental Consultant. So our battle with NOCIL was not going to be easy.

Our Committee consisted of Prof. S. B. Chandalia of the UDCT, Mr. M. S. Mirashi of the Factory's Inspectorate of the Government of Maharashtra, P. K. Ghosh of Indian Rare Earth (IRE) – a close associate of Dr. Garg, along with representatives of Department of Explosives, Department of Industries and Department of Environment and Dr. S. R. Choudhari of MPCB as the Member Secretary.

I recall we all met on the 9th floor of Benhur building at the IRE office at Marine Lines. Dr. Garg gave all of us a briefing and we were provided with documentation on NOCIL's application for Environmental Clearance as well as the objections/protests made. Dr. Garg then allocated roles and responsibilities and we decided to meet every Sunday at the Benhur to examine the case and meet key stakeholders that included some of the major environmental NGOs who had objected to the Modernization

& Expansion (M&E) of NOCIL. These meetings took place over six months after which we were able to submit our final report to the Honorable High Court.

The case of M&E of NOCIL was well made; the argument was that this upgradation will lead to greater export of chemicals and help boost the Indian chemical industry. More importantly, the pollution load on environment (both air emissions and effluents) was to remain same because the technologies to be deployed were going to be far superior and backed by Shell International. Further, the M&E would lead to the generation of new jobs creating a positive social impact. The company had impeccable record on Health, Environment & Safety (HSE) with several initiatives taken beyond compliance.

The project proposal was however controversial. The M&E of NOCIL was going to lead to expansion of several industries in the Thane-Belapur industrial area – something that was going to be hard to control. Some voiced that this was a kind of hidden agenda of the Mafatlals, backed by the Chief Minister Sharad Pawar. The M&E required closer examination in this

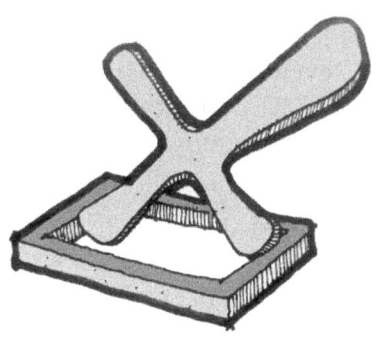

perspective and a more rigorous assessment of cumulative impacts on regional basis was needed along with an assessment of the potential hazards or risks. (Note that we are discussing a case from 1990 when there was no National EIA Notification in place and cumulative thinking of impacts/risks was simply unheard of and never applied in practice. Our work was therefore going to be path breaking to some extent.)

In those days, NOCIL was valued at Rs 482 crores. The clearance of its naphtha cracker expansion was crucial for NOCIL's survival. At that time, Indian Petrochemical Complex Limited (IPCL) was also expanding its Vadodara cracker and building another one at Nagothane in Maharashtra. The Ambani's Reliance Industries, Vijay Mallya's UB Group, Rama Prasad Goenka's RPG group and the Gas Authority of India Ltd, among others, were also setting up gas and naphtha crackers. All of them were targeting an

ethylene capacity of 3,00,000 tons a year (or more), and could take advantage of the economies of scale. So NOCIL, with its far smaller and therefore uneconomical plant operations, would be simply pushed out of the market.

With the increase in the capacity of its naphtha cracker, NOCIL's ethylene production would quadruple from the current 75,000 tons to 3,00,000 tons. NOCIL also had an advantage -- its relationship with Royal Dutch Shell Corporation, the multinational petrochemical giant. Shell's participation in the company's rights issue was expected to cover the entire Rs 400 crore foreign exchange component in the Rs 1,800 crore plan.

Mafatlal's Polyethylene India Limited's (PIL) expansion was also closely dovetailed with NOCIL's. PIL intended to raise its HDPE capacity from 50,000 tons a year to 1,50,000 tons. To do this, it needed 1,50,000 tons of ethylene from NOCIL's expanded capacity of 3,00,000 tons. PIL also had a series of other expansion plans to manufacture a whole range of polymers used in thermoplastics and rubber and to produce 20,000 tons of aniline, a raw material for rubber chemicals. So M&E at NOCIL was like waking up of a monster.

In 1989, the Department of Atomic Energy asked the BARC to conduct a risk assessment study for the Thane-Belapur Industrial Area (TBIA). Under this Inter Agency Project (IAP) the BARC carried out ambient air quality monitoring studies for 3 years. The results showed, amongst other pollutants, high concentration of non-methane hydrocarbon concentrations exceeding the limits stated by US Environmental Protection Agency (EPA). The region was found to be already in a severe pollution stress due to both industrial and traffic emissions. One could not therefore limit the environmental and risk assessment only to NOCIL and a cumulative consideration mattered.

The first step was to make a visit to NOCIL's plant in Thane-Belapur. When we visited the plant, we were received by K. Dharam and his top technical team. The idea was to tour the plant, listen to the company's presentation on M&E (and the rationale for it) and assess the existing HSE management system.

I learnt a lot from Dr. Garg on how to conduct such meetings. He was sharp and on point, asking questions that sometimes put Dharam's Team in difficult situations. I recall he even refused to have lunch on NOCIL's premises (I however, was looking forward to it!)

The tour ended at NOCIL's tank farm that had a large storage of Butadiene. Prof. Chandalia, P. K. Ghosh and I were tasked with conducting a risk assessment of NOCIL's tank farm, considering base line and the situation after M&E. I was particularly asked to do hazard assessment considering various scenarios (e.g. leaks with dense gas dispersion, BLEVES etc.) and more importantly model the domino effect to check the possible chain of blasts at the neighboring tank farms. The large gas storage at the Maharashtra Gas Cracker Complex (MGCC) was one such worry.

I asked Dharam how far the Butadiene tank was from Vashi. "Nine kilometers." he answered. Prof. Chandalia and I opened the map and we could see a direct distance of only 5km. When questioned, Dharam smiled and answered – 9km was the distance between the tank farm and Vashi by road. When I said that the Boiling Liquid Expanding Vapor Explosion (BLEVE) does not travel by road, he laughed and said that both of us were actually right – but in different perspectives! Such was the battle between us and NOCIL.

Each meeting on Sunday at Benhur was a learning experience. Since I was working on risk assessment, Dr. Garg had procured for me, copies of the famous Purple Volumes developed by the TNO, Netherlands. I had to give an undertaking of non-disclosure as we were perhaps one of the very few in India who had got access to this literature.

I had to do several calculations by hand and double check the results. Once, I submitted my calculations to P. K. Ghosh and Dr. Garg on the exceedance of Threshold Limit Values (TLVs) in the evening and when I reached home that night, I felt that I had probably made some mistake in reading the values from the risk curves. So I took a taxi at 1 am at night, reached my office at CESE, IIT and rechecked the computations till 3 am. I returned home only at 5 am when I was convinced that my calculations were correct.

(Later, TNO came up with software packages EFFECTS and RISKCURVES based on the Purple Volumes. I and my student Juzer Dhoondia, developed a computer package called MinRisk for on and off-site minimization

of risk using Dow's Fire & Explosion Index, Fatal Accident Rates (FAR), Most Probable Property Damage (MPPD) and Monds Toxicity Index.)

During the period of our assessment, I used to receive strange calls at home saying "Hello Dr. Modak, you travel to IIT by train – don't you? And hope you are aware that accidents do happen when travelling on train." Initially, I used to get disturbed and worried but later I learnt to ignore such phone calls as I had a conviction that I was not destined to die in a train mishap!

There were rumors that some of the Garg Committee members have been bought! We used to wonder who amongst us has been bought and only at the end of the journey I realized that this was simply not true and all members functioned with full independence and objectivity that the assessment deserved.

The last meeting of the Committee was held in Mantralaya in the ante-chamber room of the Chief Minister (CM) Pawar. Our final recommendation to the Honorable High Court was to say NO to NOCIL. As we were doing final reading of the draft and putting the various attachments, the door to CM's room opened and Mr. Pawar walked in. I realized for the first time how imposing was his body frame and personality. He asked, "Who are the Maharashtrians in this Committee?" When some of us raised hands like school boys in a class, he growled "Don't you feel ashamed to say NO to this very important project? If we say NO, do you realize that this company will shut down as unviable and the new project will move to Gujarat? Aren't you here to protect the interest of the State of Maharashtra? Shame on you!". There was a stony silence in the room.

But we stuck to our recommendation. We said NO to NOCIL's proposal on Modernization and Expansion.

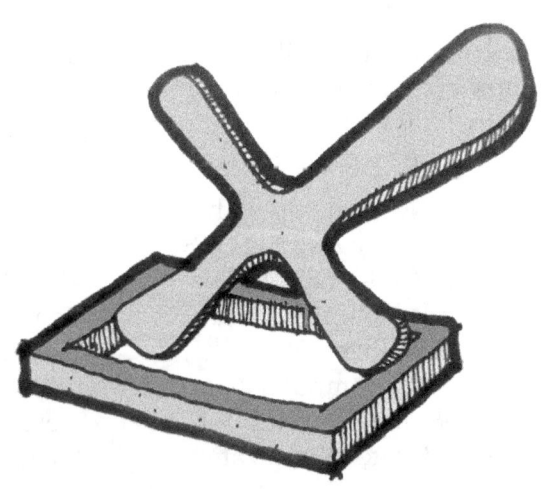

47

POLLUTION UPSTREAM, BY PRODUCTS DOWNSTREAM — AND WHO SHOULD PAY?

I was in the chamber of Member Secretary of one of the progressive State Pollution Control Boards in India. A discussion taking place was to set the effluent standard for Chemical Oxygen Demand (COD) for a pulp and paper mill upstream from a water intake point of a major city. The discussions centred around modelling of COD from the point of effluent discharge to the point of water intake and arrive at the COD limit.

I found the discussion was not focusing on the real issue. The impact of COD on the generation of disinfection by products (DBPs) leading to potential Trihalomethanes (THMs) and the associated health risks from the impacted water supply were completely missed out.

Most rivers in India today, are polluted. Untreated domestic wastes, industrial effluents and agriculture return waters have been the principal sources of this pollution. Dumping of solid wastes has also been an important contributor.

Indiscriminate withdrawal of river water for irrigation, power generation and industrial consumption has led to reduced river flows offering less dilution and low flushing velocities. The importance of maintaining "environmental flows" is usually only discussed at conferences and no serious attempts have been made towards setting the required policies. I wonder if it will ever happen?

River water quality is determined by basic parameters such as, Dissolved Oxygen (DO), Biochemical Oxygen Demand (BOD), Most Probable Number (MPN) of Coliforms and pH. Various classes of water quality are then defined based on the levels of these four parameters.

Water quality is considered to be Class A when DO > 6 mg/l, BOD < 2 mg/l, MPN <

50/100 ml and pH in the range of 6.5 to 8.5. This water is suitable for use/consumption with minimal or no treatment. However, one would hardly expect to see Water quality Class A in the river stretches of India. That is as yet a distant dream.

Water needs to be treated before used for human consumption (i.e. drinking). Water treatment plants are designed, installed and operated at locations of river intakes and only after being treated is the water transported to serve the population in our cities. We want the water we drink to be "safe."

Water treatment plants are designed to meet the drinking water quality standards that are guided by the Indian Standard IS 10500. Some of the principal parameters amongst the several listed under IS 10500 include Turbidity, MPN of Coliforms, pH, Total Dissolved Solids (TDS), Iron, and Nitrates etc.

Performance of the water treatment plant and the intensity of its treatment process depend on the quality of water it receives. The dosage of chemicals used for water purification e.g. for flocculation and disinfection increases as the pollution increases. Cleaning of the plant filters also becomes more frequent thereby generating more backwash water and longer retention times may have to be maintained in disinfection units. All this adds to the cost of operations.

More importantly, since most water treatment plants are designed as conventional; several specific pollutants such as metals, AOX etc. do not get intercepted or treated posing risks to the consumer. This risk is rarely understood and therefore not adequately addressed. In some of the Indian states, the intake works have been shifted upstream due to the problem of increasing pollution downstream. But how is this supposed to solve the problem?

Pollution of our rivers has impacted both the costs and the efficiency of the water treatment works in India. The risk of supplying safe drinking water on a consistent basis has steeply increased.

The true cost of not treating pollution upstream can be significant to the downstream population or the water users. Somewhere someone tries to saves money and somebody else pays elsewhere! This has always been a differential, skewed case of inequity requiring an inquiry into the economics of environmental management.

We need to take a systems perspective. Unfortunately, the agencies that manage pollution do not interact with the water works agencies. They need to talk and work together.

Let us consider Biochemical Oxygen Demand (BOD) as a parameter of concern for expressing the level of pollution in river water. This parameter is understood better when we connect it with the Chemical Oxygen Demand (COD). However, both BOD and COD are generally not measured at the intake of water treatment works. An associated parameter, the Total Organic Carbon (TOC) provides further insight. Only a few water treatment plants that operate sophisticated disinfection systems and tertiary treatment processes measure TOC.

BOD, COD and TOC are thus related and one can set up regression models to map one parameter from another as data is collected over time.

The higher the TOC, the greater is the dose of chlorine required for the disinfection process that ensures the destruction of Coliforms and to maintain the desired levels of residual chlorine. Therefore increased upstream pollution increases the TOC in the raw water entering the treatment plant thereby raising the cost of operation of the disinfection unit. It will be interesting to map the trend of chlorine consumed per Million Liters Day (MLD) versus the operating costs at a water treatment plant as a function of the average TOC/COD/BOD levels in the raw water at the intake works! I really wish such data is collected, analyzed and reported.

The issue is however not just the increase in the operating costs. A new dimension of health risk gets introduced. In the process of disinfection of polluted (high TOC) water, several Disinfection By Products (DBPs) are formed. These DBPs can pose significant health risks, such as the occurrence of cancer and lead to substantial medical costs[56].

Chlorinated DBPs are considered potentially

---

56 You should visit web page of US EPA http://water.epa.gov/drink/contaminants/ basicinformation/disinfectionbyproducts.cfm# that provides information on what disinfection byproducts does EPA regulate, how are they formed, and what are their health effects in drinking water at levels above the maximum contaminant level?

carcinogenic and have been associated with adverse reproductive outcomes following exposure during pregnancy. THMs are the most important/deadly group of DBPs.

THMs include chloroform, dichlorobromomethane (DCBM), dibromochloromethane (DBCM) and bromoform (BF). Organic matter in natural water, expressed as TOC, is considered as the dominant THM precursor in drinking water. The World Health Organization (WHO) has set limits on THM and the Indian Standard 10500 also specifies thresholds for THMs in drinking water.

How much do we really know about the levels of THM in our drinking water?

Research carried out in India on the formation of THMs is very limited and has shown mixed results (when water was analyzed at the water treatment plants, at the reservoirs and in the swimming pools). There is a critical need to conduct THM monitoring systematically over a year, on a national basis and at all major water treatment plants. We need to understand and assess the causes leading to generation of the THMs. Wastewater inventories at the points upstream from the treatment plants will also need to be carried out. Occurrence of cancer, especially of the bladder will also need to be examined through community health surveys. Results of this field work must be shared with the public as a preventive and corrective

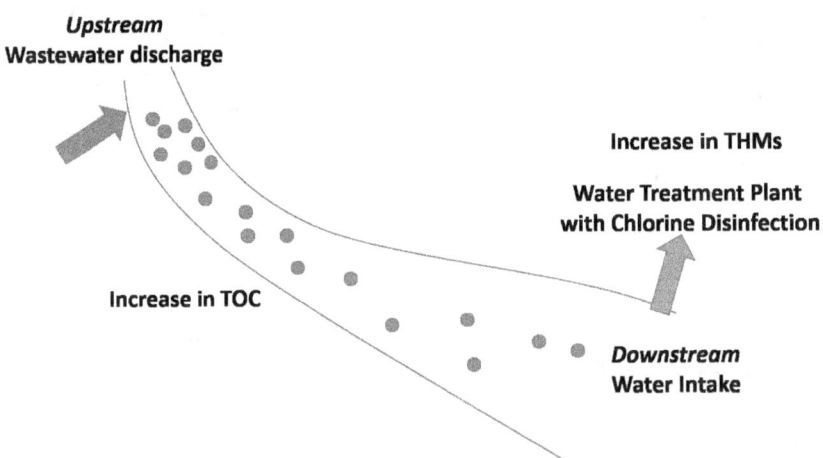

Upstream
Wastewater discharge

Increase in THMs

Water Treatment Plant
with Chlorine Disinfection

Increase in TOC

Downstream
Water Intake

The "Relationships and dynamics" of TOC and THMs from upstream to downstream

plan is launched. We need to seriously tackle the pollution upstream, optimize operation of chlorine based disinfection and even come up with substitutes to chlorine.

We could perhaps develop a Risk Index or a Score Card for a water treatment works, based on the potential generation of THMs and pay for the water accordingly. If the risk index is high then the water treatment plant will need to be compensated by the wastewater dischargers upstream. Regulators will have an important role to play as they will have to levy additional fines.

Indeed, we must address the nexus of Pollution upstream and By Products downstream. We also need to raise the question of who should pay? -- the Regulators, Wastewater dischargers upstream, the Water Treatment Plant operators downstream, Medical practioners or the Community. We need to address the problem from a more holistic perspective and not with the current narrow perspective through the mere compliance to in-stream BOD and COD standards.

48

On a Sunday morning, one of my good friends invited me for breakfast. "Dr Modak, I have a serious matter to discuss with you. Please could you bring your Professor Friend as well?" He said sounding a bit exasperated.

My friend lived in one of the tallest buildings in Mumbai -- on the 104th floor. In fact, he occupied 4 floors (from 100 to 104) and owned the complete terrace with a helipad. Few knew that he was the richest Indian on a global basis and yet he paid all his tax dues in full and on time to the Government of India in addition to several other Governments. The world economy depended on him, his business and his investments.

Some believed that his Indian tax returns were more than the annual budget of Municipal Corporation of Mumbai. To me this was rather an underestimate. Most tycoons and business houses like the Tatas, Birlas, Ambanis and Mittals were dwarfs in front of my friends "might". He however chose to remain anonymous and only PM Modi (and of course Amit Shah) knew about him. "Money is not everything in life" He used to tell me when we occasionally met. This was not surprising as he already had perhaps all the money of the world to make such a statement!

"So my friend, what's your problem?" I asked while sipping some freshly brewed Columbian coffee that was served in a solid silver mug.

"Well, you know my daughter

is getting married this year. As it is going to be an important event and one that will draw the attention of all the world, my wife and I decided to start planning. I thought of engaging the Taj group and so called on Cyrus Mistry. The first thing, Cyrus asked me whether I have obtained an Environmental Clearance (EC) from the Ministry of Environment and Forests (and Climate Change)."

"Apparently," he continued, "Union Minister Prakash Javdekar feels that the environmental impact of Indian weddings on an aggregated basis is much more than environmental impact of 100 coal fired thermal power plants put together! A report was prepared by 7 IITs to make a comparative assessment. The conclusions led to requirement of EC for Indian weddings where the number of guests or invitees exceed 500. It has now been put in the Schedule."

"Oh the 7 IITs again!" – I said, recalling the fiasco from when the 7 IITs were commissioned by the Ganga Authority to prepare the Action Plan – something the Professors had no clue about and the result of the Action Plan was inconsequential!"

But my friend continued.

"This is a terrible stipulation. I estimate at least 50,000 people will attend my daughter's wedding. This number I thought was modest – of course the event will be a little more lavish than the Weddings of Roys, Jhunjhunwalas and Mittals. But how do I get this EC? Cyrus said that it will take at least one year as it will involve baseline monitoring, some mathematical modelling (essentially a show-of) and public hearing (for name-sake)."

The requirement of EC for weddings was news to me. I knew that lately food waste had become a focus of discussions to flag the environmental impact of Indian weddings. A recent survey showed that annually, Bangalore alone wastes 943 tons of quality food during weddings. The survey showed that 22% food wasted in buffet system and 20% in served system. "This is enough to feed 26 million people a normal Indian meal!" a study by a team of 10 professors from the University of Agricultural Sciences (UAS), Bangalore, had concluded. The team, under the guidance of UAS vice-chancellor K. Narayana Gowda, surveyed 75 of Bangalore's 531 marriage halls over a period of six months. At an average cost of Rs. 40 per meal, the total food wastage in the city is estimated at Rs. 3390 million!"

I realized that my friend's plan of inviting 50,000 guests would mean that the economic implications of the food wastage could be close to annual budget of corporations of Mumbai, Delhi, Chennai and Kolkata – put together.

Given this estimated impact, I told my friend that he should hire one of the top EIA consultants in the country or for that matter in the world and get an EC on a "fast track". "Speak to the PM if Javdekar is adamant." I suggested. "The party is powerful. They just got rid of Raghuram Rajan, Governor of RBI."

"Well, I don't want to jump the queue". My friend said humbly. "I will follow the rules and get a proper EC." He then turned to Professor and asked "Sir, will you help me and be my consultant?"

Professor lit his cigar, took a deep puff and placed the cigar on an ash tray that was studded with diamond and in gold.

"I can certainly help you. We will prepare a high quality and comprehensive EIA report and follow all the required process steps"

He then started outlining his ideas.

"We will follow all the best known green wedding norms. All invitations will be e-mailed. Ministers and top administrators will however get hard copies on recycled paper as they don't read emails. We will conduct baseline monitoring at the Brabourne stadium, which will be the appropriate venue, and place continuous air quality (including odor) and noise monitoring instruments on every 15 degree sector of the stadium. These stations will collect data on a round the clock basis over 3 months, especially covering the periods of cricket matches where spikes could be observed. We will later show, through sophisticated prediction modelling; the impact on air quality and noise during our wedding will be much lower than the impact caused due to the game of cricket!"

"Regarding food, we will put placards with messages saying guests must not waste food and take only what they can consume. All those who will waste food will be tracked and fined."

"That's not a good idea." my friend said. I saw that he was embarrassed.

"OK then," the Professor continued, "we will design the menu such that there is least impact in sourcing the raw materials. All raw materials will be sourced within the 10 km impact radius (following the norm of impact assessment followed in the Indian EIA system). We will not have expensive delicacies such as beef, lobster and the ever-controversial shark-fin soup in the interest of animal welfare, sentiments and biodiversity. We will only select locally produced, organic, seasonal food, served buffet-style in order to minimize waste. This menu will influence people later to follow in other weddings. There will not be any IPR.

The bride and groom will wear only environmentally and socially responsible jewelry and cotton outfits certified by GOTS. The decorations will consist of 5,000 potted plants, reusable natural cloth, LED lights and paper flowers. Over 500 workers of a recycling firm will be deployed to segregate the excess food properly, pack

and serve the poor that are so many in Mumbai. The food waste will be promptly dispatched to a biogas processing facility. We will thus influence the vendors to go green and create in this process a huge market for green products and services. A new green wedding industry will emerge."

Now Professor took a deep puff from his cigar for a new idea.

"We will hold a 2 minute session for the Weddings vows that will be administered every one hour during the wedding ceremony. These vows will ask for making a public commitment that henceforth i.e. after attending the wedding, they will live sustainably. This vow will be administered by top Bollywood stars so that the vow will be heard, followed and practiced seriously."

"Great!" said my friend. "Any consideration on the analysis of alternatives? Cyrus said that Javdekar is very particular when it comes to alternatives He has never seen generation and analyses of alternatives in the Indian EIA reports so far and is hence very curious."

The Professor smiled and then spoke, "Our environmental and social management plan will ensure the least ecological footprint possible. We will study the addresses of invitees and come up with a decentralized strategy. The wedding will be relayed though screens of the size of a 6 storied building at multiple locations such that the overall carbon emissions are reduced. So in effect only 5000 people may attend the actual wedding at the Brabourne stadium and rest may participate remotely from say 10 locations. These locations will be carefully selected on application of Mixed Integer Zero One Programming. We will however take on cumulative impact assessment of the 10 simultaneous weddings. MoEF (& CC) is in a habit of asking such studies later as an afterthought. Further, an environmental and social management framework will be developed overarching the 10 locations emphasizing a common "green code of conduct". Separate public hearings will be executed too".

"Oh, that is very thoughtful

of you Professor", I said. "So you will assess impacts with and without "project" and with "centralized" and "decentralized" approach?"

The Professor said yes and then asked my friend, "Will you be giving any return gifts?"

"Well, I was thinking of giving 100gm gold bars to everyone who comes to bless the bride and the groom." said my friend said – "This is the least I can offer."

"Let me then come up with a high level Disaster Management Plan (DMP) as there could be possibilities of stampedes while collecting the return gifts." Professor said this thoughtfully and took down notes in his scratch pad.

I butted in. "Why don't we give 2 bars of gold if they chose to come in public transport. All they will need to do is show the manager the bus, tram or railway ticket as a proof."

"Good idea". My friend said. "I really want to do something more for all those who will attend. Why not offer a free health check up on the nearby Oval grounds and give coupons of Rs. 50,000 each to cover one year of medical expenses."

"That is very generous of

you." Professor said. He then continued, "In any case, we will publish a sustainability report following GRI G4 format post the wedding as a measure of transparency and disclosure. Importantly, I will train the media on the GRI so that there is no miss-reporting. In essence, your wedding celebrations will be low carbon-emitting, socially-responsible, energy efficient and embrace the four Rs (reuse, reduce, recycle, and repair). With all these commitments, the event will live up to the expectations of being one of the most memorable event talked about over the next 5 years (i.e. till your son's wedding)."

"Finally," concluded the Professor. "carbon offsetting, i.e., reducing greenhouse gases from other emissions sources to compensate from our own actions will be followed. We will plant trees to absorb GHGs (that will in any case be very low) and if required buy land and raise the green cover in Mumbai to 20% "

We ended the breakfast with all this inspiring conversation and the Professor was duly commissioned for getting the EC.

In few months, I received a call from my friend that the project proposal for his daughter's wedding received the EC. The Appraisal Committee was extremely happy to see the Professor's robust environmental and social management plan. The only condition they imposed was that they be invited to attend the wedding (of course for the purpose of monitoring they said and not for any other interest!)

My friend said that post getting the EC, he was asked to join Minister Prakash Javdekar for tea in his chamber. When the minister asked my friend for suggestions on his requirement of EC for weddings, my friend said that while the idea of asking EC for weddings was a right step, "how about asking for EC for holding political rallies?" He elaborated that rallies attracting thousands of people had great environmental impacts and could mean an aggregated impact equivalent to 200 coal power thermal power plants!

Apparently the Minister smiled and said, "Well, we cannot – as these events are organized to generate income for those who work for, attend and participate – For rallies, we must take a broad perspective of socio-economic benefits and not focus only on the environmental impacts."

"Why don't you and Professor join me for breakfast again?" My friend said as he ended the conversation. He once again sounded rather exasperated with the minister's explanation!

49
Silence of the Lambs

In a major reshuffle of the Ministers on July 5[57], India's Prime Minister Modi elevated the present Union Environment Minister Mr. Prakash Javdekar and inducted Mr. Anil Madhav Dave as the new Environment Minister. Mr. Javdekar would now handle the portfolio of Human Resource Development. Mr. Dave is a well-known nature conservationist and I was happy that he had been brought in.

Many said that Mr. Javdekar deserved this promotion as his performance at the Ministry of Environment & Forests & Climate Change (MoEFCC) has been outstanding and rather bold. Amongst the several changes he brought in, his reforms on fast tracking environmental clearance have been extremely innovative, tech-savvy and very much lauded. These reforms opened the gateway for large projects and investments to India – something that the Modi Government had promised and has wanted to achieve. After all, we need economic development – don't we?

Since political governance in India has a 5 year vision plan (I call this not a narrow but focused vision), what Mr. Javdekar did was rather fitting and appropriate. Many times thinking of sustainability over longer periods does not make sense. Who cares if the so called modernization of environmental governance leads to irreversible and expensive damages to India's natural assets in the future? The future is so uncertain – what with the ever increasing terrorism, economic and social disparities and above all the indifference, all of it muffles the voices on the environment. Should the environment matter at all?

---

57 See: http://indianexpress.com/article/india/india-news-india/modi-cabinet-reshuffle-know-your-new-ministers/

Just before his departure, in May, 2016 Mr. Javdekar amended the EIA Notification with a new instrument called the "Environmental Supplement Plan (ESP)[58]". The ESP focused on companies that violated India's regulations on environmental clearances. Under the ESP, these companies would now simply be fined and then allowed to continue whatever they were doing, instead of being charged with a criminal offense, as was the practice in the past.

The concept of ESP is not new. A policy on the Use of Supplemental Environmental Projects (SEPs) was introduced in the United States, as early as in February 1991. This Policy was subsequently revised in May 1995 and later in May 1998. The 2015 Updated SEP Policy supersedes earlier versions.

Under the 2015 SEP Policy[59], most federal actions against businesses or individuals for failure to comply with the environmental laws are resolved through settlement agreements. As part of the settlement, an alleged violator may voluntarily agree to undertake "an environmentally beneficial project" related to the violation in exchange for mitigation of the penalty to be paid. A Supplement Environmental Project (SEP) furthers the US Environmental Protection Agency's goal of protecting and enhancing the public health and the environment. It does not however include the activities a violator must undertake to return to compliance with the law. Some have criticized the SEP but these are short-sighted people who don't appreciate United States' philosophy of "development."

According to an investigation by the Indian Express newspaper, it is the United States' Supplemental Environments Project Policy from where India got the idea of ESP.

Jay Mazoomdar[60], the author of the article in the Indian

58 See: https://iasgs.com/2016/07/environment-supplement-plan-esp/

59 See: https://www.epa.gov/enforcement/supplemental-environmental-projects-seps

60 See: http://indianexpress.com/article/india/india-news-india/environment-ministrys-rules-for-polluters-in-india-copied-word-for-word-from-the-us-2900485/

Express, found that 2,900 words of the 3,850 that make up the Indian ESP legislation were lifted word for word from the American version. This is extremely encouraging! Such approaches of lifting words and striking commonalities should foster the relationships between India and the United States. This is what we mean when we say "being on the same pitch" or "sharing of the same thoughts." We must praise Minister Javdekar for this strategic approach!

Mazoomdar cited following instances of alleged plagiarism:

1. US (Introduction A): Supplemental Environmental Project (SEP) is an environmentally beneficial project or activity that is not required by law, but that a defendant agrees to undertake as part of the settlement of an enforcement action.   India (Clause 1): An Environmental Supplemental Plan (ESP) is an environmentally beneficial project or activity that is not required by law, but that an alleged violator of Environmental Impact Assessment Notification, 2006 agrees to undertake as part of the process of environmental clearance.

2. US (II D): SEPs provide defendants with an opportunity to develop and demonstrate new technologies that may prove more protective of human health and the environment than existing processes and procedures.

India (4 iii): Innovative Technology: Environmental Supplemental Plan will provide the proponent and the Expert Group with an opportunity to develop and demonstrate new technologies that may prove more protective of human health and the environment than existing processes and procedures.

3. US (IV A III): The project must demonstrate that it is designed to reduce:

a. The likelihood that similar violations will occur in the future;

b. The adverse impact to public health and/or the environment to which the violation at issue contributes; or,

c. The overall risk to public health and/or the environment potentially affected by the violation at issue.

India (5): The project must demonstrate that it is designed to remediate the ecological damage caused due to violations and it will reduce,

a. The likelihood that similar violations will occur in the future;

b. The adverse impact to public health and the environment to which the violation at issue contributes;

c. The overall risk to public health and the environment potentially affected by the violation at issue.

The above are only samples quoted by the Author.

The MoEFCC officials in India have defended their actions by saying that an idea such as ESP is in vogue in many western countries and the language used in the Indian draft is different. (Although they haven't stated, but I am sure that out of the 2900 words lifted from 3900 words include words like "and", "but", "however" etc. Such overlaps are unavoidable and do not really convey plagiarism. Mazoomdar has therefore been rather harsh with the Ministry).

Let us try and better understand the MoEFCC's ESP…

The MoEFCC issued a draft notification as required by sub-rule (3) of rule 5 of the Environment (Protection)

Rules, 1986 on 10th May, 2016[61].

Section 5 of the Environment (Protection) Act, 1986 empowers the Central Government to give directions which reads as:

"Not withstanding anything contained in any other law but subject to the provisions of this Act, the Central Government may in the exercise of its powers and performance of its functions under this Act, issue directions in writing to any person, officer or any authority and such person, officer or authority shall be bound to comply with such directions."

The draft notification on ESP proposes that,

"In case the projects or activities requiring prior environmental clearance under Environment Impact Assessment Notification, 2006 from the concerned regulatory authority are brought for environmental clearance after starting the construction work, or have undertaken expansion, modernization, and change in product- mix without prior environmental clearance, these projects shall be treated as cases of violations and shall be appraised for

---

61 See: http://re.indiaenvironmentportal.org.in/reports-documents/draft-notification-violation-cases-under-provisions-environment-protection-act

grant of environmental clearance and the project proponent to compensate may implement the Environmental Supplemental Plan to remediate the damage caused or likely to be caused, and take out the undue economic gain due to non-compliance and violation."

The process of appraisal of the project for granting of environmental clearance and preparation of the Environmental Supplemental Plan would be carried out simultaneously.

Any person interested in making any objections or suggestions on the proposal contained in the draft notification may forward the same in writing, for consideration of the Central Government within the period so specified, to the Secretary, Ministry of Environment, Forest and Climate Change, Indira Paryavaran Bhawan, Jor Bagh Road, Aliganj, New Delhi-110 003

Indeed, the ESP has been devised in a manner consistent to what the Government has been already doing (not just Modi Government but the Gandhi Government as well) i.e. the process of "regularization" that blesses

the corporate illegalities.

Someone overheard Mr. Javdekar in the MoEFCC corridors, saying that if Arun Jaitley is offering schemes like Dispute Resolution[62] then why not something similar for the Environment Ministry?

I like Javdekar's straightforwardness of ensuring "evenness" across the Ministries. It is really very heartening to see the congruence and consistency between the Ministries despite political and personal differences in the interest of this country.

Many argue that the ESP can be seen as a license to violate. I disagree! The violations penalized by the ESP are only mistakes made by the enthusiastic developers, eager to meet national development targets. How can we create obstacles for them by asking them to follow a timely and comprehensive EIA process? The quality of EIAs in India is in any case so poor that doing or not doing the EIA does not make any difference to the outcomes. It is very kind of Mr. Javdekar that he did not scrap the EIA process itself and thus protected the livelihoods of the many EIA consultants in India. I salute

---

62 See: http://pib.nic.in/newsite/PrintRelease.aspx?relid=136986

him for this consideration.

The ESP appears to be a crude version of a 'pay and use (or more appropriately abuse)' service. Many argue that these payments in reality may not be made. My good friends – Kanchi Kohli and Manju Menon[63] say, "Take the case of the fine of Rs.200 crores levied on the Adani SEZ in Gujarat, or Rs.5 crore fine for the Art of Living event on the Yamuna floodplains. Even if one were to be more optimistic about these collections, the government's ability to use these resources to restore the environment, or provide justice to scores of affected people, is severely lacking. The example of crores of rupees collected to compensate for forest loss, and the Comptroller and Auditor General's damning report on how these moneys have been spent, will help change one's mind."

I think that both Kanchi's and Manju's views are rather biased and incorrect as they do not know the reality. Some tell me that the moneys or fines are and will actually be paid out – but mostly for supporting the political parties. This contribution will support the sustainability and stability of the Government. So in other words fines collected from ESP will help achieve "all rounded" sustainable development in India. Most environmental NGOs don't appreciate such deep thought and consideration!

When Mr. Javdekar ushered in the new Minister Mr. Anil Madhav Dave into his cabin, Mr. Dave apparently asked him, "Prakash saab, how did you manage to introduce and implement these drastic changes in India's Environmental Governance and in such a short time? May I ask the secret of your success?"

Mr Javdekar smiled (as he often does – and sometimes without any reason) and said, "Mr Dave, there are no organized associations on the subject of Environmental Management in India who can rise and question us. They are either small or dead (like the Indian Environmental Association), or narrowed to a subject (like water – e.g. Indian Water Works Association). These associations are busy with conferences and exhibitions. Furthermore, they fight internally on matters that are petty and do not discuss the national interests. So don't worry and carry forward the good work I have started.

---

63 See: http://www.thehindu.com/opinion/op-ed/letting-them-off-easy/article8748866.ece

There is no chance of any opposition."

I must say, I appreciate Mr. Javdekar's observation. Indian environmental associations, experts and activists are yet to wake up in India on a collective basis.

I call this situation - the Silence of the Lambs.

[My wish is that one day we could form a group that the Government recognizes, honors and consults ... a Think Tank and a light house that mainstreams and improves environmental management in this country.]

50

PROFESSOR'S UNIQUE BEAUTY SALOON

I had not met my Professor Friend for quite a while. He seemed to be either abroad or on a long leave. I dearly missed conversations with him and the coffee together. I thought I had almost lost him.

But last Sunday morning, I got a call from him.

"Where have you been my Friend?" I asked or rather screamed.

"Well Dr. Modak, I was busy in setting up a Beauty Saloon." answered the Professor. "This Saloon is really unique and boutique and is set up in the interest of the Environment."

I didn't know what to say! The Professor and a Saloon?... I just couldn't understand the relationship.

In answer to my silence, the Professor suggested, "Well, why don't you drop by the Saloon right away and get a nice shave. We are in the Khan Market."

I was longing to get a shave done anyway. Sitting in a chair with a mirror in front of you, thick cream on the face, the razor blade carefully and expertly being navigated over the contours 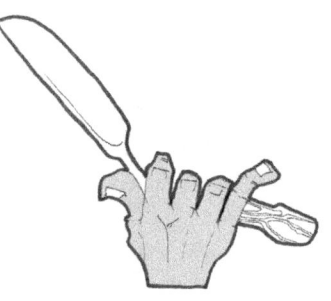 of the face and that tinge and aroma of the aftershave... Shaving has always been such a heavenly experience. I reached the Saloon with high expectations.

The Professor was waiting for me. The Saloon was already full of customers. It had a large room on the ground floor with a left wing for men and right for women. The first floor was for therapies such as massages.

The Professor explained, "Of course I don't have to tell you that the Saloon is Eco-friendly in all possible respects. The furniture, the lights, the curtains, the glass mirrors we use, all have the smallest carbon footprint. We procure the creams, sprays, solvents only if they hold a respected Eco label."

Professor said.

"Why didn't you take CII's GreenCo instead? That would have been much easier and cheaper. Someone told me that you just have to pay the fees to CII and you get the certificate." I asked the professor.

The Professor ignored my advice with a smirk on his face.

"You will have to wait a bit" He said to me in an apologetic tone. "Why don't you read newspapers in the meanwhile?" He directed me to the sofa.

I picked up a stack of newspapers from the rack. I had never come across these newspapers before. They carried only the Environmental news - Green Times of India, The Green Express were some of the English newspapers and Hara Hamara Bharat, Shashwat Dainik etc.

were the Hindi newspapers.

I started reading the Green Times. It had headlines like "20% of NPAs in the Banks are due neglecting environmental and social matters in investments"; "Most Waste to Energy Plants in India don't work!" etc. I got bored as most of these headlines were not really the news – they were the facts. Most of us knew about these issues and also knew that nothing would change or happen.

I started looking at the Green Express as I thought this newspaper might be carrying something sensational. The Green Express had headlines such as, "Did you know that 30% of drinking water at Mumbai's taps is contaminated?"; "20% of India's land will need remediation", "Air Pollution is more Indoors than Outdoors"; "Should Renewable Energy Projects need Environmental Clearance?" I liked these headlines as I saw a need for such discussions and actions. I asked Professor who published these newspapers and suggested he only keep the Green Express in the Saloon.

"Well," replied the Professor, "I edit and publish these newspapers and they are available only at my Saloon. My customers love reading these and many come to the Saloon not for the haircut but to simply to read my newspapers. I let them read and carry a copy or two back home. I print 500 copies of each newspaper every day and that stock gets exhausted by the evening."

"That's so thoughtful of you." I said. "I am sure those visiting your Saloon will inspire and transform India." I noticed however, that most of the newspapers carried advertisements from business groups such as Reliance, Ambani, Vedanta etc.

I looked around and I found that the Saloon was full with Page 3 personalities of India's (or should I say Delhi's) Green World.

I saw that the Ex-Union Environment Minister, Jayaram Ramesh having a discussion with the Professor's Chief Barber on the style of haircut he should get. Jayaram has plenty of hair, in thick and rolling curls with a mix of shining white and grey. So many options for hair styling are possible. Jayaram was not sure which style to choose and he kept changing his mind confusing the Chief Barber. The Professor took me on one side and whispered, "Jayaram Ramesh has been discussing what hair style he should get for the past one hour and has not reached a decision. He just keeps talking and my Chief Barber is now fed up."

"I am not surprised," I said and reminded the Professor of the cases of Environmental Clearance of Posco[64], the BT Basmati rice[65] and BT Brinjal[66]. These cases showed Jayaram's appetite for options and analytics and love towards switching the decisions.

As we were talking, Sunita Narain of the Centre for Science and Environment (CSE) walked in for a haircut. She asked the Professor for a catalogue. Passing her one of the latest catalogues of hair styles from Sweden (where she travels to frequently), Professor said in a mischievous tone, "Sunita,

64 See: http://www.downtoearth.org.in/news/poscos-environment-clearance-revalidated-43230 and http://timesofindia.indiatimes.com/india/After-eight-years-of-wait-Poscos-Odisha-plant-gets-environment-clearance/articleshow/28629934.cms

65 See: http://www.dailypioneer.com/columnists/edit/basmati-under-threat-gm-crops-play-foul.html

66 See: http://timesofindia.indiatimes.com/india/Challenges-posed-by-Bt-Brinjal/articleshow/5541948.cms

don't forget to get a manicure. It's a high time that you had one. You have been "nailing" the Government and the Industry a little too much lately! So do get rid of your long nails." Sunita just smiled. [Sunita has a good Swedish connection. Do you know that she received the Stockholm Water Prize[67] for the good work CSE did on water harvesting?]

Just then the Union Environment Minister Anil Madhav Dave walked in and asked the Professor for a facial. This facial was to be special. Dave wanted to change his face from a conservationist to one that is "pro-development." The Professor walked across and gave instructions to his staff about this complicated facial. "Use creams from Philadelphia and masks from Washington." He instructed them and then turned to me and said, "I will be using materials and techniques of the United States of America. This is the country where faces often change – so what you see is not what you should or want to see!"

Dr. Mukesh Khare of IIT Delhi was sitting in a chair getting his hair cut. When the hair cut was over, the Professor asked him, "Mukesh, are you satisfied?" Dr. Khare got up from the chair, pulled out a tiny air quality monitoring device that was under the chair. He looked at the reading and spoke, "I am satisfied Professor. The indoor air quality in your Saloon meets the ASHRAE standards."

Dr. Khare's monitoring of Indoor Air Quality in the Saloon

"Oh, I was asking you about the haircut." Professor said.

[By the way, do you know that India does not have Indoor Air Quality Standards? China introduced these standards as early as in 1976. Korea has introduced Air Quality Standards even for A/C Buses. In India we don't care much about the Indoor Air Quality. We show concerns only for the Outdoors even though much of our life today is indoors]

The Saloon was getting a bit

---

67 See: http://www.thehindu.com/2005/08/27/stories/2005082703431300.htm and http://www.siwi.org/prizes/stockholmwaterprize/

noisy as almost everyone was talking, except those who were undergoing steam treatments or sleeping with a mask on (during the facial). "This is rather expected." the Professor explained. "My staff consists of top doctoral students from India as well as from overseas. They are researching on the environment in India. They come to me as interns and over three months, we train them on hair styling, skin treatment etc. Once hired in the Saloon, they want to take advantage of the contact and connection they get to make with the top environmentalists, academicians, bureaucrats and industrialists of India. So while delivering saloon services, they want to talk about some of the challenges we face today and thus conversations happen. In some sense, my Saloon functions like a think tank or a workshop place. These students, as they are so habituated, post the conversations on Facebook and WhatsApp taking these conversations to the millions in the World"

"Oh, this is much more effective than the meetings that FICCI holds!" I exclaimed. "You must now work on setting up more such franchises across India."

"Do you see any action on the ground after folks leave you

Saloon?" I could not help but ask.

"Well…" the Professor said, "…It's happening slowly. But I do have a shining example to share. Our Ex-Union Environment Minister Prakash Javdekar used to visit us regularly for beard trimming. Each time, my staff trimmed his beard he trimmed the Indian Environmental Legislation. He used to say that he got all the inspiration for such trimming by listening to the conversations in our Saloon. Don't you think that India's environmental legislation has a "smart well cut look" today! " I couldn't disagree with the Professor.

Beard trimming – Secret behind India's Smart Environmental Legislation

"So why don't you get your shave done – your chair is ready." Said the Professor as he ushered me towards one of his staff, a doctoral student from UC Berkeley.

"Sir, I have the honor of performing a shave for you today." The student said with an American accent.

Then while wrapping a GOTT certified apron around my neck, he bent down and whispered in my ears, "Is it OK if I discussed my research on tree transplantations with you during the shave? I understand that you have done transplantation of trees around the roadways and there was hardly any survival."

I realized that this was something I was least expecting on a Sunday morning. I also realized that this student would be asking me questions all the time and my shave wasn't going to be as relaxing as I had expected and hoped for.

"Thank God, I am not here to do a hair transplant" I said to myself while getting off the Chair.

BLUE- GREEN FROM THE OTHER SIDE

Dr Watson and Professor Holmes

If Ibn Battuta and Confucius were rolled into one, we might find a person closely resembling Prasad Modak

Three things about Prasad's blog posts have always held a fascination for me; at the end always leaving me wanting for more.

Prasad travels far & wide in this world, with eyes, ears and all of his other senses open and an uncanny ability to capture every little minutia of his experiences with people, places and events. A raconteur par excellence with great sensitivity, his stories are so evocative that one becomes part of the play – the fly on the wall.

The multi faceted personality that Prasad is, he can speak on any subject under the sun with great authority on hither to unknown Environmental matters, while at the same time with great empathy describe the life and times of his driver. At other times, his tongue in cheek impish humour leaves you pleasantly speculating whether Prasad is all praise for the Minister or just chiding him for his decisions and actions.

And last, but not the least is his Professor friend, who is the ideal foil for many of life's unanswered questions in Prasad's mind. It is a relationship one cannot put a finger on and codify with any certainty. Prasad uses his friend skilfully to raise issues and also provide a counterpoint to his own views. It is then left to the reader to choose one from the dynamic duo. Personally, I will take Dr. Watson for his rooted to earth approach over the pipe smoking Professor Holmes and his Stratospheric flights of fantasy.

Ananth S Kodavasal
Bangalore, India

. . . .

A savoury snack bhelpuri

A decade of interactions at work, countless invigorating technical and knowledge-based discussions, interspersed with anecdotes from personal life, one would think that there would be nothing left to say. However, this is not the case with Dr Prasad Modak. And I realized this when I started reading the blog that he writes.

I like to think of the blog as the savoury snack bhelpuri, a perfect blend of tanginess, crunchiness and balance. And as a plate of bhelpuri stimulates the taste buds, the blog stimulates the mind, leaving one wanting for more. Incidentally, bhelpuri happens to be one of Dr Modak's favourite snacks. These blog posts spill over with his incredible knowledge of environmental sciences, radically different thoughts (presented mostly through his 'Professor friend'), tales of hopping across continents meeting with people (sometimes experts and at other times, incredible human beings) and his life experiences. All of it, well, most of the time, spiced up with humour.

"Shades of Blue and Green and Everything in Between" is Dr Modak's second book presenting a delectable selection of his blogs. The 'Blue' brings out the human side of Dr Modak: a mix of his life experiences presenting his various traits of spirituality, caring, giving and critical thinking. The 'Green' is about the teacher and his insatiable desire to gather and distil knowledge – presenting environmental issues and topics in ways that compel the practitioners of the field, to unlearn and relearn, providing superb insight to students as well as veterans. Some of the pieces are a must read to get an interesting commentary on the developments related to environmental governance in India, of course through the characteristic Professor friend of Dr Modak!

Every piece has a rationale to its inclusion on the blog. Sometimes it is the knowledge it imparts, sometimes wisdom and at other times, it is the experience. Knowledge about multiple environmental issues – some so common yet misunderstood, others more profound – wisdom about the multidimensional aspects of environmental sciences presented lucidly, and personal experiences (and learnings) from stalwarts in the subject, personalities in their own right, as well as from nondescript individuals. But nowhere has the knowledge or the message been preached or sermonised – it is simply embedded for the readers to recognise and appreciate.

Shantanu Roy
Pune, India

• • • • • • • • • • • • • • • •

A perfect compendium of life, the blues and sustainability

I have been reading Dr Prasad Modak's blog for a long time now. He is one of those special writers that prods and pokes at all of our preconceived notions and makes us reconsider what we are thinking. In short, just when you believe you have wrapped your mind around a complex issue on sustainability or how we should be doing in life, along comes Dr Prasad Modak to provide a very insightful and alternative perspective to the wisdom we have amassed.

However, there is more to Dr Prasad than being a Guru on sustainability. Through the posts he writes while on his own life journey, we are treated to the walk of a man on a mission to enjoy life to the full and to relish every relationship, no matter how fleeting. Whilst no one wants to live their life vicariously through another, it is impossible not to draw on Dr Prasad's life lessons, as guidance for our own life. I often find myself pondering over what for many, would be quite prosaic situations, but for Dr Prasad, a rich and fertile ground of interaction with others. I dig deep into these grounds and store away the golden nuggets that are revealed.

Dr Prasad's new book, "Shades of Blue and Green and Everything In Between" provides the perfect compendium for his writings on his life, the blue, and on sustainability, the green. I recommend this book as the perfect stimulus to reawaken our minds and as an encouragement not to ever be satisfied with the ordinary.

Balamurugan Ratha Krishnan
Melaka, Malaysia

· · · · · · · · · · · · · · · · · ·

Stories that can keep you awake at night

I first met Prof Modak in 1990. I had a new job as an Environmental Impact Assessment officer with the Ministry of Environment, Forests and Climate Change and within a few months, I was dispatched to Bangkok to attend a four-week training program on EIA at AIT, Bangkok.

Dr Modak taught us the basics of EIA at AIT. He had an effortless style. I thoroughly enjoyed his sessions. We never realised we were being taught. Today when I read his blogs, I feel the same patience and wisdom in his prose. Dr Modak's blogs sustain a balance even when discussing serious stuff. I particularly like his way of blending the personal with the scientific, the exotic with the ugly.

His humor and satire stitch seamlessly and his characters seem familiar and believable. I thoroughly enjoyed reading all the stories. The one on EIA for Indian weddings took the cake .....

Dr Modak's stories are great at evoking emotions. Some of them have kept me awake at night... Government corridors, pollution control boards, projects, projects and more projects and never ending discussions and decisions are disturbingly familiar .... Dr Modak tells stories that need to be heard not once but again and again. Keep going.

Meenakshi Kakkar
Calgary, Canada

. . . .

A Learning Experience with Fun

Storytelling is not only an effective way of understanding, it can be fun. The readers (or listeners?) live out the events the storyteller proposes through the prism of their own personal experiences. They ask questions such as 'what would I have done here,' or 'I wonder how this would work for me?'. Prasad Modak's stories give this learning experience a humorous twist that makes us enjoy the storyline right up to its inevitable conclusion; sometimes highlighting the delights of human folly, sometimes suggesting useful solutions to universal problems. I loved the New Year Resolution, his attempt to reconcile the private electric car within a larger sustainability context, and the environmental assessment of Indian weddings. The amusing scenarios where various Hindu deities try to intervene (in a good direction, of course) in the environmental affairs of humans, illustrate our inability to come to grips with our temporal regulatory complexities.

Prasads's stories can be read just for fun. But at a deeper level they also touch upon the various aspects of the sustainability challenge which our societies are trying to address. They demonstrate clearly, why progress is sometimes so slow, but also point clearly, to where progress is possible. Never moralising or preaching, they help us understand, and contribute to, organising our own lives and personal philosophies.

Fritz Balkau
Paris, France

. . . .

Manoj Karmarkar : *Very Informative and thought provoking article as always*

Shantanu Roy : *This piece is simply superb!! Modelling otherwise sounds so abstract for the learners. Pedagogy like this is needed for the teaching of environmental science so as to get professionals who understand modelling, not just the application of the modeling software. And this is true for so many other concepts of environmental science. It's so frustrating when even practitioners in the field get confused on basic things like organic pollutants and COD, using the terms interchangeably.*

Zarasp Irani : *Well written article and very informative in the way you have linked the progression of the practice of assessment. I fully agree that the practice in this country is weak and has been further diluted by unethical, short term, bottom-fishing approach*

Pradeep : *Great reading. Fantastic style of narration to explain a complex issue of maintenance in an EFT*

Nayan Khambati : *Very thought provoking article.I hope everyone realizes the urgency and we start on the path chalked out by you.It could be in the smallest possible way.I think we all owe that much to our future generations*

Aparna (Nahar) Sethi : *You have an amazing array of knowledge and experience in doing interesting things. Though I have no knowledge about GMDH, I was definitely interested to read about it. Each and every post of yours is so interesting to read as it offers a new understanding about your experience and knowledge. We are enriched just to be reading them. Thanks for sharing your old and new experiences.*

Pravina parikh : *Good idea! Generation of new business avenues! May be getting EC report would eventually become a status symbol and a fashion to gossip about in high class clubs and social events!! Depending upon the propaganda, there may be a prize announced for the family which spends highest amount and / or best EIA report for wedding-events. Wow! ECO WEDDING!!*

Mythili Ravi : *Absolutely hilarious!! Prof Modak, I didn't know that you write literary masterpieces as well. Thought you are an expert basically on the drab EIA!!*

V S Balasubramanian : *Good analysis. I need not read so many books to understand the status of EIA and ESP in India, thanks Modak Sir...*

Nayan Khambati : *Good observations and excellent interpretation of current happenings in the present Indian environmental scenario. I do not see in the near future any of our professional associations rising above their petty squabbles and contributing positively to the future policies. But, obviously we can blame ourselves for not participating and showing spine at the right time on subjects concerning issues beyond our daily routine. Inaction by good people at* the right time, is more damaging than destructive action by the "not-so-good" people. Let's wake up, try and make a difference in the future.

Pradeep : *Great piece of writing. Delightful blend of fantasy, science, reality, politics with your softly biting comments. Enjoyed thoroughly Prasad! !!*

Jillian Kane Bhambhani : *A touching story Dr Modak. So often we tend to neglect the obvious around us whether at work, in our personal lives or even during meetings with strangers. Many times we read too much into something. But life has a way of turning out just the way it should be. Am so glad the envelope was never opened.*

Pranay Krishnan : *Brilliant article Sir, a must read. I don't know if I got all the underlying messages but there is much I take out of this article.*

Manoj Karmarkar : *Amazing and amusing!! I certainly believe in the occult. Would in fact start researching on the subject and which I feel shall become very handy. Although this is fascinating and amazing, there is a scary side as well. I mean if one can read future of self and near & dear ones. Doing so can be a boon and a bane.*

Arun Balan : *I had a opportunity to attend your class at NITK Surathkal. Your way of story telling is really interesting.I am very impressed with your presentation and story telling…*

Rajeshwari Dholakia Antani : *Wow! Thought provoking! Very well written. I love the ending note: Many of us don't have options in life so we live the way others want us to. But some of us who have, should live life differently and if required change the course of life*

Kshaumesh Antani: *Lovely article Sir!!. A lesson for those being interviewed and those who are interviewing!!*

Paritosh Tyagi : *Another good one from a master story-teller ! Good lessons to learn, more for the interviewers than the candidates. By the way, how do you manage to remember so much of detail including the names of so many persons who you met more than thirty years ago?*

Akhilendra : *Teachers with tunnel vision could be lethal to the society as generations may get affected. All I can say is my repeat statement "Some are wise. Then how about others? They are "other"wise.*

Sudhirvj : *Adventures such as these become lessons in life for those who read it!*

Ananth S Kodavasal : *Again at your brilliant best Prasad. Experience and practical knowledge cannot be supplanted by mere reading of books, articles and reports.*

Sunil Herat : *Dr Modak, Your story is well beyond any person can think and write in a serious situation like this. Humor in the story is such that one can easily forget the serious situation you're in. Classic demonstration on how to handle such difficult situations in life*

Sujata virdhe : *You have a wonderful style of writing. Truly enjoyed the article. It is emotionally thought provoking.*

Thank you. It made my day

Panneerselvam : *Indeed very emotional art of Giving …. Unfortunately for whatever reason, we simply forget this important aspect of "life" and get carried away by materialistic life, which in any case is so temporary…. sad but true….*

Environmental Management Centre (EMC) LLP

Environmental Management Centre (EMC) LLP was established in 1996. EMC's consulting services are essentially strategic, knowledge driven and supported through research and training. In all consulting assignments, EMC's expertise lies in harmonizing economic, environmental and social considerations (often called triple bottom line) in business logic, development plans and policy frameworks.

Since inception, EMC has built together a team of environmental professionals trained in engineering, science, economics and planning. This core team is supported by Associates that work from India as well as from abroad on a part or full time basis. Associates bring in skills and experience in specialized areas. EMC operates a unique environmental internship programme that is sought after by top students from reputed universities in India as well as overseas.

Over the past 20 years, EMC has conceived, developed and executed a number of national, regional and international assignments that have set several "firsts". Many of these assignments have stimulated action leading to policy reforms, sustainable investments and led to long term capacity building. EMC is perhaps one of the very few Indian companies that operates from India and offers services globally.

Visit www.emcentre.com

Ekonnect Knowledge Foundation (Ekonnect)

Ekonnect is a nonprofit section 8 company set up with the aim of increasing understanding and imparting education to address challenges and offer solutions in arena of Environmental Management and Sustainablity. Ekonnect is an initiative of Dr.Prasad Modak who is Founder and Director of this company.

All programs at Ekonnect are designed for action: each ensures that participants apply solutions to real world problems and leverage on opportunities. Ekonnect invests time and thought in custom designing learning programs for the intended audience making the best of resources available. The pedagogy, armed with an E-learning platform, is unique providing flexibility and practical applications.

Ekonnect believes in collaboration; pooling in resources, people, associates and organizations as and when required in the best interest of the program/project at hand. Examples of Ekonnects programs are Disha - a career counselling program, Finishing School, Anvaya - a short film contest, Not Just Walk in the Park - targeting children and Tree Revival campaign in cities.

Ekonnect hosts Green Purchasing Network of India and works closely with the International Green Purchasing Network to promote Sustainable Consumption and Production (SCP). An Ekocalendar is brought out each year to raise awareness and promote positive action *every day.*

Visit www.ekonnect.net

www.ingramcontent.com/pod-product-compliance
Lightning Source LLC
Chambersburg PA
CBHW070104290526
45789CB00005B/1921